The Menace of Multiculturalism

THE MENACE OF MULTICULTURALISM

Trojan Horse in America

ALVIN J. SCHMIDT

Foreword by Dinesh D'Souza

Westport, Connecticut
London

Library of Congress Cataloging-in-Publication Data

Schmidt, Alvin J.
    The menace of multiculturalism : Trojan horse in America / Alvin
J. Schmidt ; foreword by Dinesh D'Souza.
        p.   cm.
    Includes bibliographical references and index.
    ISBN 0–275–95598–2 (alk. paper)
    1. Multiculturalism—United States.   2. Pluralism (Social
sciences)—United States.   3. United States—Race relations.
4. United States—Ethnic relations.   I. Title.
E184.A1S345   1997
305.8'00973—dc20   96–24462

British Library Cataloguing in Publication Data is available.

Library of Congress Catalog Card Number: 96–24462
ISBN: 0–275–95598–2

First published in 1997

Praeger Publishers, 88 Post Road West, Westport, CT 06881
An imprint of Greenwood Publishing Group, Inc.

Printed in the United States of America

The paper used in this book complies with the
Permanent Paper Standard issued by the National
Information Standards Organization (Z39.48–1984).

10   9   8   7   6   5   4   3

To my dear sons
Timothy John
and
Mark Alvin
May they do their part
in keeping multiculturalism
from destroying their great nation
and their future.

Contents

Foreword

If multiculturalism in American schools and colleges were, as many of its advocates insist, nothing more than a program for teaching young people about other cultures, merely a broader alternative to "monoculturalism," then it would be uncontroversial. Who could be against hundreds of thousands of undergraduates going beyond Plato and Shakespeare and energetically grappling with the *Analects* of Confucius, the *Muquaddimmah* of Ibn Khaldun, and Rabindranath Tagore's *Gitanjali?*

The reason for the controversy over multiculturalism—both as an educational program and as the basis for identity—is that in practice it offers a specific paradigm for understanding both Western and non-Western cultures. Similarly, it provides an ideological lens for interpreting conflicts about race, gender, and sexual orientation in the United States. Consequently, the multicultural debate is a civil conflict within the West about competing ways to understand ourselves and the world beyond.

Alvin Schmidt's *The Menace of Multiculturalism: Trojan Horse of America* is a powerful indictment of multiculturalism in practice, yet it is written from the point of view of one who is supportive of a broader, more integrated concept of learning, as well as one who is committed to America as a more inclusive society. Schmidt's attack on multiculturalism is so unrelenting and effective precisely because he sees it as betraying its goals, dividing the nation into warring factions, promulgating lies instead of truth, and thus undermining the prospects for citizens of different backgrounds living together and adjudicating differences in a rational and civil manner.

Schmidt accurately diagnoses cultural relativism to be the hidden hand guiding much of what passes for multiculturalism today. After all, as its name suggests, multiculturalism is a doctrine of culture. All cultures are presumed to be equally worthy of study and respect; no culture is considered to be superior or inferior to another. In this view, the standards for evaluating a culture must come from within that culture. No culture has the right to impose its values on another. For all their variety, contemporary approaches to multiculturalism are united in their denial of Western cultural superiority.

One reads Schmidt's tough exposé with a mixture of amusement, revulsion, and regret. There is amusement at the hypocrisies of the political left, such as the genuflections to racial diversity, gender diversity, and every other form of diversity except the one form that matters most in an educational setting, namely, philosophical or intellectual diversity. Thus, as Schmidt shows again and again, religious and political conservatives are rarely welcome at the multicultural picnic.

Schmidt is unsparing in his portrait of the unseemly practices of other cultures, such as the bloodthirsty enthusiasms of some American Indian tribes. Most of us have internalized the moral standards of Western modernity, which include a visceral distaste for enforced physical suffering. Consequently relativists have an uphill battle demonstrating that torture and human sacrifice constitute legitimate adaptations to local circumstances. Even today, there are few American defenders of genital mutilation in parts of Africa and the Arab world. Yet it is hard to read about the barbaric practices of other cultures without a sense of regret and chagrin; set against the historical backdrop of colonialism and conquest, this guilt too is distinctively Western.

Ultimately, Schmidt is concerned with more than saving a generation of American students from ignorance and delusion about their own culture and that of others. His stakes are even higher, because he knows that ideas have consequences, and he recognizes that, taken to its extreme, multiculturalism threatens to weaken legitimate American institutions, indeed the very mediating institutions of church and family that are the best hope for a confused nation to recover its moral and civic moorings.

I welcome Schmidt to the club of writers who are routinely denounced not because what they say is false and dangerous to society, but because what they say is true and dangerous to the pretensions of an intellectually and morally bankrupt ideology. This ideology is loosely leftist, although it masquerades as liberal. Schmidt is right to sound the alarm, so that this time the Trojan horse will be recognized, the looters will be turned back at the gates, and the city on the hill will be preserved from destruction.

Dinesh D'Souza

Preface

In writing a book critical of the current sociopolitical movement known as multiculturalism, I have obviously not taken a popular stance. Many Americans today accept multiculturalism, but many of these same people do not know what it is or what its objectives are. This book is an attempt to give Americans a better understanding of this phenomenon that is now in their midst.

Given my extensive survey and criticism of multiculturalism in this book, it might interest the reader to know that I am not unfamiliar with multicultural experiences. I was not born an American but a Canadian, and I lived the first four years of my life (in the 1930s) in what sociologists call a culture of poverty. My parents lived in a small, primitive two-room (kitchen and one other room) log house. It was located on poor farmland with no running water or indoor plumbing. Underneath its crude, noncarpeted wooden floor, which rested on the ground rather than on a concrete foundation, resided dozens of rats. These filthy creatures had daily access to our two rooms through holes they had gnawed through the floor. While I slept, as both an infant and a toddler, the rats ran over my tiny bed virtually every night; sometimes they took a sock or two with them. Frequently, they robbed us of food items that they cleverly stole off the table when no one was in the house. Covering the items with substantial lids did not help.

My father and mother would get the mail or go to church, both four miles away, not with a Model A Ford but with a team of horses and a hayrack. My parents had no money to buy groceries. Our diet consisted of vegetables, chickens, eggs, and meat, all raised and prepared at home.

We had no radio or newspapers. My father spoke some broken English; my mother knew not a word. Thus I recall being quite proud of myself for literally knowing two English words when I started grade school, a one-room rural school with eight grades. Every pupil in this public school, except one, spoke German. In the current vernacular, English is my second language. My parents, reflecting personal experience and community values, saw no real value in education, at least not beyond the eighth grade. For them, anyone who went to school beyond grade school was a deviant.

I, and some of my schoolmates, often experienced real ethnic bigotry and discrimination during World War II, especially during third grade. Our teacher, an elderly woman of Scottish descent, had a strong dislike for Germans. Perhaps she even hated them; I'm not sure. Soon after she came to the school, she firmly outlawed the speaking of German during recess periods, which most of us did. She reprimanded and punished us—keeping us for an hour after school—when we spoke German. To be sure, this soon ended the speaking of German on school property.

My early years, as multiculturalists like to say, were lived in two different cultures, one of poverty and the other of an ethnic nature. Through these early life experiences, I believe that I have some insight into the lives of people who are not part of the mainstream culture. I have also learned that had I been permitted to retain my early culture, I would have remained deprived and culturally isolated from the rest of the world. Assimilating Canada's majority culture, which began with school attendance, did not demean or deprive me. Nor was I a victim of "cultural imperialism," as multiculturalists would say. I lived in the country and therefore had an obligation to absorb its culture. Assimilation was a blessing, not an oppressive evil.

Based on substantial data, this book shows that multiculturalism is a modern Trojan horse in America's culture. So those looking for a "politically correct" viewpoint need read no further. Of course, I expect strong reactions from those multiculturalists who have learned to silence the opposition by hurling the epithet "bigot" or "insensitive" at anyone questioning their values and practices.

Unlike many American white males, as I have just noted, I have personal experience of prejudice and bigotry. Thus for more than thirty years, I have worked hard to remove prejudice and bigotry by teaching my students in college that America must become color blind; that we Americans must judge each other, as Martin Luther King, Jr., said, not by the color of our skin but by the content of our character. Our character, however, is being threatened by the exponents of multiculturalism who are reviving some of America's past sins as they promote the importance of race, ethnicity, and cultural separateness among Americans. This approach has already spawned prejudice and discrimination. Multiculturalism, rather than ending prejudice and bigotry, is creating new forms of it. Anger about past injustices in America will not be rectified by bringing back old prejudices and separatist practices draped in new garb.

I am very sympathetic to the plight of minorities in America's past. The treatment that America accorded the American Indians, blacks, Irish, Italians, the Germans during World War I, and the Japanese during World War II was indeed unjust and shameful. I also regret the way women have been treated prior to their receiving suffrage and even after the 19th Amendment was ratified. A few years ago, I showed my sympathies regarding discrimination against women by publishing a book: *Veiled and Silenced: How Culture Shaped Sexist Theology* (Macon, Ga.: Mercer University Press, 1989). Moreover, while some minorities, especially blacks, endured more injustice than others, in this context it is fitting to note the words of Thomas Sowell, the renowned black scholar. In his book, *Ethnic America* (1981), he shows that virtually every ethnic group in the United States, at one time, suffered some form of discrimination. On the other hand, no nation has done more to correct the unjust treatment of minority groups than America, and it is still working hard to do more.

Being concerned about the invasion of multiculturalism and its long-range effects on America is not to say that I find everything acceptable in the present-day culture. Many things in American culture—and some are already the result of multiculturalism's influence—are incompatible with the traditional Euro-American culture. It is the Euro-American culture that has made America great, and it is this culture that multiculturalism stands to destroy.

I do not believe that a planned conspiracy is at work to undermine and destroy the Euro-American culture. Rather, the current promotion of multiculturalism seems to be the result of it being "in the air," so to speak, spread by social contagion. Many see it as an idea whose time has come, one that will solve all major social problems. In accepting multiculturalism, people are showing that they are conformist and tend to follow new philosophies, fashions, and fads without critical thought or evaluation. It is "trendy" to identify with multiculturalism. All these factors, I am sure, are involved in multiculturalism's current looming presence.

Finally, I wish to say a word about the vast amount of evidence I present in this book in order to warn Americans about multiculturalism. A critic might say that I could have made the argument with less evidence, but my response is no, not really. The response to those who have criticized multiculturalism has usually been the claim that such incidents are isolated, anecdotal exceptions. The book's numerous citations, taken from across the nation, should put that argument to rest.

Acknowledgments

The writing of this book could not have been achieved without the co-operative support of my loving wife, Carol. She not only did various chores around the home that I should have done, but she permitted and supported me as I "holed" myself up in my home study, enabling me to sift and organize several years of research notes to write this book. She also faithfully read the manuscript before it went to the publisher. Her mind and eyes often alerted me to see the need to recast or reword some parts as the manuscript was in process.

As a sociologist, I am acutely conscious of the social isolation that writing a book requires. As every writer knows, writing is a solitary, lonesome task. It cannot be done in the presence and company of others. To a degree, it compels one to become a modern monk for months on end with very long days. And, again, my wife endured it all. So, Carol, many kind thanks!

Considerable gratitude is also due to my friend and colleague James E. Davis, professor of history at Illinois College. Being an avid reader of current periodicals, he often drew my attention to pertinent books and articles that dealt with the phenomenon of multiculturalism and its radical disciples. And not to be overlooked are the many helpful comments and suggestions that Brad Stetson offered. He not only read the manuscript for the publisher in its early stages, but whenever I called him in California, he always responded in the most helpful manner. Needless to say any and all of the book's content is my responsibility.

I also thank the library staff at Illinois College, especially Laura Sweatmen, Mike Westbrooke, Pat Schildman, and Martin Gallas, head librarian. Laura never tired of requesting inter-library materials, books, and articles; Mike was always nimble on the internet, searching for the answers to unusual research questions that I often gave him; Pat often helped me with the library's existing holdings; and Martin often granted me other privileges. To all of these great people, I am extremely grateful.

Chapter 1

Introduction

These are the times that try men's souls.

Thomas Paine

MULTICULTURALISM'S TRAGEDIES DISCOVERED EARLY: A PERSONAL NOTE

The concerns and warnings regarding multiculturalism delineated in this book reflect a variety of my experiences: my birth and upbringing in a foreign country, my acquisition of English as a second language, my profession as a sociologist, my study of cultures and history, and my visits to many foreign countries. Long before the word *multiculturalism* was coined, I, as a young boy in the 1940s, heard about the tragic effects of this then-unnamed phenomenon from my father, a German who had immigrated to Canada from Poland.

Born in Poland, my father in his early youth moved with his parents to West Prussia, that part of Germany where the Germans and the Poles were in continual conflict with each other, both before and after World War I. How well I remember the horrible stories he related during my grade school years of bodily assaults and actual ethnic killings. The stories were astonishing to me, for at the time I really did not understand the enmity between the Germans and the Poles.

The conflict between them was rooted in cultural and ethnic hostilities and was not the product of a social movement or ideology now known as multiculturalism. The German-Polish animosities were natural consequences of people who failed to adopt one culture, common to both. The two groups stubbornly adhered to their individual cultural prejudices and differences, much as multiculturalists do today by encouraging cultural minority groups not to assimilate into their host country's culture.

At the youthful age of sixteen, my father and two teenage neighbors were ruthlessly grabbed and pushed against a wall to be shot by some neighborhood Poles. The reason was simple: they were Germans who lived in territory now (1919) claimed by Poland after Germany lost World War I. My father and his two friends were rescued by an American military officer who had fortuitously chanced upon the scene and ordered that all violence cease. Had the officer arrived five minutes later my father and his companions would have been brutally murdered. Just five years later, my father and his family migrated to western Canada, seeking to escape the ongoing ethnic and cultural tensions of their native land.

Despite my father's first-hand experience of the painful costs attached to clinging to one's ethnicity and culture, he learned little from it. Once in Canada, he and his relatives tried their best to avoid the country's English-speaking culture. At that time (the 1920s), Canada (except for Quebec), much like the United States, wanted its immigrants to assimilate. Living in isolated Manitoba, where interaction with English-speaking residents during the 1920s and 1930s was extremely minimal, and where radio broadcasts or English newspapers were nonexistent, he and his relatives were easily able to sidestep assimilation.

My father did not like to hear English spoken at home and disapproved of Germans marrying non-Germans. When English church services were introduced in the local Lutheran church, he and some of his friends saw this practice as especially unfortunate. Church services in English were seen as a type of "ethnic cleansing." I sometimes responded: "Dad, if you don't like to see the disappearance of the German language, why then did you come to Canada?" My questions made no impact. He disliked anything that resembled a melting pot, much as the multiculturalists do in America today.

The obvious is frequently difficult to see. Thus, in spite of my father's personal experiences with ethnic and cultural strife in Europe, he and his relatives both failed to see that resisting cultural assimilation invariably produces the cultural tension, enmity, and conflict from which he escaped in Europe. Similarly, it is not obvious to countless Americans today as they lend their support to multiculturalists who do not want immigrant and minority groups to relinquish their foreign cultures.

Nor is it obvious to countless Americans that their nation avoided the ethnic fights of other societies, such as the conflict between the Germans and the Poles in West Prussia, or even worse, the present bloodshed in Bosnia, because fortunately America never became a multicultural society. Instead, it melted (assimilated) millions of immigrants and their children into a new, dynamic culture. It made them Americans by dissolving their foreign cultures in the melting pot. The nation practiced Teddy Roosevelt's dictum: "We have no use for the German or Irishman who remains such."[1]

MULTICULTURALISM DEFINED

Multiculturalism is a leftist political ideology that sees all cultures, their mores and institutions, as essentially equal. No culture is considered superior or inferior to any other; it is merely different. Criticism of other cultures, especially non-Western/minority cultures, is labeled "insensitive" or "bigoted." There is one major exception, however. The Euro-American culture with its Judeo-Christian underpinnings is not only criticized but often condemned, being accused of racism, sexism, and classism.

The term "Euro-American culture" refers to those components of American culture that are derived from the beliefs and practices of England and, to some degree, of Northern Europe and adapted to American needs. Briefly, these beliefs are as follows: God created human beings and the world; human behavior is to be judged as right or wrong, moral or immoral, in light of the Ten Commandments of the Bible; objective knowledge is attainable; the rights, freedoms, responsibilities, and dignity of the individual take precedence over those of groups; people are governed by the rule of law; laws are formulated democratically; every man or woman is equal before the law; every accused individual is innocent until proven guilty in a fair trial where he or she can face the accuser; people have the right not only to succeed but also to fail; and a free society that provides equal opportunity does not guarantee equal outcome.

Multiculturalism encourages immigrants and other minorities to retain their foreign cultures by not assimilating into the Euro-American culture. Even the word "foreign" is deemed politically incorrect, for it does not conform to the political values and ideology of multiculturalism. Government is urged to legislate and fund bilingual education for immigrant children in public schools. Cultural assimilation is disdained because it is tantamount to cultural imperialism.

Multiculturalism must not be confused with multicultural education, as it often is. Multicultural education presents and examines the values and practices of other cultures objectively and critically in a nondoctrinaire manner. It recognizes that American culture has always had some diversity, especially religious and ethnic differences, but it views such diversity as subcultural and subordinate to America's majority culture rather than standing separately alongside of it. Thus the present volume does not use the term *multiculturalism* or *multiculturalist* to mean multicultural education.[2] Instead it focuses on the effects and ramifications of multiculturalism as an ideology.

The existence and recent growth of multiculturalism has been fueled by cultural relativism, the concept that each culture is to be judged relative to its own standards, and not to those from another culture. This idea can be traced back to the German philosopher and court preacher, Johann Gottfried von Herder (1744–1803), who argued that each society's culture was to be judged "without foisting any set pattern upon it."[3]

Cultural relativism gave birth to the idea that the moral behavior of another culture was culturally relative too, and not to be judged by someone *outside* of that culture. Soon this notion expanded, stating that one's behavior may not be judged even *within* one's own culture. This belief has now filtered down to the average man and woman in America and to individuals in other Western societies as well.

In the 1960s and 1970s the ideology of postmodernism took hold. While this ideology is difficult to define with precision, certain recurrent themes can be discerned, notably: the attainment of objective truth or fixed verities is impossible; no truth or ideas are transcendent; all ideas are socially or culturally constructed; ideas or truths are true only if they benefit the "oppressed"; and the facts of history are unimportant. Briefly expressed, postmodernism is cultural relativism with political overtones, and multiculturalism is really the marriage of cultural relativism and postmodernism.

True to postmodernism's ideology, multiculturalists see Western culture or Euro-American culture in the United States as not having benefited non-Western/minority cultures, and so its values or truths must be considered specious. This helps explain why multiculturalism, as Dinesh D'Souza has observed, "represents a denial of all Western claims to truth."[4] It also explains why its disciples denounce Western and Euro-American culture, which they seek to undermine and even dismantle by introducing into American culture a variety of non-Western cultures with equal honor and rights.

The coming together of cultural relativism and postmodernism in multiculturalism has been fortified by an allied ideology: Marxism (see Chapter 3). Marxism has given multiculturalism its rationale and its concepts (e.g., oppression, inequality, imperialism, and revolutionary change) to devalue and dismantle America's 300–year-old culture. All aggressive-minded multiculturalists employ these concepts to attack the Euro-American culture.

MULTICULTURALISM IN THE FORMER YUGOSLAVIA

The news media report the bloody conflagration in the former Yugoslavia in great detail, but they are strangely silent on one central issue:

they consistently fail to tell Americans and the world that the horrors and atrocities being witnessed almost daily in this benighted land are the bitter fruits of multiculturalism. The word "multiculturalism" never appears in the news reports. But in fact the human hatred and bloodshed in the former Yugoslavia are largely the product of failed multiculturalist practices that operated there for decades and in some instances for at least two centuries.

Why do the media consistently avoid mention of the failed multicultural policies of the former Yugoslavia as the underlying cause of its civil breakdown? Being avid supporters of multiculturalism at home, are the American media afraid to report the truth about the tragic effects of multiculturalism away from home? Do they fear that Americans might get the message and reject this ideology, so dear to many reporters? Or do they perhaps think that the Serb and Croats simply do not know how to implement multiculturalism, but that its advocates in America would do better with their version of a multiculturalist society?

MULTICULTURALISM IN AMERICA

This book is an attempt to break that silence, for clearly, America has a dangerous problem on its hands. This work cites numerous illustrations that show multiculturalism is a modern Trojan horse and that Americans neither see nor understand the danger it hides.

A number of parallels can be made between ancient Troy and present-day America. The residents of Troy were intrigued with the large, unusual wooden horse outside of the city's gates; Americans have become intrigued with the phenomenon of multiculturalism, a modern Trojan horse. The Trojans were warned not to take the wooden horse into the city, but they did so nevertheless; Americans, urged not to take multiculturalism into their midst, failed to heed all warnings. And, once inside the nation, the occupants of this modern Trojan horse have opened the gates to let their fellow warriors into the nation's schools and universities, businesses, government, and churches. Yet one more step remains to complete the analogy of the ancient Trojan horse. Troy was destroyed after its own people brought the wooden horse into their city. Will America complete the analogy by also suffering defeat for taking the Trojan horse of multiculturalism into its midst?

Chapter 2 alerts the reader to the many false portraits of multiculturalism that its clever-minded promoters have put before the public to gain its acceptance. Chapter 3 focuses on the Marxist and neo-Marxist assumptions that are operative in multiculturalism. The fourth chapter attempts to disprove the claims of multiculturalists that all cultures are of equal value.

Multiculturalists often damn facts of history (see Chapter 5) by publishing "noble lies" that will make minorities and ethnic groups feel good, as well as make their cultures appear equal, or perhaps even superior, to the Euro-American. This tactic is motivated by the Marxist-Leninist principle that the end justifies the means. So, for instance, if the goal is defined as worthy, presenting false accounts as authentic history in school textbooks is justified. And consistent with postmodernism's argument that truth is only true when it benefits minority groups, false accounts are not false if they will contribute to the well-being of minority or underprivileged groups.

Multiculturalism's denial of the existence of objective truth and morality has the potential for dire consequences. Once this posture is taken, it opens the door for some totalitarian group or ideology to seize power and define "truth" consistent with its values. That is precisely what happened in Germany in the 1930s when Hitler and the Nazis came to power, and a similar phenomenon occurred under communism in the former Soviet Union in the 1920s. The Nazis and the communists, though bitter antagonists, both defined truth and morality as whatever served the party's interest.

Americans are being sold a false bill of goods by the propaganda peddlers of multiculturalism with regard to what they call diversity. Thus Chapter 6 shows that their concept of diversity is not diversity at all but a form of reverse bigotry. Views and opinions that do not mesh with the leftist ideology of multiculturalism are *ipso facto* barred from being expressed, especially on many university campuses where free speech putatively is a cardinal tenet. Most diversity is considered diverse only insofar as it departs from Judeo-Christian principles and morality.[5] The quest for multiculturalist diversity is also creating new forms of racial segregation, separating racial and ethnic groups on the basis of their different cultures. This ideology is especially being promoted on American college and university campuses.

Chapter 7 focuses on the apostles of multiculturalism who are seriously engaged in changing the nation's mode of thought and speech by forcing individuals to conform to their "politically correct" ideology. Individuals expressing ideas, words, and behaviors that are not seen as politically correct are often severely punished. Many university students, for example, are disciplined or expelled. The politically correct enforcers function as the police of multiculturalism.

In numerous elementary schools, multiculturalists are actively promoting bilingualism. If the push for bilingualism is not checked, America will invariably become the dis-United States.[6] Efforts to introduce bilingualism (mostly Spanish) in many American schools cost the taxpayers billions of dollars each year. In effect, the Bilingual Education Act of 1968 is paving the way for the eventual shattering of America's melting pot. One need only look to Canada to see what havoc bilingualism has created there; it is tearing the Great White North apart. As discussed in Chapter 8, America does not need a Quebec in its midst.

Multiculturalism's premises of moral and cultural relativity even threaten the traditional nuclear family by rejecting the Judeo-Christian code[7] of sexual morality that has been the foundation of the traditional family for thousands of years (see Chapter 9).

Americans need to know that multiculturalism is attacking and even eradicating the foundation of their nation's morality, laws, and ethics, for the multiculturalists have an intense hatred of anything that reflects biblical values. On occasion, the multiculturalist, antibiblical forces have been aided by the United States Supreme Court as it removed and outlawed biblical values and norms, for example, banning the posting of the Ten Commandments in public schools. In addition, special efforts have been made to expunge Christian symbols from all public properties. As pointed out in Chapter 10, such efforts amount to "the multiculturalist purge."

Multiculturalism has been aided by many liberal educational administrators, unwary business executives, zealous governmental bureaucrats, and unsuspecting church leaders. This topic is taken up in Chapter 11, "With Friends like These . . ."

The final chapter urges America to fight for its soul. If multiculturalism continues to infiltrate America's basic institutions with its potentially divisive ideology, neo-pagan principles, and multi-morality, it will surely lose its soul. To be sure, the country will still be on the globe, but it will no longer be America, "the home of the free and the brave." In the eyes of the world, America has always been the land where people came to be free—*free* to practice their religious beliefs, not to be free *from* them, as multiculturalists would have it. It is a land whose people always believed they were "one nation under God" and whose people said "in God we trust." Countless Americans believed that their nation was the "Promised Land," the land that God selected and preserved for them. Evidence for this belief is not lacking. Against unusual odds, the nation gained its independence, grew and prospered economically, abolished slavery, survived the Civil War, won two world wars, assimilated and united millions of immigrants for three centuries, and overcame the internal strife of the Vietnam War. But will it win its most insidious war, the war against multiculturalism?

Many multiculturalists seem to be plagued by the white man's guilt— a feeling of remorse that many white Americans have regarding their nation's past sins, relative to the discrimination against racial minorities and women, for example. The amends and corrections that the United States has made in the past thirty years have not assuaged their guilt. Many advocates of multiculturalism, most of whom are white, still feel guilty and see American culture as racist, sexist, classist, and oppressive.

But if America is so racist and oppressive, why do millions continue to see America as a beacon of hope? If America's gates were opened fully, millions more from all over the world would enter. Indeed, millions of immigrants, representing numerous races, enter the country, legally and illegally, every year. People do not voluntarily come to a country whose culture is oppressive and racist.

Implicit in much of the multiculturalists' disdain for Western or Euro-American culture is their conviction that multiculturalism will usher in a cultural utopia. It will create a world wherein all kinds of cultural and ethnic groups will live in peace and harmony. To posit such a vision is to forget the etymology of the Greek word *utopia* (*ouk* = no; *topos* = place). In plain words, there is no such place.

Only individuals who reject the fallen nature of human beings can believe in a utopia. Empirically, however, the propensity for evil in human nature, and the impossibility of utopia, can no more be denied than the law of gravity. Thus, sooner or later, every multiculturalist dream inevitably results in a Balkan nightmare.

NOTES

1. Theodore Roosevelt, "True Americanism," in *American Ideals and Other Essays: Social and Political* (New York: G. P. Putnam's Sons, 1898), p. 26.

2. I am indebted to Brad Stetson for some of his comments relative to distinguishing multiculturalism from multicultural education.

3. Cited in Patrick Gardiner, "Herder, Johann Gottfried," in *The Encyclopedia of Philosophy*, ed. Paul Edwards (New York: Macmillan and Free Press, 1967), 3: 488.

4. Dinesh D'Souza, *The End of Racism: Principles for a Multiracial Society* (New York: Free Press, 1995), p. 344.

5. The concept of the traditional family in Western or American culture refers to the marriage of two heterosexual adults, who from such a union have children by birth or adoption, who are responsible for the nurture, education, and welfare of their children, and who are sexually and economically faithful to one another.

6. The term *dis-United States* is derived from Arthur M. Schlesinger, Jr. See his book *The Disuniting of America: Reflections on a Multicultural Society* (New York: W. W. Norton, 1992).

7. The term *Judeo-Christian ethic* refers to that system of values and morality derived from the Bible which Jews and Christians have in common. Much of this ethic stems from the Ten Commandments that spell out people's duties and relationship to God and their fellow human beings.

Chapter 2

False, Deceptive Portraits

Propaganda does not deceive people; it merely helps them to deceive themselves.

Eric Hoffer

Prior to 1990, the *Reader's Guide to Periodical Literature* had no entry for multiculturalism; by 1993 it had forty-one entries. Today the term *multiculturalism* can be found in innumerable indexes, newspapers, and magazines and is commonly heard on radio and television. Indeed, it has become a household word. Its methods and objectives are not so well known, however. This ideology with strong political overtones is promoted and advocated by college/university professors and administrators, elementary and secondary school teachers and officials, governmental bureaucrats, textbook publishers, the mass media, and a host of church leaders. Some states even have a full-time Office of Multicultural Affairs.

Some advocates of multiculturalism are often uninformed as to the true nature of this new *ism*. Its zealots are anything but uninformed about the objectives. In their way of operating, they fit Karl Mannheim's description of ideologues, whom he described as being "so intensively interest-bound to a situation that they simply are no longer able to see certain facts."[1] It is the multiculturalist's failure to see the bitter fruits of this ideology that commonly results in ethnic and cultural conflict, and often bloodshed.

To a large degree multiculturalism has gained its present foothold because many Americans have been presented false portraits of what it is and does. Sometimes it is the well-intentioned promoters of multiculturalism who present some of these false claims. For the most part, however, they are the work of the clever advocates who know that if they were to reveal the true nature of multiculturalism most Americans would reject it out of hand, as happened in the recent (1995) *Enola Gay* incident at the Smithsonian Institution, discussed later in this chapter.

"MULTICULTURALISM HELPS PEOPLE APPRECIATE CONTRIBUTIONS OTHER CULTURES MADE TO AMERICAN CULTURE"

One false portrait often presented by multiculturalists, especially in educational circles, is that multiculturalism helps students and others to appreciate the contributions other cultures have made to our own culture. Well-meaning citizens ask: "What can possibly be wrong with learning about other cultures?" The answer of course is nothing, but that is not a true picture.

If multiculturalism merely taught individuals about the contributions other cultures have made to American culture, there would be no problem. No one would object to teaching students in elementary schools, high schools, and colleges that the United States, for example, borrowed some cultural practices from a number of other cultures.

This approach, for instance, might teach students that the names of half of the fifty states in the United States are derived from Indian names. Minnesota, Nebraska, Ohio, Kansas, Massachusetts, Illinois, Michigan, and Utah are some examples. Countless American towns and cities also have Indian names—Chicago, Tacoma, Omaha, Wichita, Milwaukee, and Saginaw are just a few of them. American counties with Indian names are also abundant: Catawba, Choctaw, Iroquois, Cherokee, Suwanee, Okaloosa, and so on. In addition, many American English words are derived from American Indian cultures; these include hurricane, muskeg, caribou, moose, tomahawk, and coyote. One researcher estimates that some 200 American words owe their existence to Indian names.[2]

Teaching and informing students that the Indians' cultural contributions are part of American culture is necessary to show that such contributions have enriched the nation's culture. Such teaching should be part of every school's curriculum. As I have pointed out earlier, that kind of teaching is simply multicultural education, and it must not be confused with ideological multiculturalism. As stated in Chapter 1, mere multicultural education that informs students about other cultures and critically evaluates them as well is not what the zealous disciples of multiculturalism have in mind.

As a professor, I find some of the above examples from American Indian cultures, as well as others, useful in my classes to show how they contributed to today's American culture. But good educational practice also requires that the instructor alert students to the flaws, inadequacies, and especially the barbarous customs that existed in many of these and other cultures. Multiculturalists, however, ignore the negative aspects of other cultures, particularly the practices of minority or non-Western cultures. They prefer to highlight only the flaws in American culture. By doing the latter multiculturalists encourage Americans to become xenocentric and non-Western minority groups ethnocentric, really promoting cultural separatism. As Robert Hughes noted: "But you do not have to listen to the arguments very long before realizing that, in quite a few people's minds, multiculturalism is about something else. Their version means cultural separatism with the larger whole of America."[3]

Hughes and many others like him have made such comments not because they oppose teaching and learning about other cultures, but rather in order to respond to what ideological multiculturalists have said and are doing. Here is a case in point: In 1973 the American Association of Colleges for Teacher Education boldly declared: "Multicultural education rejects the view that schools should seek to melt away cultural differences or the view that schools should merely tolerate pluralism . . . to endorse cultural pluralism is to endorse the principle there is no one model American."[4] This kind of education is not merely learning about other cultures, but about creating cultural separatism. Ultimately, such education undermines America's national identity. In the words of Arthur M. Schlesinger, Jr.: "They [multiculturalists] would have our educational system reinforce, promote, and perpetuate separate ethnic communities and do so at the expense of the idea of a common culture and a common national identity."[5]

Multiculturalists are not interested in teaching students to appreciate the contributions of different cultures in part because such an approach might lead to a greater appreciation of American culture. They find little to appreciate in American culture, believing it to be oppressive and imperialistic. Their main goal, as Lawrence Auster has observed, is apparently to find fault with America: "[M]ulticulturalism should be understood as an attempt, undertaken in our own schools, to tear down, discredit, and destroy the shared story that has made us a people and impose on us a different story which tells us our civilization and past history are essentially evil."[6] Lilian and Oscar Handlin have expressed similar sentiments: "The multiculturalist assault on the core themes of American education [is] part of a wider effort to redefine American civilization and genuinely to alter the country's character."[7]

"MULTICULTURALISM HONORS ALL CULTURES"

Multiculturalists' writings do *not* honor *all* cultures. They commonly portray Western or Euro-American culture in a negative light, and they selectively ignore prominent cultural contributions made by groups that are out-of-favor with their ideology.

Many multiculturalist school textbooks conspicuously overlook the immensely important contributions the Germans, for example, made as members of the Union Army during the American Civil War. Illinois, Indiana, Wisconsin, and Missouri in particular furnished many German regiments. One historian, William Burton, says that New York supplied seven German regiments and Ohio "created six to twelve German regiments."[8] According to Mrs. Jefferson Davis, the wife of the Confederate president, the Germans were vitally important to the northern cause: "without the Germans the North could never have overcome the armies of the Confederacy."[9]

The German contributions in the Civil War are ignored, however, and the Irish, Italians, and Swedes fare no better. They too added greatly to the Union army's success in defeating the Confederacy through their service in the military.[10]

While ignoring the significant contributions of large ethnic groups in America, multiculturalist textbooks often laud selected individuals from the "forgotten" groups. Such individuals often played relatively minor roles in American history. A fifth-grade text *United States and Its Neighbors* (1993), in discussing the Civil War, states: "Many black and white women fought another kind of war—with bandages and medicine. Nurse Clara Barton risked her life to tend to the wounded during fighting."[11] The new and highly controversial publication *National Standards for United States History* (1994), a landmark of multiculturalism attempts to demonstrate that women played a major role in the American War of Independence by showing a picture of Molly Pitcher, the hero of Monmouth, firing a cannon in place of her sunstricken husband. But no mention is made that Molly was a German descendant. Thus through mention of figures such as Molly Pitcher and Clara Barton special efforts are made to give attention to "neglected" folks, but to ask the question of comparative significance vis-à-vis the German and Irish contributions is considered politically incorrect.

Certainly, texts need to make amends for so long ignoring the accomplishments of women and black Americans, but in compensating for past omissions, multiculturalists commonly commit two errors. First, they exaggerate the role of women and some minority groups in historical events, and second they sometimes cite incidents and give credit to individuals that cannot be scholarly documented. (Chapter 4 discusses this problem in greater detail.) If the participation of one person, Clara Barton, for instance, merits inclusion as contributing to the successful conclusion of the Civil War, then on what basis do texts exclude the large numbers of Germans and Irish who participated in this war? This question is pertinent because multiculturalism portrays itself as appreciating *all* cultural and ethnic groups.

Individuals familiar with the multiculturalist's agenda know why they ignore the Civil War contributions of the Germans, Irish, and other participants of European descent: Since they are now part of the Euro-American culture in America, they need no accolades. As assimilated Americans, they have become the oppressors of America's underprivileged. Hence, the claim that multiculturalism appreciates all groups is false.

Actually, it is quite appropriate, especially in grade and high school textbooks, to omit reference to the Germans and Irish in discussions of the American Civil War because these people fought as Americans for an American cause, not as Germans or Irish. For more than 100 years the matter of what racial or ethnic groups participated in the Civil War was unimportant to textbook writers, and rightly so. But now that the multiculturalists have arrived, the idea is to highlight the contributions of groups not previously credited in order to raise their self-esteem. Critics like Arthur Schlesinger, Jr., call it "feel-good history."[12] However good their intentions, this can only make the nation overly race and ethnic conscious.

A SIMPLISTIC VIEW OF CULTURES

Numerous multiculturalists are seemingly unaware of the extreme complexity of cultures including those cultures that are illiterate and lack a highly developed technology. Richard J. Perry recently noted that multiculturalists, "despite their genuflection to the validity of other cultures, . . . fail to comprehend their complexity."[13] Multiculturalists often present other cultures uncritically, as though they were utopian entities. This is evident in the recent book *The Conquest of Paradise* (1991) by Kilpatrick Sale who portrays North American Indians as having lived in a virtual Garden of Eden until the white man came from Europe and ruined it all.

Multiculturalists also share the simplistic belief that the mere mention or showing of a few practices from other cultures to children in a textbook or on television will help them develop an understanding of such cultures. Consider the following. In a kindergarten school in Waterloo, Iowa, pupils are taught to count to ten in Swahili so that students will appreciate and understand the African culture of Swahili. Such a simplistic approach can give children no more appreciation or understanding of the Swahili culture than having them say *Gesundheit, wunderbar,* and *aufwiedersehen* will give them an understanding of the German culture.

The simple fact is that many multiculturalists are ignorant of other cultures, as most Americans have never been very interested in studying and learning about other cultures. It is for this reason that their portrayals of foreign cultures are so simplistic. If the proponents of multiculturalism really understood the complexities involved in learning about and understanding other cultures, they would realize that next to nothing is learned by focusing on some isolated practice of a largely unknown society. Cultures are extremely complex. They can rarely be understood by merely highlighting one or two cultural traits as many purportedly multiculturalist textbooks do. In reality, another culture can be understood only by immersing oneself in it for an extended time period, and often this requires learning the spoken language of that culture as well.

Multiculturalism's simplistic approach to other cultures may also be a way to compensate for failure to study and learn foreign languages. For years, colleges and universities have been jettisoning foreign language requirements from their degree programs. Gone are the courses in Latin or Greek, which were once required to earn a bachelor of arts degree. Since the 1970s graduate students in numerous American universities have not needed to take any foreign languages, not even for the doctor of philosophy (Ph.D.) degree. The scuttling of foreign languages in university undergraduate and graduate programs especially in the humanities and social sciences has produced students, teachers, and professors who today are some of the most vocal promoters of multiculturalism. It is in these academic areas that multiculturalism is most pronounced.

If multiculturalists are genuinely interested in having students gain a greater understanding of other cultures, they might begin by urging colleges and universities to bring back foreign language requirements for all degree programs. Those who have seriously studied foreign languages know that knowledge of a foreign language provides considerable understanding about the culture of which the language is an integral part. Perhaps if college and university students had not been deprived of studying foreign languages for so long, we might today have less simplistic portrayals of other cultures done in the name of multiculturalism. Individuals can learn little or nothing about other cultures by participating, say, in ethnic food fares. Such events, though interesting and entertaining, can hardly be considered multicultural.

American ignorance of other societies and cultures has evidently made multiculturalists feel guilty. What better way to absolve such guilt than to climb onto the multicultural bandwagon, which is seen as making amends for cultural ignorance. Moreover, the current push for multiculturalism is appealing because it does not demand acquiring any in-depth knowledge about other cultures. Having students read about the selected cultural practices of another society seems quite sufficient. In line with the current frenzy for purportedly learning about other cultures, kindergarten children in Iowa, for instance, are taught to count to ten in Swahili, as noted earlier. Apparently, learning a few Swahili words is considered adequate to make students aware of African culture. But how many teachers know that Swahili is also the language spoken by many nonblacks, the Arabs, in that part of Africa? And how many teachers know where the other countries of Swahili-speaking people are located on a world map? In a geography test published by *National Geographic* in 1989, twenty-three percent of Americans were unable to locate the Pacific Ocean on a blank globe and 51 percent did not know the location of South Africa.[14]

Teaching students a paltry sum of Swahili words reveals a simplistic view of culture, and it also fails to give a holistic view of the culture of which the Swahili language is a part. Moreover, it can give students the false impression that Africa has only one culture and one language, especially since the Swahili language is intended to present African culture. That Africa has at least 800 languages and about as many cultures does not appear to be important.

EQUATING CULTURE WITH RACE OR SKIN COLOR

In their eagerness to publicize multiculturalism, the popular print media and television try to present multiculturalism in colored pictures. The message here is that people with different skin colors represent different cultures. Such presentations give a distorted picture of culture; one might even call such attempts racist. Culture does not stem from people's genes or skin color. Rather culture consists of society's institutionalized values, beliefs, and practices that are *learned* through human interaction, not biologically inherited.

There is no such thing as a white, black, brown, or yellow culture, and yet multiculturalists are getting more and more Americans to think in these terms. Black Americans, for instance, have a very different culture than that of black people in African countries. Japanese descendants in America have absorbed cultural practices that are quite different than those of their relatives or friends in Japan. The same is true of Chinese descendants in the United States. When any of these life-long American residents visit the countries of their ancestors, their foreign friends or relatives see them as products of the American culture. The skin color might be the same, but the cultural habits they display are conspicuously different.

In order to promote minority or non-Western cultures, multiculturalists, like racists in America's past, are once again making people color-conscious. One publisher of multiculturalist materials advertises a video titled "Teaching Indians to be White." Linda Chavez says it well: "In the multiculturalists' world view, African-Americans, Puerto Ricans, or Chinese-Americans living in New York City have more in common with persons of their ancestral group living in Lagos or San Juan or Hong Kong than they do with other New Yorkers who are white. Culture becomes a fixed entity, transmitted, as it were, in the genes, rather than through experience.[15]

Consider this recent example. Robert Woodson, a black analyst of social problems, states that equating culture with skin color is penalizing black students. As proof, he cites an incident in which six black high school students were afraid to go up to the platform at graduation time to receive their academic awards of excellence because they did not want their black peers to think they were accepting "white" culture.[16]

NON-WESTERN CULTURES AS SACRED

The United States, like other societies, has benefited from constructive criticism of some of its cultural practices. But ardent multiculturalists scorn criticism of non-Western or minority cultures because to do so is being "bigoted" or "insensitive." Thus other cultures are never criticized, no matter how dysfunctional or inhumane some of the practices might be or have been. Foreign or non-Western cultures are almost sacred.

If cultures cannot be criticized, then how can bad, evil, or unjust practices be changed or eliminated? It was cultural criticism that led Americans to recognize that their segregation practices were unjust and had to be eliminated. This resulted in the comprehensive civil rights laws of the 1960s by which the country outlawed institutionalized racism. It became a better nation as a result.

To see any culture as sacred and beyond criticism is to treat it as an end in itself rather than as a means to an end. Culture exists to serve people, not the other way around. Thomas Sowell, the black American critic of multiculturalism, states: "Cultures exist so that people can know how to get food and put a roof over their head, how to cure the sick, how to cope with the death of loved ones, and how to get along with the living."[17]

Finally, culture is the product of human beings; as noted earlier, it is their society's institutionalized values, beliefs, and practices. These cultural elements are not necessarily more sacred, but they are often less so than the people to whom they belong. If people are flawed, for which we have centuries of evidence, then components of culture will also be flawed and thus in need of criticism, adjustment, or perhaps elimination.

MULTICULTURALISM AS A SOCIAL PANACEA

Multiculturalists are convinced that their philosophy will usher in a new millennium, enabling people to overcome cultural prejudice and discrimination. When prejudiced Americans, for example, finally learn something about cultures, they will drop their prejudices regarding other cultures, races, and ethnic groups. They will accept the customs of the other "peoples" on equal terms with their own. ("Peoples," rather than people, is a favorite multiculturalist term; it implies that each group keeps its own culture in contradistinction to assimilation.)

This multiculturalist stance, based on wishful thinking, comes primarily from the intellectuals, or the "overeducated,"[18] who frequently are self-appointed leaders of multiculturalism's propaganda. As alienated individuals, they are not interested in learning from the history of failed multiculturalist practices in other countries.

For example, multiculturalists promote their ideology even as daily they see the tragic events unfolding on television in the former Yugoslavia, whose multiculturalist practices so clearly demonstrate that such practices lead only to human hatred and bloodshed. The former Yugoslavia has long rejected cultural assimilation, retained ethnic consciousness, and kept multilingualism alive. It even operated with two alphabets, Latin and Cyrillic. The deleterious effects of these multicultural practices were already noted by Albert Bushnell Hart in 1915, more than a decade before the confederation of Yugoslavia came into being in 1929 and seventy-five years before the Balkan atrocities of the 1990s: "Nowhere . . . is there such a terrific feeling of hatred and determination to put down neighboring peoples."[19] The additional years of multiculturalist practices since 1915 have only intensified the Balkan rivalries. Thus today the Serbs, Croats, Bosnians, and other groups are killing each other with a vengeance. Only Slovenia, with its homogeneous (nonmulticultural) population, has been able to avoid the bloody conflagration by seceding early in this Balkan crisis.[20] The region is a veritable laboratory of failed multiculturalist practices.

In light of the Balkan disaster, why do intelligent people still promote multiculturalism? Why do they not see that multiculturalism does not work? It never has, and it never will, for as long as human nature remains what it always has been, multiculturalism will produce more ills than it will cure.

The promoters of multiculturalism in America are unhappy with their country's culture. They are alienated from its capitalistic, Eurocentric values, a culture that has given its people—including those who despise it—more prosperity, creature comforts, freedom, rights, and opportunity than any other culture in the world, past or present. Having lavishly benefited from the abundant fruits of this culture, often without real toil or effort on their part, they evidently see no challenges left for them. Life has been too easy, especially when compared to the Third World, for instance. Thus meaning and satisfaction lie in championing the cultures of other "peoples" and minority groups, who are "oppressed" by the Euro-American culture.

Multiculturalism's advocates believe that its ideology will usher in a noncapitalistic, non-Eurocentric, and nonoppressive society, and create a multicultural country, a utopia, one without "inequality" and "cultural imperialism." Working toward that goal gives the alienated more meaning in life. Moreover, if the multiculturalist utopia is not attained and America becomes culturally disunited in the process, multiculturalism will at least have ended the hegemony of that culture.

SUBCULTURES AND CONTRACULTURES EQUATED WITH CULTURE

When multiculturalists use the word "multicultural," they fail to define what they mean by "culture." They ignore longstanding definitions of culture presented by anthropologists and sociologists. Again, culture consists of a society's established and institutionalized values, beliefs, knowledge, and practices that are learned through human interaction. According to this definition, culture is the property of a society or a nation, an aggregate of people within given geographic boundaries. But multiculturalists apply the word "culture" to almost any group that has some behavioral variations from that of another. This is an ambiguous concept of culture. A group that has some behavioral variations vis-à-vis another does not necessarily make it a separate culture any more than some behavioral variations on the part of family members make them another family.

More specifically, by applying the word "culture" to any and all groups, multiculturalists fail to distinguish between the culture of a country and that of its subcultures and contracultures. Thus multiculturalists talk about the culture of minority groups as though they were entities separate from their country's culture at large, when in fact they are only subcultural groups, and thus are still part of their nation's common culture as well.

Distinguishing subcultures and contracultures from a country's majority culture was first done by Milton Yinger in 1960.[21] Subcultures, he said, are groups that hold to some values and practices that are different from the society's culture at large, but they also share many of the values and practices of their country's culture. Orthodox Jews in New York, the Amish in Pennsylvania, and the Hutterites in South Dakota are subcultural groups. All of them, however, are still part of their society's culture at large. They are not separate cultures.

Contracultures (or countercultures), though somewhat similar to subcultures, are groups whose beliefs and practices are largely illegal, harmful, and opposed to the society's majority culture. Some religious cults, Hells' Angels, neo-Nazis, and street gangs are contracultures.

Equating subcultural and even countercultural groups with culture on a societal level also ignores an important fact of American history, namely, that most subcultural groups in the United States in time relinquished their differences as the nation's culture assimilated them. Subcultural groups of immigrants in America in time gave up their subcultural ways as they became assimilated Americans. This demonstrates the premise that equating subcultural groups with a country's culture is neither historically nor conceptually accurate.

Equating subcultures and countercultures with the culture of a society also lends legitimacy, at least implicitly, to their deviant values and practices that are often detrimental to the society's majority culture. This is especially true with regard to countercultural groups.

Finally, if subcultural and even countercultural groups are equated with the culture of a country in which they exist, one must ask how long will that country's majority culture remain viable? Logic would indicate that such an equation will eventually weaken and diminish the country's common culture and perhaps lower it to the level of its subcultures or, worse, to its countercultures.

AMERICAN REGIONAL (STATE) VARIATIONS EQUATED WITH CULTURE

Multiculturalists falsely picture regional variations in the American culture—and most of these are minor—as different cultures. Thus they speak about the culture of Oklahoma versus the culture of Illinois, or the Southern culture opposed to the Northern culture. Such expressions are misleading. Doing certain things differently in different regions within the United States does not necessarily reflect different cultures but only minor variations within the same larger American culture. Such variations usually are not even equal to differences found in subcultures. They certainly are not marks of separate cultures.

Equating regional (state) variations of American culture within the country's culture conveys a tacit multiculturalist message—namely, if the variations among the fifty American states or regions are not problematic, then why might there be any problems in accepting multiculturalism? This portrait softens resistance to the promotion and implementation of multiculturalism's agenda.

"MULTICULTURALISM IS DEMOCRATIC"

This statement, often bandied about by multiculturalists, is an extremely deceptive portrait, for it gives the impression that multiculturalism is truly a democratic philosophy. Because Americans see democracy in a rather sacred light, anything that is associated with democracy is thus accepted without question.

Individuals who think that multiculturalism is a reflection of democracy should know that multiculturalists are actually opposed to traditional democracy. As John Fonte notes, "Multiculturalists are extremely uncomfortable with any form of majoritarianism [rule by a majority] and even with the very idea of an American people."[22] They are determined to use the term *peoples* rather than *people.* The term *people* connotes a unified, assimilated population, a phenomenon that multiculturalists do not favor. The term *peoples,* on the other hand, accents separate cultural groups. Thus in New York State's curriculum guide the United States, as Fonte shows, is pictured as "one nation, many peoples." This guide, produced in 1991, attempts to indoctrinate public schools with multiculturalist ideology. This sixty-five-page document uses the word "peoples" over and over, but it never uses the expression "the American people." Fonte points out that "If there is no people (as in 'We the people . . . '), but rather many 'peoples,' the concepts of popular sovereignty and majority rule become meaningless."[23]

To champion the rights of "peoples," as multiculturalism does, is contrary to the foundations of traditional democratic freedoms which have their roots in individual rights, not group or peoples' rights. The suppression of individual rights in history, for example, in Nazi Germany and the former Soviet Union, also brought the death of democracy and freedom. Thus the rhetoric of multiculturalism that portrays its goals as democratic is false. Once individuals and their rights are subordinated to a group or some collectivity, democracy becomes an empty term. That was the situation in the former communist countries of Eastern Europe. Each one of these countries in the post–World War II era used the word "democratic" in its official name, but there was no democracy. It was a cruel charade. Individual rights were suppressed in favor of the ultimate group's rights, the Communist party; in Nazi Germany, group rights meant the rights of Nazi groups.

"AMERICA IS A MULTICULTURAL SOCIETY"

This oft-repeated assertion simply does not square with the facts. When foreigners who have observed Americans, either in the United States or overseas, are asked whether Americans convey multicultural behavioral patterns, all see Americans conspicuously revealing a decided monoculture, not a multicultural image.

Those who are unfamiliar with multiculturalism can be forgiven for accepting the false claim that America is, and always has been a multicultural society. But what are we to make of those who know better and still try to paint this false portrait? For instance, Ronald Takaki, a Berkeley professor, uses the subtitle *A History of Multicultural America* for his book's main title, *A Different Mirror* (1993).

It is far more accurate to say that the United States is a multiethnic, not a multicultural, country. It has received and assimilated large numbers of ethnic groups which, after a couple of generations, still retain some ethnic awareness. Often that awareness, however, is rather vague. The country, of course, also has ethnic groups who arrived more recently. These have a stronger ethnic identity than did earlier migrants. But America has never been, nor is it now, a multicultural society in the sense of the former Yugoslavia or the former Soviet Union.

All sorts of ethnic groups (Germans, Irish, French, Italians, Poles, Czechs, Ukrainians, Swedes, Russians, Greeks, African ethnics) came to America, bringing with them their unique cultural customs and habits. By the third generation, however, their ethnic ways were commonly abandoned in favor of the American culture.

The United States is not a multicultural society with a German culture, Dutch culture, Greek culture, African culture, or the like. They do not exist. There may indeed be an annual German Oktoberfest, a Greek festival, or a Dutch tulip festival, but these and other ethnic festivities only reveal a "symbolic ethnicity," as Herbert Gans appropriately calls such events.[24] These "ethnics" do not see themselves as having or maintaining a foreign culture. Rather, they all see themselves as Americans. Nor do their friends or relatives in the country of their ancestors see them as one of their own culturally.

Finally, to argue that the United States is a multicultural society is also a puzzling assertion. If that were true, then why do the multiculturalists say American schools, universities, churches, and businesses need to introduce and establish multicultural programs and policies? One cannot introduce something that already is in existence.

"MULTICULTURALISM IS NON-ETHNOCENTRIC"

For years social scientists have defined ethnocentrism, a key concept in introductory sociology textbooks, as the belief of individuals that their group or culture is superior to all others. Some would also add that ethnocentrism prevents individuals from examining their group's shortcomings, thus depriving them of realizing that their group could benefit from necessary and meaningful change.

Multiculturalists themselves may not be ethnocentric, in that they so frequently find fault with their own society's (American) culture, but they unwittingly encourage ethnocentrism as they urge groups from minority cultures not to give up their non-American values and practices. America is to accept their culture. With such urging, these groups sometimes claim that their culture is superior to the American culture. The current phenomenon of Afrocentrism is one such example.

Ideological multiculturalists have a real blindspot, being quick to label those who disagree with them as ethnocentric, but failing to see ethnocentrism operating in the behavior they promote on behalf of non-Western or minority cultures. Thus one rarely, if ever, sees textbooks in sociology or anthropology—which now are strongly biased in favor of multiculturalism—apply the concept of ethnocentrism to minority cultural beliefs or practices.

Multiculturalists do their utmost to get school textbooks to cast the best light on the accomplishments of non-Western or minority ethnic groups. Harriet Tubman, for instance, is lauded as having been a courageous black woman who helped black Americans escape to the North by way of the Underground Railroad. Squanto is cited in textbooks for the help he gave the Pilgrims. And so on. While this approach has some merit, it also is fraught with the potential of producing ethnocentrism.

Contributions made to American culture by individuals from different minorities should not cast glory on any group, but rather should honor the nation that produced and nourished such individuals. That kind of approach would be far more beneficial to children of minority and non-minority groups than aiming for self-esteem on the basis of cultural or ethnic identity.

MULTICULTURALISM'S REAL PORTRAIT

The recently constructed (1995) exhibit of the *Enola Gay* at the Smithsonian Institution is a pertinent illustration of multiculturalism's real portrait. This exhibit was scrapped just before its official unveiling, because World War II veterans, concerned citizens, and members of the U.S. Congress voiced their objections upon seeing what the multiculturalist revisionists were doing to historical facts as well as to U.S. integrity. The display stated that the Americans, in the war with Japan, victimized the Japanese and that it was a war in which the Japanese had " 'to defend their unique culture against Western imperialism.' "[25]

Shortly before his death in 1994, Russell Kirk stated:

Multiculturalism is animated by envy and hatred. Some innocent persons have assumed that a multicultural program in schools would consist of discussing the latest number of *National Geographic* in a classroom. That is not at all what the multiculturalists intend. Detesting the achievements of Anglo-American culture, they propose to substitute for real history and real literature—and even for real natural science—an invented myth that all things good came out of Africa and Asia (chiefly Africa).[26]

A similar assessment is offered by Diane Ravitch. She notes that multiculturalists and their sympathizers "seem to celebrate everything that is non-white, non-Western, and non-male, while criticizing everything that isn't."[27] Another observer, Dwight Murphey, states that the current phenomenon of teaching multiculturalism in our schools "is far from a mere academic exercise; it is a struggle for our heart and soul—for our collective memory and self-perception."[28]

Finally, let us hear from another multiculturalist, George Gheverghese Joseph, who thinks that even mathematics must become a multicultural exercise. Like other pro-multiculturalists, Joseph does not want multicultural education to teach merely about other cultures. Instead, multicultural education should bring about "a form of *affective* [sic] commitment, even involving 'initiation' into other cultures."[29]

These observations, along with those already cited, show that the ideology of multiculturalism is not a benign phenomenon. Many of America's current racial tensions may already be the result of multiculturalism's propaganda that urges various groups to become race and color conscious. As noted in Chapter 6, numerous colleges and universities have in recent years fostered and implemented separate housing, graduations, and even yearbooks for different racial groups. The emphasis on racial integration which was so prominent in the early 1960s, and justly so, is being replaced by a growing racial/color consciousness. Martin Luther King's plea that Americans judge one another on the content of character is being rapidly subverted.

The false portraits discussed in this chapter have enabled multiculturalists to move their Trojan horse into the schools, universities, churches, and businesses of America. Whether enough Americans will see the true portrait of multiculturalism before it is too late remains to be seen.

NOTES

1. Karl Mannheim, *Ideology and Utopia: An Introduction to the Sociology of Knowledge,* Trans. Louis Wirth and Edward Shils (New York: Harcourt, Brace, 1936), p. 40.

2. Jack Weatherford, *Native Roots: How the Indians Enriched America* (New York: Crown, 1991), p. 204.

3. Robert Hughes, "The Fraying of America," *Time,* 3 February 1992, 47.

4. AACTE *Bulletin,* 1973.

5. Cited in "Schlesinger Assails Multicultural 'Mystique,' " *American Experiment* (spring 1994): 6.

6. Lawrence Auster, *The Path to National Suicide* (Monterey, Va.: American Immigration Foundation, 1990), p. 34.

7. Lilian Handlin and Oscar Handlin, "America and Its Discontents," *The American Scholar* (winter 1995): 35–36.

8. William L. Burton, *Melting Pot Soldiers: The Union's Ethnic Regiments* (Ames: Iowa State University Press, 1988), p. 92.

9. John W. Burgess, *The European War of 1914: Its Causes, Purposes, Probable Results* (Chicago: A. C. McClurg, 1915), p. 121.

10. Burton, *Melting Pot Soldiers*, pp. 112–154.

11. James A. Banks et al., *United States and Its Neighbors* (New York: Macmillan/McGraw-Hill, 1993), p. 441.

12. Arthur Schlesinger, Jr., *The Disuniting of America* (New York: W. W. Norton, 1991), p. 98.

13. Richard J. Perry, "Why Do Multiculturalists Ignore Anthropologists?" *The Chronicle for Higher Education*, 4 March 1992, A52.

14. "Take the Gallup Geography Test," *National Geographic* 176 (December 1989): pp. 818–821.

15. Linda Chavez, "Demystifying Multiculturalism," *National Review*, 21 February 1994, 26.

16. Joseph G. Conti and Brad Stetson, *Challenging the Civil Rights Establishment: Profiles of a New Black Vanguard* (Westport, Conn.: Praeger Publishers, 1993), p. 159.

17. Thomas Sowell, "A World View of Cultural Diversity," *Society* (November/December 1991): 43.

18. I am indebted to James Q. Wilson for this label for those who pride themselves as intellectuals. See his article, "Against Homosexual Marriage," *Commentary* (March 1996): 36.

19. Albert Bushnell Hart, "Antecedents of the Balkan Crisis," *The Outlook*, 27 October 1915, 516.

20. Misha Glenny, *The Fall of Yugoslavia* (New York: Penguin Books, 1993), p. 177. See also Vladimir Dedijer et al., *History of Yugoslavia* (New York: McGraw-Hill, 1974).

21. J. Milton Yinger, "Contraculture and Subculture," *American Sociological Review* (October 1960): 625–635.

22. John Fonte, "Ill Liberalism," *National Review*, 6 February 1995, 49.

23. Ibid., p. 49.

24. Herbert Gans, "Symbolic Ethnicity: The Future of Ethnic Groups and Cultures in America," *Ethnic and Racial Studies* 2 (1979): 1–20.

25. John Leo, "The National Museums of PC," *U.S. News and World Report*, 10 October 1994, 21.

26. Russell Kirk, *America's British Culture* (New Brunswick, N.J.: Transaction Publishers, 1993), p. 92.

27. Cited by Karen J. Winkler, "Who Owns History?" *The Chronicle for Higher Education*, 20 January 1995, A11.

28. Dwight D. Murphey, "The Historic Dispossessions of the American Indian: Did It Violate American Ideals?" *Journal of Social, Political, and Economic Studies* 16 (fall 1991): 349.

29. George Gheverghese Joseph, "A Rationale for a Multicultural Approach to Mathematics," *Multicultural Mathematics*, ed. David Nelson et al. (New York: Oxford University Press, 1993), p. 3.

Chapter 3

Multiculturalism's Leftist (Marxist) Concepts

False words are not only evil . . . but they infect the soul with evil.
Plato

Communism may be dead, but the leftist (Marxist) ideology is still alive and well. Thomas Sowell recently said: "Marxism . . . continues to flourish on American college campuses, as perhaps nowhere else in the world."[1] Sowell's remark is corroborated by a 1992 conference, "Marxism in the New World Order: Crises and Possibilities," held at the University of Massachusetts at Amherst. Only 300 were expected to attend, but 1,500 registered. Nearly all were professors. The conference's attendees were diehard believers of Marxism,[2] not realists who recognized that the most inefficient, cruel, and inhumane socioeconomic system had come to an end.

Marxism flourishes in the ideology and politics of present-day multiculturalism. Some multiculturalist advocates, including many well-meaning teachers and school administrators, are not aware of the leftist (Marxist) concepts and assumptions operative in multiculturalism. Unwittingly, they often give aid and comfort to a radical leftist philosophy. If the unsuspecting advocates of multiculturalist practices were aware of the Marxist threads in the fabric of multiculturalism, they would be a lot less eager to advance its principles and policies. Most, I suspect, would resist the phenomenon outright. Marxist concepts and principles, even during the Great Depression of the 1930s, had no real appeal to most Americans. Thus those promoters of multiculturalism who know that their movement is imbued with Marxist assumptions are careful not to make this known to the American public, for that would squelch their efforts to create a multiculturalist society.

"DOWN WITH INEQUALITY"

One Marxist concept operative in multiculturalism is its belief that all inequalities, including cultural inequality, are evil. Thus in the eyes of multiculturalists all cultures are to be equally valued. To believe and argue that some cultures are superior or inferior to others is heresy to all true-believing multiculturalists.

Karl Marx saw inequality in the context of economics, and for him it was one of the greatest evils of mankind. Extending the concept of inequality to culture, multiculturalists argue that cultural inequality is evil, the product of "cultural imperialists." (Imperialism is another Marxian concept.) Thus multiculturalism sees the inequality of cultures as an evil that must be uprooted by teaching students in grade and high schools, as well as in colleges, that all cultures must be equally valued. The expression "equally valued" was used by the multiculturalist promoters of New York City's proposed Curriculum of Inclusion (also known as the Rainbow Curriculum) of 1993.

Textbooks that promote multiculturalism deliberately overlook any empirical data and examples that show cultures of many different societies to be highly unequal. For instance, textbooks in the humanities and social studies commonly fail to cite inhumane cultural practices such as the torturous sun dance of the Plains Indians which was performed during the 1700s and 1800s until the United States government outlawed it in the 1880s. Nor do most texts mention the cannibalism or human sacrifices once practiced by many Indian tribes. Thus multiculturalists sanitize those cultures that have prominently unequal cultural practices and report only those customs that make minority cultures look good.

Intent on promoting their point of view, multiculturalists often manage to get administrators and faculty in high schools and universities to introduce highly particularistic, ethnocentric course offerings into the curricula designed to lead students to see all cultures, subcultures, and even countercultural groups as essentially equal. For instance, Duke University now offers courses in "Queer Theory" and "Feminist Criticism." At Syracuse University (New York) students can no longer enroll in a conventional Shakespeare course; it is now listed as "Shakespeare and the Boundaries of Genre." These offerings and many others like them are preferred to traditional courses and will supposedly remove inequality.

In recent years, multiculturalists have attacked the educational canon in universities and colleges, as well as in grade and high schools, for fostering inequality. Traditional, even classical works by authors who have been the staple of Western education for centuries—among them Homer, Sophocles, Plato, Aristotle, St. Augustine, Dante, Luther, Locke, Shakespeare, Hobbes, Milton, and Bunyan—are being replaced, either in part or totally. Multiculturalists have dubbed these authors "dead white European males" (DWEMs) because they purportedly have nothing meaningful or helpful to say to minorities, women, and homosexuals, the defined victims of inequality. The literature of DWEMs is labeled sexist, racist, class-biased, and homophobic.

Ironically, the disciples of multiculturalism, who worship at the shrine of Marxism, conveniently forget that Marx, too, was a DWEM. In making this observation, I am guilty of a major multiculturalist sin: logocentrism. That is, I am using logic whose roots are in "Eurocentric" reasoning and thus contrary to the norms of multiculturalism. Many people of other cultures that we are asked to recognize and accept don't think logically like Westerners, say the multiculturalists.

By focusing on courses that are extremely ethnocentric, however, when and where will students learn about human experiences that transcend the trinity of race, gender, and class? That is what the classics are all about. As George Will states, the classics "instruct us in history, irony, wit, tragedy, pathos, and delight."[3] They prepare students to understand, appreciate, and cope with life's challenges. W.E.B. Du Bois also was conversant with the multiculturalists' despised canon but spoke movingly of the spiritual solace it provided: "I sit with Shakespeare and he winces not. Across the color line I move arm in arm with Balzac and Dumas. . . . I summon Aristotle and Aurelius and what soul I will, and they come all graciously with no scorn nor condescension. So, wed with Truth, I dwell above the veil."[4] To him, the timeless wisdom of the classical works spoke to all people and races, not just to whites of European ancestry. Were he alive today, it is not very likely that he would favor the ethnocentric course offerings that focus on the underclasses or minority cultures advocated by today's multiculturalists.

"DOWN WITH WESTERN IMPERIALISM"

Multiculturalists frequently invoke the Marxian concept of imperialism but have given the concept a neo-Marxian meaning. They state, for instance, that Western or Euro-American culture in the United States has been imperialistic because it has displaced the American Indian cultures.

They also apply the concept of cultural imperialism to societies that have a monolingual culture as opposed to one that is bilingual or trilingual. The United States is guilty of cultural imperialism because its monolinguistic culture displaced the prior existing linguistic and cultural groups of the American Indians. Tony Hall, a Canadian multiculturalist, maintains that cultural imperialism is at work whenever countries such as Canada and the United States do not officially uphold and support the prior-existing languages and cultures of the North American Indians.[5]

FALSE CONSCIOUSNESS

Marx contended that the working class (the proletariat) was unable to see the misery and inequality that capitalists (the bourgeoisie) imposed on them because of the working class's false consciousness. The Marxist-influenced multiculturalists have adapted this doctrine to condemn their opponents: that is, anyone who fails to see that the American culture has oppressed women, immigrants, and minorities is living in a state of false consciousness. To excise this major social problem, multiculturalists are introducing culturally diverse course offerings into the university curricula. Such courses are intended to remove the false consciousness on the part of women and cultural minorities.

"DOWN WITH 'OPPRESSION' "

The multiculturalists have taken another concept from Marx's lexicon, namely, "oppression." They argue that a society's majority culture—like America's "Eurocentric" culture—oppresses minority, immigrant cultures by expecting these cultures to relinquish their beliefs and customs and to be absorbed into the greater society's national culture.

In 1991, the Department of English at the University of Texas in Austin proposed revising its required freshman composition course by having the course focus on reading and writing about diversity and difference, two favorite multiculturalist buzzwords. The new course proposal caused considerable shock and consternation among many faculty members, one of whom lamented: "Where we used to have chapters devoted to grammar, we now have chapters devoted to oppression."[6] Also in 1991 a professor at Duke University, an opponent of multiculturalism, criticized the university for engaging in "oppression criticism."[7] But separating the so-called oppressed from the oppressors is not practiced just at the University of Texas and at Duke University. It has become common on many college and university campuses.

Oppression is a favorite word for multiculturalists and so is used freely and sometimes inappropriately. In a work on integrating women into the educational curricula, one writer asks: "Who oppressed women, and why were they oppressed?"[8] Writing about power disparities in educational settings, this author concludes that women are oppressed because men have deprived them of power and influence in shaping school curricula.

Another multiculturalist, William R. Jones, asserts that oppression exists "whenever one group accumulates a surplus of power and is able to use that power as the basis for institutionalizing whatever their [sic] prejudices or their [sic] biases are."[9] One way to fight oppression, Jones advises, is to take required courses in multiculturalism, as every student now must, for instance, at Florida State University. As Jonathan Rauch says, the word "oppression" has become "a one-size-fits-all political designation," and it is "used by anyone who feels unequal, aggrieved or even uncomfortable."[10]

"REVOLUTIONIZE AMERICA"

In his *Theses on Feuerbach*, Karl Marx preached revolution: "The philosophers have only interpreted the world differently; the point is, to change [revolutionize] it."[11] While many multiculturalists may have never heard or read this statement, they have definitely been influenced by his revolutionary thoughts. They have a tremendous dislike, even hatred, for the United States and for its history of cultural assimilation. Their goal is to transform the United States from a culturally assimilated (melting pot) society to an unassimilated multicultural society with a wide variety of cultures, subcultures, and linguistic groups spread across the country's landscape and accorded equal status. Multiculturalists seek to create and "celebrate diversity" and are not concerned that their diversity methods may ultimately balkanize and divide the United States.

Multiculturalists, influenced by Marxist thinking, appear to want America to become a divided country. The reason goes back to the Marxists' hatred of capitalism, especially in the United States which has practiced it with such eminent success. American capitalism, with some modifications, has clearly outperformed and defeated Marxist socialism (communism) in Eastern Europe and the former Soviet Union, and no true Marxist is thrilled with that outcome. Thus it is neither paranoia nor conspiratorial thinking to imagine that true Marxists, unable to destroy the United States through Soviet communism, desire to achieve their goal by some other method. And the method they have used is to inject multiculturalism into America's schools, universities, churches, and businesses. This conclusion unequivocally fits the Marxist paradigm for radically changing the world to conform to its founder's words: "Our task is not to interpret the world but to change it." America is not exempted.

In keeping with Marx's goal of changing the world, Marxists have traditionally favored disruptive, revolutionary tactics. Ponder the following words of Karl Marx and his cohort, Friedrich Engels: "The Communists [Marxists] everywhere support every revolution movement against the existing social and political order of things."[12] Empowered by the spirit of Marxism, multiculturalism is a revolutionary movement. Its devoted followers know their movement has the potential of destroying cultural assimilation in the United States, an objective very much desired by them.

THE ROLE OF ALIENATION

According to Marx, the proletariat was alienated from the goods it produced as well as from the capitalistic system that was the cause of its alienation. Whether the workers really were alienated in Marx's day remains an unanswered question, for no empirical studies show that they were. Some scholars of Marx say that Marx knew this too. That is why he insisted that workers would never do certain things themselves, but that changes would have to be done for them by their socialist leaders. Knowing this to be true, why did he write so dogmatically about alienation? Marx himself was extremely alienated, a nonproletariat, and he projected his own dislike for the capitalist system and his alienation from it onto the working class. Here we can point out a striking parallel among the true believers of multiculturalism. They too are alienated; they hate the American culture, which like capitalism in Marx's eyes, must be replaced. Marx wanted capitalism replaced by communism, which would end alienation and produce a worker's utopia of equality in which everyone would work "from each according to his ability, to each according to his need." The alienated multiculturalists want to replace the assimilated American culture with a multiplicity of other cultures, which they say will create a utopia of cultural equality with no more alienation, in which people of many different cultures—a "salad bowl" as they call it—will no longer be dominated and oppressed by the dominant Euro-American culture.

Educators, businessmen, and church leaders everywhere have naively accepted and promoted the multiculturalist movement under the guise of democracy and toleration. Are they aware of the movement's Marxist underpinnings? Have they any inkling that it will eventually destroy the nation's traditional culture? Indeed, if multiculturalism continues to grow, America will become an arena of ethnic-tribal groups, each intolerant of other ethnics, each group seeing itself as superior to the others. Each group's different values and lifestyles will invariably clash with those of other entities. Gone will be America's common cultural bond that has been the envy of the world. Though imperfect, the melting pot has worked remarkably well for more than 300 years. What the American Civil War, the two world wars, and the "Evil Empire" of communism were not able to do, the multiculturalists may yet accomplish—that is, destroy American culture, especially its many freedoms, its Judeo-

Christian value system, its economic prosperity, and, of course, its melting pot.

"KNOWLEDGE AND TRUTH ARE SOCIALLY CONSTRUCTED"

The Judeo-Christian/Western tradition has for centuries maintained that the world was purposefully created by God, who posited universal, objective knowledge and truth that were discoverable by and applicable to all humans. This knowledge and truth were not bound to any social class, group, or culture, and they were indeed discernible through sound human reason and logic if people would seriously examine the evidence. Finally, all human beings were subservient to this objective knowledge and truth. This understanding of knowledge and truth held sway until Marx came along and argued that there was no God and thus no objective knowledge or truth: "It is not the consciousness of men that determines their existence, but on the contrary, their social existence determines their consciousness."[13]

If one substitutes the word "consciousness" for objective knowledge or truth, it becomes apparent that Marx jettisoned the Judeo-Christian/Western concept of knowledge and truth. For Marx, knowledge or truth arises only out of people's social existence. Thus different social situations (social classes, as Marx would say) produce different knowledge or truth, and so truth is always relative; it is never absolute. Truth neither transcends nor applies to all people's social experiences or to their cultures; truth, knowledge, or morality are all culturally relative. And since knowledge or truth arises from people's social existence, it is a product of their interaction and thus created by them. Knowledge or truth is therefore a servant of the people just as is any other product created by them. This means that people no longer are servants of the truth, as Western philosophy has held for centuries. Now, as multiculturalists say, truth must serve the "peoples."

NOTES

1. Thomas Sowell, "The Road to Hell Is Paved with Good Intentions," *Forbes*, 17 January 1994, 62.

2. Andre Ryerson, "Whither Marxism?" *Academic Questions* (spring 1993): 71–75.

3. George Will, "Commencement at Duke," *The American Scholar* (autumn 1991): 500.

4. W.E.B. Du Bois, *The Souls of Black Folk* (1903; reprint, New York: Alfred A. Knopf, 1993), p. 89.

5. Tony Hall, "Imperialism and Canada," *The Canadian Forum* (October 1994): 47.

6. Gary Gregg, "Campus Wire," *Campus* (winter 1991): 13.

7. Ibid., p. 13.

8. Mary Kay Thompson Tetreault, "Integrating Content about Women and Gender into the Curriculum," in *Multicultural Education: Issues and Perspectives,* ed. James A. Banks and Cherry McGee Banks (Boston: Allyn and Bacon, 1989).

9. William R. Jones, "Oppression, Race, and Humanism," *The Humanist* (November/December 1992): 7.

10. Jonathan Rauch, "Beyond Oppression," *The New Republic,* 10 May 1993, 18.

11. Karl Marx, "Theses on Feuerbach," *The German Ideology,* Parts I and II (1846; reprint, New York: International Publishers, 1947), p. 199.

12. Karl Marx and Friedrich Engels, *The Communist Manifesto,* ed. Samuel H. Beer (New York: Appleton-Century-Crofts, 1955), p. 46.

13. Karl Marx, *A Contribution to the Critique of Political-Economy* (1859; reprint, New York: International Publishers, 1970), p. 21.

Chapter 4

All Cultures Are Not Equal

I am ... convinced that all that one gets from studying foreign culture is a token understanding.

Edward T. Hall, *The Silent Language*

The doctrine of cultural relativity has led multiculturalists to the conclusion that all cultures are essentially equal and thus to be equally valued. They sometimes use the term *cultural interdependence* to convey their notion of cultural equality. This notion was largely responsible for New York City's proposed Curriculum of Inclusion, the so-called Rainbow Curriculum, in 1993. Its proponents tried to persuade the school board and parents that all cultures, including subcultural groups such as homosexuals and lesbians, deserved equal educational consideration because they were to be equally valued.

EXAMINING CULTURAL EQUALITY

The multiculturalist theory of cultural equality underlying the Rainbow Curriculum was rejected by a majority of New York City's school board after large numbers of irate black, white, and Hispanic parents protested its content. The board also fired the curriculum's chief architect, Joseph Fernandez.[1]

The argument that all cultures are essentially equal does not stand up under empirical scrutiny and is plainly contradicted by people's everyday experiences. In this connection, Allan Bloom has aptly observed:

Culture means a war against chaos and a war against other cultures. The very idea of culture carries with it a value: man needs culture and must do what is necessary to create and maintain culture. There is no place for a theoretical man to stand. . . . [T]he political or moral cultural relativist of the ordinary sort is doomed to have no culture.[2]

Evidently, the parents in New York City understood what Allan Bloom was saying when they rejected the proposed curriculum and its cultural equality posture.

Multiculturalists simply ignore any culture that contradicts their claim that all cultures are of equal value. If they are indeed equal, then no one can make a logical objection to the culture of the Ku Klux Klan, to Hindus in India burning a widow on her husband's funeral pyre, to the Neo-Nazis, or to any cultural custom or belief, no matter how outlandish or horrid. To say that all cultures are of equal value is to give these particular cultures equal honor and respect. The following section cites some cultures and their practices to test the validity of the cultural equality theory. Interestingly, such examples are commonly omitted from textbooks authored by multiculturalists.

The Dobuan Culture

The Dobuans live in Melanesia, a series of islands northeast of Australia. A child in the Dobuan culture enters a world where the father resents his or her birth because he must now abstain from sexual intercourse with his wife until the child is weaned.[3] The child commonly receives care and love not from the father but from the mother's brothers. Frequently, the mother offers very little nurturance as well. Early in life the child is exposed to sorcery and witchcraft, which is taken with the utmost seriousness. The Dobuans believe that all human events are the result of sorcery. Thus, everyday associates are seen as sorcerers who threaten one's daily life and affairs. Yam crops grow only if they have been successfully stolen from one's neighbors through magic and witchcraft. Benedict says: "A good crop is a confession of theft."[4] Thus gardens are physically guarded. Trust among the Dobuans is essentially nonexistent; they see suspicion and deception as virtues. It is taken for granted that every good man has stolen, deceived others, and killed children. Theft and adultery are "valued charms of the valued men of the community."[5] Every Dobuan lives in fear of being poisoned. Even husbands and wives do not trust each other.

Dobuan life is virtually devoid of humor or mirth. Arguments and conflict are seen as heightening the possibility of being poisoned. All the same, avoiding conflict is no assurance that one is safe. Friends may be polite and calm in order to catch off-guard the one they want to harm.

The Dobuans have other macabre cultural practices. For instance, when a person dies, the brothers and sisters of the deceased are required to sleep by the corpse, each holding on to the cooking pot that is placed over the corpse's head.[6] For the Dobuans the concept of accidents is nonexistent; therefore, all unfortunate events and incidents are attributed to witchcraft or sorcery.[7]

Dobuans are not born distrustful, hostile, deceitful, jealous, suspicious, and sorcery minded. They learn and internalize these characteristics from their culture.

The Alorese Culture

The Alorese are inhabitants of the East Indies. Research published by Cora Du Bois in the 1940s revealed that the Alorese mothers feed their infant children irregularly and inconsistently. Crying is sometimes heeded and sometimes totally ignored. After age one children are responsible for their own feeding, which forces young toddlers to beg from other children. Mothers commonly try to arouse jealously among their children. By brandishing knives the mother will, on many occasions, threaten to slice off her children's ears or hands. Between the ages of two and five, the average child engages in frequent and violent temper tantrums.

One Alorese nursery tale conveys parental dislike, even trickery, with regard to children in their primary years. It depicts a mother telling her child to get some water with a bamboo tube that has a hole punctured in it by the mother, secretly and deliberately. As the child desperately attempts to fill the tube with water, the mother and father desert the child, telling him that his bad behavior prompted the desertion. At the son's wedding, the parents reappear and present him and his wife with a basket of rice and some bamboo tubes that appear to be filled with blood sausage. Later as the young man and his wife open these gifts, they discover that the tubes contain only feces, and the basket of rice has only empty hulls. Speaking of children's behavior, Du Bois says: "Rages are so consistent, so widespread, and of such long duration among young children that they were one of my first and most striking observations."[8]

The Kukukuku Culture

New Guinea has numerous cultural groups, one of which is the Kukukuku culture, whose people not only terrorize neighboring tribes but also take many of them as prisoners. Once taken captive, prisoners' legs are broken, and then they are killed by the captors' children. The prisoners also have their legs and arms cut off, after which the flesh is cut into small pieces, wrapped in bark, cooked, and then eaten. "The young men," says Jens Bjerre, "are not really considered worth while until they have killed somebody."[9] And when twins are born, one is killed and thrown away.[10]

When a wife dies, the husband and daughters sleep with the corpse. According to the mourning ritual, the bereaved beat themselves with sharp flints until blood flows. Their dead are not buried but are instead taken to a rock hill, where their heads are propped up by arrows so that they look down on the green valley below.[11]

The "Giraffe" Women of Burma

In Burma (Myanmar) the Padaung tribe (numbering about 7,000 members) fashions several loops of a brass rod (about a third of an inch in diameter) around the neck of a girl when she is about five years old. As she gets older, more loops are added. Each added ring (loop) creates downward pressure on the vertebral column, pushing the chest, the collarbones, and the ribs downward. The net effect of about twenty pounds of coils is the creation of an extremely elongated neck. In addition, women are required to wear another thirty pounds of brass coils on their arms and legs. These brass rings severely impede the women's ability to walk, and when they do walk, they invariably waddle. Given their stretched necks, women cannot drink water in the normal manner, and so they are forced to sip with a straw. Their voices sound like noises in the shaft of a well, one observer noted.

The Padaung culture argues that the brass rings serve to protect the women from tigers. In reality, however, the practice enhances tribal identity. It has also served as a way to punish adulterous women: when the brass rings are removed the woman's head drops forward, causing her to suffocate. In 1979, the custom of giraffe-like necks among Padaung women was very much alive and growing in popularity.[12] Even today (1996), this rather inhuman practice is culturally intact.

Female Clitoridectomy

In recent years, much has been written about the practice of female clitoridectomies in many African countries. To some degree, it is also being practiced in Europe and in America by many recent African emigrants. Many Western countries such as Canada, France, Sweden, England, and some American states have outlawed the practice.

Clitoridectomy is an age-old cultural practice. One source says that it is done in twenty-six African countries with a prevalency rate ranging from 5 to 99 percent.[13] Even in medicine, the act is sometimes erroneously called female circumcision. Whatever criticism has been made regarding male circumcision, and there is a considerable amount, it is in no way similar to the controversy over clitoridectomy. Minimally, clitoridectomy involves the removal of a girl's clitoris. Frequently, however, the act also includes removing the inner and outer labia, and sometimes "almost all of the girl's genitalia are cut away and the remaining flesh from the outer labia is sewn together, or infibulated, and the girl's legs are bound from ankle to waist for several weeks while scar tissue closes up the vagina almost completely."[14] One physician states that even in its mildest form the operation "is anatomically equivalent to amputation of the penis."[15]

The act is commonly done by forcing a young girl to submit by tying her down, for instance. One author reports that viewers cringe when seeing the act on a television video. Often it is done by one of the parents using a razor blade.[16] It is performed largely for cultural reasons. Sometimes, especially in America, immigrant mothers want their daughters to have the operation because they believe it will make them less desirous of having sex in their teenage years. Physiologically, the operation makes it impossible for the female ever to experience sexual orgasm.

Sati (The Burning of Live Widows)

For hundreds of years, India's cultural practice of *sati* (or *suttee*), the burning of an alive widow on her husband's funeral pyre, was an integral part of India's culture. The practice existed until the British outlawed it in 1829, when India still was part of the British Commonwealth.

After India gained its independence in 1947, it continued the ban against *sati*. But cultural practices, whether humane or not, do not die easily or quickly. In 1987 a widow was burned to death in the village of Deorala, India. Her husband died at age 24, and his wife, 18 years old, chose to be burned alive. "Dressed in bridal finery, she walked at the head of the funeral procession to the centre of the village where in the presence of a crowd [of about 4,000] she ascended the pyre and was reduced to ashes with the body of her husband."[17] After she was cremated, thousands came to receive "blessings" from this dead widow, who in their eyes was a goddess.[18]

The Aztecs

The Aztecs of Tenochtitlan (now Mexico City) were a war-waging people who fought primarily to acquire prisoners whom they needed for human sacrifices. Prisoners were commonly led up stairs, through thick clouds of incense, to the top of the Great Pyramid. Here, according to Richard Townsend, the victim was laid on a sacrificial block; then an obsidian knife cut open his chest, from which the heart was torn out.

"Streams of blood [from the many sacrificed warriors] poured down the stairway and sides of the monument [pyramid], forming huge pools on the white stucco pavement."[19] The heads of victims were commonly "strung up on the skull rack as public trophies, while the captor-warriors were presented with a severed arm or thigh."[20] With great rejoicing, the severed body parts were taken home, where they were made into a stew for Aztec meals. The eating of human flesh was a ceremonial form of cannibalism.[21]

Other Cultures

The Auca Indians in east Ecuador don't like crying babies. While this does not distinguish them from most other societies, they are set apart, according to Rosemary Kingsland, by what they often do with the crying infants. A chronically crying baby is put in a hole dug in the ground and then trampled on, while saying: "The next baby will cry less."[22]

The Siriono Indians of eastern Bolivia, the anthropologist Allan R. Holmberg has shown, constantly argue about food. Accusations abound with regard to not sharing food, hoarding it, and secretly eating it in the forest. Not infrequently, food is hidden even from family members, and men accuse women of hiding food items in their vaginas.[23] Human excreta surround their houses, which after some time, says Holmberg, "become rather unbearable to the unaccustomed [non-natives]."[24]

In the culture of the Chuckee of Siberia, women are required to skin slaughtered reindeer, cut them up, and then prepare the meat. After the men have eaten, the women eat what is left over, which is often only scraps. The Chuckee men have a saying, says Frederick J. Simoons: "Being woman, eat crumbs."[25] Among the Hudson Bay Eskimos, as Peter Freuchen found in the 1950s, men rather than the women ate the boiled meat because it was "too good for women to have."[26]

CONTINENTAL CULTURAL DIFFERENCES

Michael Novak convincingly shows that cultures also are unequal on a broad continental basis.[27] As he notes, Latin America has more natural resources than North America, being rich in oil, gold, silver, rubber, farm products, and other commodities necessary for a prosperous economy. But South American countries are poor, and some desperately so. Both American continents received their first European settlers during roughly the same period—in the sixteenth and seventeenth centuries; yet, North America is far more prosperous than South America. The reason why is a cultural one. The British and Northern Europeans brought a different culture to North America than that brought to Latin America by the Spanish and Portuguese. As Novak states, the culture of

"Latin America places more emphasis on luck, heroism, status, and *figura* than the relatively 'Protestant' ethic of North America which values diligence, regularity, and the responsible seizure of opportunities."[28] Lawrence Harrison makes a similar point relative to the differences between the two Americas.[29]

IMPLICATIONS OF CULTURAL EQUALITY

Even the ordinary citizen knows that the Aztec sacrifices of human beings is not just different; that the burning of widows is not just a different cultural practice; and that placing brass rings around the neck of a young girl is not just another cosmetic custom. People know that these and similar cultural practices are not only different but also morally wrong. Indeed, even some supporters of multiculturalism at times admit indirectly that not all cultures are equal. A case in point is the matter of female clitoridectomies. Gender feminists, who are strongly supportive of multiculturalism, have a real problem in dealing with the subject of clitoridectomy, given the doctrine of cultural equality. On this one issue they have been forced to take issue with the multiculturalist doctrine of cultural equality, denouncing the practice as female genital mutilation (FGM). The United Nations' Conference on Women widely condemned the practice at its fourth conference in Beijing, China, in September 1995.[30]

Even as multiculturalists try to promote other cultures in the name of cultural equality, countless nonmulticulturalists insist that many cultural practices are far from equal, even when no moral implications are involved. No one can dispute that smoke signals once practiced in many American Indian cultures are not merely different from radio signals; that witch doctors or shamans treating patients are not only different but also less successful in treating illnesses; that the one-time travois of American Indians was not equal to the wagon or motorized vehicle for transporting goods; and that a wigwam or longhouse was not equal to a European castle. The list is endless.

Whereas countless ordinary people understand that cultures are not equal and not just different, but often also immoral and inhumane, why do multiculturalists continue to teach their doctrine of cultural equality? There are three possible answers as to why they keep promoting this false ideology.

The first reason might be their ignorance of other cultures, but this may be true for only some multiculturalists. Second, ideology is so powerful for some individuals that they cling to it even in the presence of contradictory empirical evidence. The third possibility is the strength of their alienation from Euro-American culture, which impels them to push this faulty notion. This fanaticism is perfectly illustrated by an incident that occurred at Stanford University a few years ago: as multiculturalists paraded on campus, they shouted: "Hey hey, ho ho, Western culture's got to go."

Multiculturalists overlook at least one inherent contradiction within their argument of cultural equality. If cultures truly are equal, then there is no need to change the American culture by introducing the values, beliefs, and practices of other cultures. The fact that so many multiculturalists degrade the American culture vis-à-vis non-Western or minority cultures belies their argument that all cultures are equal.[31] To use an expression in business: "There is no gain in exchanging one dollar bill for another dollar bill."

Finally, if America were to fully accept the multiculturalist doctrine of cultural equality, it would undoubtedly have the effect of drastically diluting its present national and cultural pride. Such a posture in all likelihood would dismantle the nation's 300-year-old culture and its worldwide influence. It would end America. Indeed the Trojan horse of multiculturalism is more than a minor nuisance in the life of America's culture.

NOTES

1. Stephanie Gutman, "The Curriculum That Ate New York," *Insight*, 15 March 1993, 1–11.

2. Allan Bloom, *The Closing of the American Mind* (New York: Simon and Schuster, 1987), pp. 202–203.

3. R. F. Fortune, *The Sorcerers of Dobu* (New York: E. P. Dutton, 1932).

4. Ruth Benedict, *Patterns of Culture* (Boston: Houghton Mifflin, 1934), p. 148.

5. Ibid., p. 169.

6. Fortune, *The Sorcerers of Dobu*, p. 180.

7. Ibid., p. 150.

8. Cora Du Bois, *The People of Alor: A Social Psychological Study of an East Indian Island* (Minneapolis: University of Minnesota Press, 1944), 1:51.

9. Jens Bjerre, *The Last Cannibals*, trans. Estrid Bannister (New York: Drake Publishers, 1974), p. 70.

10. Ibid., p. 91.

11. Ibid., p. 89.

12. John M. Keshishian, "Anatomy of a Burmese Beauty Secret," *National Geographic* (June 1979): 798–801.

13. Nahid Toubia, "Female Circumcision as a Public Health Issue," *New England Journal of Medicine*, 15 September 1994, 712.

14. Linda Burstyn, "Female Circumcision Comes to America," *Atlantic Monthly* (October 1995): 32.

15. Toubia, "Female Circumcision," p. 712.

16. Burstyn, "Female Circumcision," p. 33.

17. Sakuntala Narasimhan, *Sati: Widow Burning in India* (New York: Anchor Books, 1990), p. 2.

18. Ibid.

19. Richard Townsend, *The Aztecs* (London: Hudson and Hudson, 1992), p. 100.

20. Ibid., p. 92.

21. Ibid.

22. Rosemary Kingsland, *A Saint Among Savages* (London: Collins, 1980), p. 44.

23. A. R. Holmberg, *Nomads of the Long Bow: The Siriono of Eastern Bolivia* (Garden City, N.Y.: Natural History Press, 1969), p. 155.

24. Ibid., p. 99.

25. Frederick J. Simoons, *Eat Not This Flesh* (Madison: University of Wisconsin Press, 1961), p. 110.

26. P. Freuchen, *Book of the Eskimo* (New York: Fawcett, 1961), p. 97.

27. Michael Novak, "Why Latin America Is Poor," *The Atlantic Monthly* (March 1982): 66–75.

28. Ibid., p. 71.

29. Lawrence Harrison, *Who Prospers? How Cultural Values Shape Economic and Political Success* (New York: Basic Books, 1992).

30. Robin Morgan, "Dispatching from Beijing," *MS* (January/February 1996): 17.

31. I am indebted to Brad Stetson of the David Institute for this observation. As he says, the multiculturalist argument of cultural equality is "self-referentially incoherent."

Chapter 5

The Facts Be Damned: Omissions, Distortions, and Noble Lies

Facts are stubborn things; and whatever may be our wishes, our inclinations, or the dictates of our passions, they cannot alter the state of facts and evidence.

John Adams

The nineteenth-century German philosopher, Georg Friedrich Hegel, responding to a student's interjection "But sir, what you say does not agree with the facts," replied: "Let the facts be damned." Undoubtedly, Hegel made this remark because he wanted his views to prevail. He might even have had good reasons for wanting to ignore or damn the facts. This might also be true of some multiculturalists, who frequently damn the facts in promoting their ideology.

Historical omissions and distortions abound in multiculturalists' publications. As noted in previous chapters, the negative or harmful practices of non-Western or minority cultures are typically omitted, and in the rare instances when they are noted, they are presented in an innocuous manner. On the other hand, the Euro-American's cultural shortcomings, or negative cultural practices, are cited wherever possible and are often portrayed at great length. The great achievements of the Western world are portrayed as being no more important than the far less spectacular accomplishments of non-Western societies. Sometimes even new "facts" are created, for example, the multiculturalists claim that Crispus Attucks, killed in the Boston Massacre in 1770, was black; that Western civilization was stolen from Africa; that the American Indians were highly conscientious ecologically; that the Constitution of the

United States was shaped by the Iroquois Indians; and others. This tactic is reminiscent of the "noble lies" that Plato talked about in *The Republic* in which such lies were intended to persuade kings and the populace to achieve worthy objectives. Thus the multiculturalists who publish their revised histories present as significant and authentic history undocumented and highly dubious accounts about minor persons or events, usually with some ties to some minority group. The idea is to appease and please, apparently to help such groups overcome the "oppression" that has been imposed on them by the "Eurocentric" American culture.

THE PRACTICE OF SLAVERY

As shown in Chapter 2, multiculturalism essentially consists of teaching students about other cultures, including the positive and negative components of given cultures. But as we have noted, the promoters of multiculturalism primarily illustrate the negative cultural practices of the Euro-American culture.

When present-day textbooks discuss slavery, they only cover slavery as it existed in America or other Western societies, and they consistently ignore the practice of slavery in non-Western cultures. For example, textbooks say nothing about the many American Indian tribes who practiced slavery long before Columbus and other Europeans came to America. The widely used grade school text, *United States and Its Neighbors* (1993), authored by James Banks et al., discusses slavery on at least twenty pages, but makes no mention of the American Indians' practice of slavery. The same is true of another widely used grade school text, *The American Nation* (1995).[1] Nor is there any reference to it in *National Standards for United States History* (1994), one of the three books highly publicized as a national school guide for teaching multiculturalism.[2]

Nontextbooks favoring multiculturalism also omit slavery in non-Western societies. One such example is Kilpatrick Sale's book *The Conquest of Paradise* (1992) which contains no reference to slavery as it was practiced by numerous American Indian tribes, long before the white man arrived. Nor does it make any reference to Almond W. Lauber's book *Indian Slavery in Colonial Times* (1913). Lauber describes many instances of slavery among America's Indians before the Europeans arrived. For instance, in the St. Augustine area of Florida in 1565 some natives held Cuban Indians as slaves, and in 1616, the Dutch navigator, Henrickson, encountered slaveowning Indians in the Schuylkill River area of Pennsylvania. The Illinois Indians at times bartered their slaves with the Ottawa Indians and the Iroquois. The Pima of Arizona enslaved Apache and Yuma Indians. Lauber is not the only source for data on the institution of slavery among the Indians. The multivolume publication by Reuben Gold Thwaites's *Early Western Travels, 1748–1846* (1904) also documents slavery among many Indian tribes. Thwaites states that the Pawnee Indians, for example, were so "frequently enslaved by their [Indian] enemies, [that] the term 'Pani' [Pawnee] became equivalent to Indian slave."[3]

Slavery is a moral evil, and that fact does not change, regardless of what group practiced it. Textbooks provide a necessary and valuable public service by discussing the immorality of the practice, and they need to emphasize that it is evil in every society and not just in American culture. But Americans, of course, will never know anything about the past slavery habits of American Indians if such facts are omitted.

Lack of reference to the slavery customs of American Indians is not the only omission in multiculturalist texts. When the importation of slaves from Africa to America is described, only rarely is it mentioned that native Africans sold their own people to the Europeans. Multiculturalists especially ignore John Thornton's recent book (*Africa and Africans* [1992]) which notes the cooperation of African slave captors: "The Atlantic slave trade" Thornton claims, "grew out of and was rationalized by African societies who participated in it and had complete control over it until the slaves were loaded onto European ships for transfer to Atlantic societies."[4]

Another omission pertains to the slavery that existed in many African countries long before the Europeans ever practiced it, as shown by David R. James.[5] When one does find such a reference, it is mentioned only tangentially or minimized. The school text *The World Past and Present* (1993) is a case in point. This book does briefly note African slavery, but it quickly minimizes it by saying that under this system of slavery "enslaved people were not treated as harshly and could sometimes gain their freedom after working for many years. The practice of slavery changed dramatically when the Europeans became involved."[6]

Grade school textbooks also fail to mention that slavery lasted much longer in African and Asian countries than in the British empire or in the United States. For instance, Ethiopians did not outlaw slavery until 1942, India not until 1976, and Mauritania, an African country, waited until the 1980s.[7] In March 1996, an article appeared in *Reader's Digest* showing that slavery exists even today in the African country of Sudan.[8]

Granted, textbook space is limited, and it is impossible to include everything that is important in a given volume. But lack of space does not prevent the inclusion of negative incidents involving Western or American culture. If multiculturalist writers of texts were truly interested in teaching students about all cultures, they not only would include negative incidents of non-Western cultures, but would also note how Western and American culture eliminated unjust practices such as slavery.

Early in the life of the Christian church (about A.D. 55), St. Paul told Philemon to take back his runaway slave, Onesimus and to treat him "no longer as a slave but more than a slave, as a beloved brother" (Philemon 16). Many biblical scholars see this New Testament document by Paul as the first Christian seed that eventually grew to abolish slavery, first by the British and then by others.

St. Paul was not the only early Christian leader who opposed slavery. St. Gregory of Nyssa (fourth century) preached on the evils of slavery,[9] as did St. Chrysostom, a contemporary of St. Gregory, often called the golden-mouthed preacher. He said that in Christ no one was a slave.[10] Two other church fathers in the fourth century, Lactantius and St. Ambrose, voiced similar exhortations.

Unfortunately, the institutionalized church sometimes ignored St. Paul's and many of its early leaders' directives, by condoning and sometimes even supporting slavery in many countries. Throughout the church's existence, however, some Christian leaders continued to condemn slavery. One such person was St. Olaf, who in the eleventh century banned slavery in Norway. In more recent times, it was the influence of William Wilberforce, a British member of Parliament, who, moved by Christian teachings, fought to outlaw slavery. After twenty years of labor and toil, his arguments led England to ban slavery in 1833 throughout the expansive British empire. This, and similar evidence, is of no significance to multiculturalists. They ignore observations such as the following one by Suzanne Miers: "The great blossoming of Protestant and then Catholic missionary activity in the nineteenth century was intimately connected with the abolition of the slave trade."[11] If multiculturalists were truly interested in pointing out the merits of all cultures, they would emphasize the motives and forces in Western and American culture that led to the abolition of slavery.

VIOLENCE IN AMERICAN INDIAN CULTURES

Human Sacrifices

While it is appropriate and necessary to discuss American Indian cultures in American history textbooks, it would also be appropriate to include some of the negative or evil customs of American Indian cultures, just as it is necessary to note the negative aspects of Western or American culture. But school texts billed as multicultural do not include material about negative non-Western practices. The young therefore receive a very inaccurate view of many Indian cultures. For instance, the school text *The American Nation* portrays the Maya as people "who built great civilizations in the Americas." Similarly, another text, *The World Past and Present,* says that the Maya "created America's first great civilization."[12] But neither text speaks of the gruesome, bloody human sacrifices routinely conducted by the Maya. Howard La Fay describes the Maya's ghastly human-sacrifice ceremony: "a priest ripped open the victim's breast with an obsidian knife and tore out the still-beating heart." The priests also drew blood from the victim's genitals. La Fay continues: "priests and pious individuals cut holes in their [prisoners'] tongues and drew rope festooned with thorns through the wound to collect blood offerings."[13]

The authors of these texts might be forgiven if they were squeamish about including bloody incidents in grade school texts. But earlier in this same text, when discussing the Crusades of the Middle Ages, they have no qualms in stating that during the Crusades "many innocent people, both Christians and Muslims, died as a result of the 'holy wars,'" and that "at the Temple of Solomon men rode in blood up to their knees."[14]

Human sacrifices were an integral part of the Maya culture, yet multiculturalist writers omit them. Why? We may hazard a guess that they are disregarded because they fail to support the cultural equality principle.

One recent book (not a school text) does briefly mention the Maya's ritual slaughter of humans, but the authors try to make the practice seem culturally acceptable by comparing the Maya bloodletting ritual to the "wine and wafers [in] the Christian communion."[15] Whether they intend to draw a parallel to the body and blood of Christ in the Christian celebration of the Lord's Supper is not clear. If so, any intended parallel is specious inasmuch as the wine and wafers in the Christian communion are not parts of human beings whom Christians sacrificed.

The Aztecs are also pictured in *The World Past and Present* (1993) as having "created great civilizations as impressive as those found anywhere in the world."[16] Yet what did these "great civilizations" accomplish? Where is there a Magna Carta type of freedom or bill of rights such as is found in the American Constitution? Did they invent anything comparable to the movable-type printing press? Did they produce a Beethoven, a Mozart, or a Bach? What great advances in medicine or in food production and its distribution can be credited to the Aztecs?

School texts make no mention that the Aztecs had no concept of right or wrong. Nor do they note that they had "no religious guidelines for moral behavior."[17] Yet young, malleable minds are led to believe that the Aztecs had a civilization on a par with America's present day society.

United States and Its Neighbors (1993) does refer to the human sacrifices of the Aztecs, but does not point out that this torturous ritual was a significant part of the Aztec culture. Instead, it tries to cast a good light on this macabre practice by telling the school children: "The Aztecs believed that the only way to prevent this [the failure of sunshine] from happening was to offer the gods a human life."[18] In other words, their good end(s) justified their means, their murderous behavior. Using this kind of logic, one could argue that the American South was justified in practicing slavery because it kept the cotton industry from failing.

Scalping

Another act of human violence, the scalping of prisoners by American Indians, is also omitted in multicultural textbooks. Some books have even made the outrageous claim that scalping was actually introduced by the European settlers and that the Indians copied the practice from the white man. The respected scholar Georg K. Neumann has shown conclusively, based on prehistoric skulls of Indians of the Middle Mississippi culture in the Spoon River area of Illinois, that the Indians practiced scalping long before the Europeans landed in America.[19]

Cannibalism

Given that human sacrificing and scalping are not mentioned in school books, it is not surprising that cannibalism in many tribes also is not cited. A little known fact is that the Mohawk tribe derived its name from its habit of eating human flesh. Alpheus Hyatt Verill writes: "The Mohawks were notorious eaters of human flesh, and were called *Mohowauock* or man-eaters by the Narragansets."[20] William Warren, a native of the Chippewas, noted in his *History of the Ojibways* (1852) that his people occasionally ate human flesh.[21] In 1853 John Palliser wrote that the Sioux and Minitares had their women cut pieces of human flesh from slain enemy warriors. These pieces were then broiled and eaten.[22] Eskimos, especially during times of stress, also consumed human flesh.[23] The Pawnees would roast their prisoners for food.[24] And the French explorer, La Salle, reported that he encountered an instance in which the slaves of Indians were forced to eat their own.[25]

In the 1670s Father Chrestien Le Clercq described some Iroquois cruelties that often included forcing prisoners to eat their own flesh. The Roman emperors, Diocletian and Nero, the two savage persecutors of the early Christians, "would hold in horror the vengeance, the tortures, and the cruelty of the Indians of New France [Quebec], and above all the Iroquois, towards their prisoners." Le Clercq noted that the Iroquois cut off the prisoners' fingers, burned them with firebrands, tore away their nails, and made "them eat their own flesh."[26]

The Sun Dance

When multiculturalists talk about the Plains Indians in modern textbooks, they do not mention the excruciating ordeals of the sun dance. This dance commonly occurred during the summer. A young man had two pegs pierced through the muscular portion on each side of his chest. Tied to each peg was a leather rope which in turn was fastened to the top of a pole, considerably taller than the dancer. This ritual required the subject to lean back so that the ropes would be taut as he circled (danced) round the pole three to four days in the hot sun without drink or rest, commonly causing him to hallucinate. Given the stress of this ordeal, the pegs would often tear out of the flesh. The United States outlawed this torturous ritual in the 1880s.

This chapter emphasizes the violence of some Indian customs for two reasons. First, these violent acts were an integral part of many Indian tribes whose cultures today are often accorded moral equivalence (or even superiority) to the Euro-American culture. Second, if these or similar violent acts were part of the Euro-American culture, they would certainly be mentioned. For instance, in one of the textbooks for the primary grades, in which the Pilgrims in Massachusetts are discussed, the authors not only described the stocks as a form of physical punishment, but also included a picture of a person locked in one of these devices.[27] Double standards are commonplace in multiculturalist textbooks and do not bode well for American education.

THE MORTUARY CUSTOMS OF AMERICAN INDIANS

Multiculturalists have had much success in convincing the general public, including legislators, that America in the past grossly violated Indian burial rights. Across the United States, the bones of dead Indians are either returned to various tribal groups for burial or they are no longer available for public viewing in museums. The Dickson Mounds in Illinois is one such example. The bones of deceased Indians, sometimes those of dogs too, as well as artifacts once housed in museums are being "repatriated."

Multiculturalist propaganda, along with ignorance and self-inflicted white guilt, has prompted state and federal legislators to enact laws that often violate the public trust of numerous museum donors as bones and artifacts are returned to Indians. But many items were legitimately purchased from Indians, and in many instances scientific data are being destroyed as well. Even the world-famous Smithsonian Institution has capitulated. In 1991 it returned bones from hundreds of individuals, some over 2,000 years old, to be buried at Larson Bay, Alaska. Idaho's Historic Preservation Office relinquished a skeleton estimated to be over 10,000 years old, perhaps the oldest human skeleton in existence.[28]

In all this furor, another significant historical fact has been omitted: Many, perhaps most, American Indians did not bury their dead. Disposal of deceased members varied from tribe to tribe and from one geographic area to another. The Indians in the Northern Plains, in the Mackenzie subarctic region, and elsewhere practiced scaffold or tree "burials" rather than inhumation. In parts of the Yukon, California, and the Great Basin area, some tribes cremated their dead. The Choctaws skeletonized their dead and then stored the bones in bone houses. Some of the Pueblo buried their dead in refuse mounds. The Iroquois and many others bundled the bodies after the bones were disarticulated. In other parts of North America, the dead were left to be eaten by dogs or wolves. In parts of Alaska, the late Aleut culture (A.D. 1100–1750) sometimes removed given organs and then placed the remains in a hollow log. During the pre-Koniag era (A.D. 500–1100), the Eskimos dismembered the dead person's bones and then broke them, evidently so that the marrow could be used for food. The Teton Dakotas wrapped the dead in cloth and then placed them in the forks of trees.[29]

To argue that the bones of deceased Indians are now to be given earth burial is somewhat ironical because this argument is largely a "Eurocentric" one. As we just saw, numerous Indian tribes did not bury their dead. Are Indians and their multiculturalist provokers aware that they are conforming to a Western cultural practice, while at the same time despising much of what that culture represents?

Countless Indians did not give earth burial to their deceased simply because they had no effective digging devices. It is exceedingly cumbersome to dig graves with digging sticks, especially in some geographic regions where the soil is extremely arid or stony. Harold Driver once stated that it is unknown how much inhumation actually took place before Columbus arrived. He also noted that the inhumation that Indians practiced after the arrival of the Europeans may well have been the result of Christianity's influence.[30]

STATUS OF MINORITY WOMEN

American Indian Women

Many non-Western cultures had major flaws in other areas of human life, notably the pronounced, longstanding discrimination of women. The status of white American women 300 years ago was considerably lower than what it is today, but still it was far superior to the treatment American Indian women received from their men. Women had to do all the menial labor: plant and harvest corn; convert animal hides into garments; prepare food; gather firewood; nurture the children; and even set up and move the tepees and wigwams. Apparently that is why the early white settlers often spoke of American Indian women living in virtual slavery.

Hispanic Women

Part of the multiculturalist agenda is to promote the Hispanic culture in the United States, but remarkably no mention of *machismo* can be found in grade school or high school textbook sections that discuss American Hispanics. When the rare writer does mention *machismo*, usually in a college-level text, the reference is brief and not accompanied by any critical assessment.

Machismo is the cultural practice whereby an Hispanic husband acts as lord over his wife. It means the Hispanic husband expects, and usually gets, full compliance from his wife. She ungrudgingly tolerates his sexual liaisons with other women, for having extramarital relationships is considered a sign of virility and wholesome aggressiveness for him. A good wife not only accepts her husband's philandering, but she also is sexually faithful to him. She teaches her daughters that someday they too should imitate her submissive role. She tells them that adultery for a married-Hispanic woman is a disgrace, whereas her sons hear no such message from her or their father. Moreover, a husband may abandon his wife if he believes she has committed adultery. Widowers, but not widows, are expected to remarry.[31]

Islamic Women

Multiculturalists are equally taciturn regarding the status of Islamic women. The school text for sixth graders, *Eastern Hemisphere* (1995) by Kenneth S. Cooper et al., devotes eight pages to Islam but makes no reference to the low status of women in Islamic countries, where women are veiled and allowed only restricted public social activities.[32] This kind of portrayal of Islam is typical in most grade school texts.

During the Gulf War of 1991, many Americans were shocked to hear that women in Saudi Arabia were not permitted to drive automobiles. But how could they know when multiculturalist textbooks commonly omit making any reference to women's low status in Islamic countries? The multiculturalists ignore their status because noting it would make American culture look better and would violate the premise of cultural equality.

NO MENTION OF ISLAM'S JIHAD

Multiculturalists do not mention the Islamic belief of *Jihad* ("holy war") in grade school textbooks because to do so would be "politically incorrect." But *Jihad* is not an idle or innocuous belief among faithful Muslims. The Koran (Qu'ran) enjoins them: "When ye encounter unbelievers, strike off their heads, until ye have made a great slaughter among them" (Sura XLVII). *Jihad* has lost some of its original meaning, but according to Robin Wright, it is still evidently operative in the struggle against Israel.[33] Thus, when textbooks devote several pages to Islam, one would think that *Jihad* would merit some mention.

THE IROQUOIS AND THE AMERICAN CONSTITUTION

Excising the negative or morally evil practices of non-Western cultures is just one way in which the multiculturalists obscure facts. Some of their distortions or noble lies are as follows.

In recent years, the advocates of multiculturalism claimed that the Founding Fathers borrowed ideas for the Constitution of the United States from the Iroquois Indians (the League of Five Nations), organized in the late 1500s. The fifth-grade school text *United States and Its Neighbors* (1993) uncritically proclaims this historical fiction. The book has a two-page "Traditions" section titled "We, the People." In pictorial form it shows the Iroquois holding a council meeting, and it makes the undocumented claim: "The Iroquois League was a living example of what American leaders wanted to create when they set out to write the Constitution."[34] The grade school text *The American Nation* (1995) says even more. It asserts that the opening words of the United States Constitution, "We, the people," were borrowed directly from the Iroquois treaty.[35]

In 1991, Arthur M. Schlesinger, Jr., showed that this same distorted piece of "history" had made it into a New York eleventh-grade American history book because of the powerful Iroquois lobby in New York State.[36] That lobby's power, with its multiculturalist-political clout, has now reached far beyond New York. This same noble lie is now in textbooks published by a number of publishers and is sold across the United States. The two textbooks cited above are merely two examples of many similar school texts.

Along with the myth that the Iroquois confederacy helped shape the American Constitution is the fabrication that the League of Five Nations was a prototype of democracy. Multiculturalists fail to note that Lewis H. Morgan, the foremost nineteenth-century authority on the Iroquois, and someone who lived among them, reported that the Iroquois had no minority or majority voting process. Debates and political give-and-take also were not part of the League's procedures. The confederacy was not a democracy; rather, Morgan called it an oligarchy.[37] An oligarchy consists of the rule of an entrenched few who typically are replaced by individuals like themselves. Yet the myth persists—and is even taught to school children—that the Iroquois were sophisticated practitioners of democracy. It is another attempt to make American Indians appear to have been highly advanced politically. This kind of erroneous history is not confined to school texts. Recently (1992), a nontextbook appeared making a similar false claim in its title: *Indian Roots of American Democracy* (1992) by Jose Barreiro.

THE EXAGGERATED STATUS OF IROQUOIS WOMEN

United States and Its Neighbors (1993) also falsely asserts that the Iroquois council members, male sachems (chiefs), "were chosen by the women of each group."[38] In a similar manner, *The American Nation* (1995) declares: "The eldest women from each family chose the man who would serve as leader of the clan."[39] Again, let us see what Morgan found. He notes that council members were chosen by *men and women*, not just women. The sachem was selected "by free suffrage of males and females of adult age."[40] Nowhere does Morgan say women alone did the electing. Exposing grade school children to noble lies, as illustrated by these textbooks, is an enormous departure from acceptable educational standards.

GREENING THE REDMAN

Several years ago, television aired a public service message featuring an American Indian with tears in his eyes as he saw polluted items floating down a river. The message was obvious. The Indians were ecologically minded, whereas the white descendants of European ancestors have been polluters, causing the Indian to weep. This impression appears to be widespread. Television is not the only medium that has given the public a false picture of the Indian as a model of environmental consciousness. Magazines have also contributed to this new myth. One magazine, for instance, published an article quoting a Pueblo Indian, Jose Lucero, saying: "Only the indigenous peoples have demonstrated efficiency in taking care of the Earth [*sic*]."[41]

Having personally asked numerous college students how they perceive American Indians with regard to environmental concern, I received the response that they are more ecologically minded than Americans as a whole. No doubt this perception stems in large part from items such as the television ad described here and accepting them uncritically. But the impression that Indians have always been environmentally minded, goes beyond mere perceptions: It is now presented to young students as absolute truth. Once again, the school text *United States and Its Neighbors* (1993) serves as an example. Under its subchapter heading, "Living in Harmony with Nature," it declares: "Wherever Indians lived, they lived in harmony with their environment. . . . And after thousands of years in North America, they left the land as beautiful as it had appeared to the first Americans."[42] The picture of Indians as ecologically minded, in harmony with nature, is accepted as true only by the uninformed or ideological multiculturalists. Many American Indians, both before and after Columbus, were anything but protectors of the environment. In many parts of the United States, they destroyed millions of forested acres by using fires to hunt and to fight enemy tribes. Often these fires went out of control, devastating thousands of acres of forests. In addition to uncontrolled fires, Indians also engaged in broadcast burning of forests. This practice kept the forests free of shrubs, and it fostered more herbal growth. It also made hunting easier by providing grassy areas for the game, and it made the animals more visible.[43]

Over extended periods of time, these burnings took their toll. In 1633, Andrew White complained that the broadcast fires opened forests so that one could "freely drive a four-horse chariot in the midst of the trees."[44] Columbus made similar observations more than a century earlier. Broadcast fires on the American prairies, from northern Texas to Minnesota, kept land free from encroaching tree growth. In short, the prairies were kept treeless as a result of man-made fires. Without them "the forests of the Rocky Mountains would extend across the plains to meet hardwood forest spreading from the Mississippi River."[45] H. Maxwell has argued that if the Europeans had arrived 500 years after Columbus the entire eastern part of the United States would have been treeless and prairie-like.[46] In addition, the early settlers often found large open (treeless) areas in the eastern and southeastern United States which were the result of man-made burnings, practiced for centuries.

After the Indian fires ceased, many forests grew in Wisconsin, Illinois, Nebraska, Kansas, and other states. The Virginia forests, for instance, developed mainly after 1600.[47] Contrary to the current multiculturalist myth, Michael Williams says that the Indians had no "pristine state of equilibrium" with nature.[48]

Another myth states that the Indians never killed more game than they needed, but the literature on Indian hunting practices shows this to be false. Paul S. Martin and H. E. Wright maintain that 10,000 to 15,000 years ago, prehistoric hunters engaged in overkill to the extent that some species became extinct. These hunters "exterminated far more large animals than has modern man with modern weapons and advanced technology."[49] Even Calvin Martin, who finds fault with the overkill hypothesis, notes that "decades of over-hunting" by American Indians, as late as the 1700s, caused many fur-bearing animals and other wild game to become "alarmingly scarce."[50] As all students of Indian hunting habits know, when given tribes exhausted an area's supply of game, they moved to another area. Given that the continent had a relatively sparse population of humans, they were able to do so, finding game in another locale.

THE "HELPLESS" EUROPEAN SETTLERS

The multiculturalists generally picture the settlers as having been helpless and claim that they would not have survived had it not been for the expert help of the "natives." In telling students how the Indians helped the Europeans, one high school textbook, *United States History* (1988), after displaying a picture of Indians girdling trees, audaciously asserts: "The Indians . . . taught the colonists an easy method of felling trees. It was known as girdling. They stripped the bark off of the trees and waited for them to die. In time the trees fell; the land was cleared for fields and houses."[51] This illustration can have only one meaning, namely, that the Europeans did not have the faintest notion of how to fell a tree. This kind of statement is patently false. After all, the Europeans had to cross the Atlantic to come to America, and they did so only through ships made primarily of wood. And, of course, the wood was derived from trees they felled with steel axes.

Europeans, of course, downed trees for centuries, long before they came to America. Moreover, they felled them by methods that were far more efficient than by girdling. There was no need to wait for the trees to die as girdling requires. They did not have to learn the Indian's inefficient method of downing trees.

The text *Regions Near and Far* (1993), a fourth-grade book, teaches lower grade school children that the Pilgrims were a helpless lot who "probably would not have survived the next winter without the help of Squanto." The book goes on to say: "He [Squanto] taught them how to plant, hunt, and fish."[52] Perhaps the Pilgrims needed some advice on how to hunt, but to say they had to be taught how to plant and fish is another factual distortion. Europeans knew how to plant various grains and other crops centuries before they encountered the Indians. The same was true with fishing.

IGNORING MULTICULTURAL CONFLICTS

As multiculturalists push their agenda, they consistently ignore the historically reoccurring phenomenon of severe cultural conflicts, whether it is in Sri Lanka, Bosnia, the former Soviet Republics, or Canada. Were they to discuss cultural or ethnic strife, people would soon realize that multiculturalism does not work and often leads to severe strife, even bloodshed. The textbook *United States and Its Neighbors* (1993), in trying to cast a positive light on Canada's multiculturalism, falsifies the recent political divisiveness in Canada. This text says: "In the past, language and customs have separated British and French Canadians. But this is changing. Today both groups are learning to speak each other's language and work together. The future of Canada is bright and full of promise."[53]

This is an extremely erroneous statement. In fact, Canada is a political mess as a result of its multiculturalist policies. Ever since the Canadian government officially embarked in the early 1970s to make the country multicultural, it has exacerbated its problems with the French in the province of Quebec and more recently with the Canadian Indians.

Only 16 percent of the Canadians—primarily governmental bureau-crats—know how to "speak each other's language," English and French. The vast majority have no interest in becoming bilingual, and they never will. Moreover, although Quebec has been crusading to get Canada's other nine provinces to adopt French as a language equal to English, it severely restricted the use of English within its own boundaries when it enacted Bill 101 in 1978. This law requires all business to be transacted in French. In 1988 the Canadian Supreme Court, on the basis of the new Charter of Rights, declared parts of Bill 101 null and void. In response, Quebec passed a new law, Bill 178, which "reinstated the primacy of French in commerce and made it illegal to display signs in any language other than French."[54] Quebec now has language police patrolling shops and offices, making sure that any signs in English (which are allowed indoors if its letters are smaller than the accompanying French letters) conform to the law. One analyst says: "Bill 178 is the most strikingly illiberal measure in a strikingly enlightened society."[55] Canada's future is anything but "bright and full of promise."

As a former Canadian, I visit Canada at least once a year and see the country's multicultural troubles first hand. Clearly, the country is becoming balkanized. (See Chapter 8 for an extended discussion of Canada's current multicultural problems.) American school children deserve to be told the truth about what multiculturalism is doing to Canada; instead, they are taught distortions and falsehoods.

OMITTING WESTERN CULTURE'S GREAT ACHIEVEMENTS

Multiculturalist texts are loath to mention the great inventions and discoveries of Western culture, much less give presentations on how these improved human life and added to the longevity of millions. On the other hand, multiculturalists love to cite some inconsequential cultural artifact or practice of some non-Western cultural group—past or present—as being equal to any accomplishment of the West.

Even when multiculturalists note some outstanding Western invention or discovery, it is rarely identified as a Western or European achievement. The reader is left to infer whether or not a given discovery or invention is a Western achievement. Given the declining standards of today's American education, it is anyone's guess as to how many will make the correct inference.

FEEL-GOOD HISTORY FOR MINORITIES AND WOMEN

The multiculturalists' role is to make non-Western minority groups feel good about themselves, and they try to do this in two ways. One method is to slight the Euro-American culture. If members of minority cultures read about the sins and shortcomings of the Euro-Americans, they will conclude that the cultural practices of their ancestors were free of such sins, and thus they will feel good about themselves and their ancestors.

The second method is to cite some example or incident that a minority member, or his or her ancestral group, reportedly contributed to American culture. Such favorable mention will enhance the self-esteem of present members who identify with the group in question. Empirically, this is a flawed argument. Most people's self-esteem comes from doing something worthwhile themselves rather than receiving it vicariously from their ancestors. The second tack conveys a certain amount of irony because it implies that the maligned Euro-American culture perhaps is not so bad as multiculturalists would have people believe—that is, if minorities made some contribution to it.

This second method frequently ignores the facts of history to accomplish its goal. This is not surprising inasmuch as multiculturalists operate according to the Marxist principle that the end justifies the means. A few examples of teaching feel-good history follow.

One study by Robert Lerner and associates found that textbook writers in the 1970s and 1980s cited individuals and historical events that involved minority characters who previously (in the 1960s) did not merit historical mention, much less extended discussion of them. In fact, they often receive more page space than individuals who made immensely greater contributions. In one textbook, for instance, Crispus Attucks (one of several Americans killed in the Boston Massacre in 1770) receives more extensive coverage than Paul Revere.[56] Attucks, by some authors, is said to be a black man, even though his racial identity has never been positively ascertained.[57] W.E.B. Du Bois, a black writer, is more prominently covered than Booker T. Washington,[58] whose reputation has suffered among minorities for his conservative views. Harriet Beecher Stowe, author of *Uncle Tom's Cabin*, who exposed the evils of slavery to millions of Americans, is now often cited less frequently in texts than is Harriet Tubman,[59] the black woman who helped about 300 black slaves escape by way of the "Underground Railroad." That she was assisted by white abolitionists is totally ignored.

In another article, Robert Lerner and his colleagues show that one textbook, in discussing the Civil War, provides photographs of three female nurses but none of General Grant or General Sherman. Still another account praises a 16–year-old female, Sybil Ludington, who in 1777 undertook "an urgent mission" in a "daring" ride to alert the state militia during the American Revolutionary War. She is portrayed as cold and tired, but nevertheless she continues her ride. Even though she managed to rouse the militia, the British troops still escaped. Her failure is not noted. All the same, she received two and a quarter inches of page space, while Paul Revere received only faint mention.[60]

In the history textbook *American Odyssey* (1991), a book of 880 pages, Paul Revere also is totally ignored, but one-half page is devoted to a picture showing Mrs. Schuyler burning a wheat field on the approach of the British soldiers.[61] This textbook is authored by Gary Nash, one of the authors of the highly controversial and avidly pro-multiculturalist three-volume *National Standards* (1994). These volumes also exclude Paul Revere from American history.

Excluding Paul Revere is a big loss, for he was no ordinary Patriot. Not only was his ride to Lexington highly successful, but also he successfully completed a ride to Lexington two days before the well-publicized one. In the earlier ride, he informed John Hancock and Samuel Adams about British plans to march on Concord to capture the Patriots' arsenal. This ride helped the Americans prepare for the eventful day of April 19, 1775. Seven months earlier, September 11, 1774, he left by horseback from Boston to ride to Philadelphia, where he arrived on September 17, to deliver the Suffolk Resolves to the first Continental Congress. It was a ride of 315 miles. One historian says: "He traveled thousands of miles on horseback during troublesome times."[62] He also set up a gunpowder mill after he made a mental picture of the manufacturing process on his tour of a mill in Philadelphia. Some historians also list him as a member of the Boston Tea Party.[63] Nonetheless, today he is either completely ignored or has been relegated to obscurity in favor of relatively minor figures. This revisionism has been motivated to please women and minority groups, as well as to minimize accounts devoted to white males who too closely reflect Western standards and values.

Note, for instance, a question asked of students in grades 9 through 12 in the *National Standards* (1994): "How did Native American societies such as the Pueblos, Catawbas, Iroquois, and Lenni Lanape respond to European *land hunger* [emphasis added] and expansion?"[64] In another place, students are told to "Debate why so few church leaders and non-slave holders in the South spoke out against the internal slave trade."[65] No mention is made of the many church leaders who did speak out and were prominent leaders in the abolitionist movement.

At every opportunity the *National Standards* (1994) draws attention to the negative aspects of American culture. The Ku Klux Klan is cited seventeen times and McCarthyism of the 1950s nineteen times, and almost an entire page is devoted to Cotton Mather's defense of the Salem witch trials. But not a word is written about the new McCarthyism of the 1990s—political correctness.

In addition to Paul Revere, other prominent Americans, including Cyrus McCormick, Thomas Edison, John Deere, and the Wright brothers, all great inventors, are eliminated. In their place are Sojourner Truth, Harriet Tubman, Cesar Chavez, Susan B. Anthony, Rosa Parks, Mary McLeod Bethune, Mother Jones, Jane Addams, Thurgood Marshall, Martin Luther King, Jr., and W.E.B. Du Bois. Some of these names are found in all three volumes of the *National Standards*.

THE "WHITE-MALE HEGEMONY"

Those who seek to give Paul Revere and other well-established American heroes the honor they deserve and once received are said to support "white-male hegemony." In keeping with Marxist ideology, multiculturalists believe that people's race, sex, or ethnicity determine and shape their view of reality. Multiculturalists therefore judge historical figures by this standard. The existing values and practices of Western societies are seen to be the product of white males. The longstanding Western position that ideas transcend people's race or ethnicity is also seen as a white-male construct that needs to be eliminated. Whenever complaints are voiced about the frequent distortions of history that are reflected in today's school texts, the multiculturalist response is that such criticisms are merely desperate acts of white males, intent on protecting their vested interests.

The multiculturalist disgust for the white-male hegemony has recently spread to attacking science for being sexist and culturally biased. Science, it is argued, is socially (culturally) constructed and is another example of institutionalized, white-male thinking. In short, science is relative and class based, incapable of yielding objective truth. Society therefore needs to recognize and encourage the development of "feminist science," "feminist algebra," "Afrocentric science," and the like. This argument is not merely one of "higher superstition," as Paul R. Gross and Norman Levitt show in their recent book by that title,[66] but it also reminds one of the Nazi belief that "German physics" was seen as superior to "Jewish physics." Nazi physicists in the 1930s, it should be recalled, refused to let Albert Einstein, a German citizen of Jewish descent, lecture at the University of Berlin.

AMERICA THE UGLY

To some multiculturalists, America is not the beautiful but the ugly, a view that is evident in almost everything they promote. Thus the Smithsonian Institute in Washington, D.C., inspired by multiculturalism, recently (1994) erected the *Enola Gay* display depicting the United States as having fought an anti-multicultural war in World War II in which the Japanese were compelled "to defend their unique culture against Western imperialism."[67] That Japan started the war by its attack on Pearl Harbor is not mentioned, for this would make Japan's culture look less than honorable. So again, the truth is sacrificed in favor of multiculturalism's agenda.

Regarding this exhibit and other, recent Smithsonian displays, John Leo states: "On a recent two-hour trek through the history museum, I noticed very little celebrating American achievement, nothing about the Founding Fathers, the idea of America or what Americans have in common."[68] Leo also notes that throughout the World War II displays, heroism is minimized, with one notable multiculturalist exception: the Japanese kamikaze (suicide) pilots receive a place of honor. Because they are non-Western, an exception to multiculturalism's anti-hero message can be made.[69]

Children in the primary grades are also given a negative view of America. A 1993 children's book, *The Bracelet*, for example, is about a girl named Emi, whose Japanese-American family, along with others, is being relocated to different parts of the United States during World War II. The book reveals that Emi's family was taken "to a prison camp because they were Japanese-Americans."[70] Accompanying this statement is a colored-sketched drawing that shows people at a railroad station as military police stand guard, poised with bayoneted rifles. It is certainly appropriate for students to be told that America violated the civil rights of Japanese-Americans during the war, but why show this kind of picture to young children? Ordinarily, textbook authors are squeamish about showing rifles, but here bayoneted rifles are pictured for children in the earliest grades. As with the Smithsonian display of the *Enola Gay*, this biased text fails to make any reference to the fact that Japan first attacked the United States at Pearl Harbor and that it was this act that ignited the war between the two countries. It is hard not to conclude that the authors want to make America look ugly.

Another book, *Sweet Clara and the Freedom Quilt*,[71] also intended for the primary grades, focuses on the Underground Railroad and describes how it took the slaves to Canada rather than primarily to the northern states. Most assuredly, children need to read about the Underground Railroad to learn about the horrors of American slavery, but this book seems to convey a hidden message—namely, that America was so evil that the black slaves went to Canada and the northern states did not offer any freedom. It is difficult to see how such an approach can prepare students to make America a better place tomorrow. The facts of history are not incompatible with the goals of social and civil justice.

NOTES

1. James A. Banks et al., *United States and Its Neighbors* (New York: Macmillan/McGraw-Hill, 1993); James West Davidson and Michael B. Stoff, *The American Nation* (Englewood Cliffs, N.J.: Prentice Hall, 1995).

2. This volume is designed for grades 5–12. See Charlotte Crabtree and Gary Nash (Project Coordinators), *National Standards for United States History* (Los Angeles: University of California National Center for History in the Schools, 1994).

3. Reuben Gold Thwaites, *Early Western Travels, 1741–1846* (Cleveland: Arthur H. Clark, 1904), 6:61.

4. John Thornton, *Africa and Africans: In the Making of the Atlantic World, 1400–1680* (New York: Cambridge University Press, 1992), p. 74.

5. David R. James, "Slavery and Involuntary Servitude," in *Encyclopedia of Sociology*, ed. Edgar F. Borgatta and Marie L. Borgatta (New York: Macmillan, 1992), 4:1792.

6. James A. Banks et al., *The World Past and Present* (New York: Macmillan/McGraw-Hill, 1993), p. 430.

7. Robert Sawyer, *Slavery in the 20th Century* (New York: Routledge and Kegan Paul, 1986).

8. Brian Eads, "Slavery's Shameful Return to Africa," *Reader's Digest* (March 1996): 77–81.

9. See his "In Ecclesiasten: Homilia IV," in *Patrologiae Graecea*, ed. J. P. Migne (Parisorum [Paris]: Petit-Montrouge, 1863), 44:664–665.

10. See his "In Epistolam Ad Corinthios: Homilia XL," in *Patrologiae Graecea*, ed. J. P. Migne (Parisorum [Paris]: Petit-Montrouge, 1862), 61:354.

11. Suzanne Miers, *Britain and the Ending of the Slave Trade* (New York: Africana, 1975), p. 153.

12. Davidson and Stoff, *The American Nation*, pp. 48–50; Banks et al., *The World Past and Present*, p. 611.

13. Howard La Fay, "The Maya: Children of Time," *National Geographic* (December 1975): 738.

14. Banks et al., *The World Past and Present*, p. 223.

15. Linda Schele and David Schele, *A Forest of Kings: The Untold Story of the Ancient Maya* (New York: William Morrow, 1990), p. 90.

16. Banks et al., *The World Past and Present*, p. 615.

17. William Norman Grigg, "Vilifying Columbus," *The New America*, 5 October 1992, 26.

18. James A. Banks et al., *The United States and Its Neighbors* (New York: Macmillan/McGraw-Hill, 1993), p. 85.

19. Georg K. Neumann, "Evidence for the Antiquity of Scalping from Central Illinois," *American Antiquity* (1940): 287.

20. Alpheus Hyatt Verrill, *The Real Americans* (New York: G. P. Putnam's Sons, 1954), p. 37.

21. William W. Warren, *History of the Ojibways* (1852; reprint, Minneapolis: Ross and Hines, 1957), pp. 500–501.

22. John Palliser, *Solitary Rambles and Adventures of a Hunter in the Prairies* (London: n.p. 1853), p. 286, cited in Alfred W. Bowers, *Hidatsa Social and Ceremonial Organization* (Washington, D.C.: Smithsonian Institution Bureau of American Ethology, 1965), p. 277.

23. Robert F. Spencer and Jesse D. Jennings, *The Native American* (New York: Harper and Row, 1977), pp. 111, 308.

24. Verrill, *The Real Americans*, p. 37.

25. Almon Wheeler Lauber, *Indian Slavery in Colonial Times Within the Present Limits of the United States* (Williamstown, Mass.: Corner House, 1913), p. 40.

26. Chrestien Le Clercq, *New Relation of Gaspesia* (1910; reprint, New York: Greenwood Press, 1968), p. 271.

27. James A. Banks et al., *Regions Near and Far* (New York: Macmillan/McGraw-Hill, 1993), p. 111.

28. Clement W. Meighan, "Bury My Bones at Wounded Knee," *National Review*, 27 May 1991, 34, 35–36. See also Meighan's "The Burial of American Archaeology," *Academic Questions* 6 (summer 1993): 9–19.

29. For further information on how Indians disposed of their dead, see Paul S. Martin et al., *Indians Before Columbus* (Chicago: University of Chicago Press, 1947); Thomas Morton, *The New English Canaan* (1632; reprint, New York: Burt Franklin, 1883).

30. Harold Driver, *Indians of North America* (Chicago: University of Chicago Press, 1961), p. 451.

31. For a good discussion of *machismo* and Hispanic family life, see Bron B. Ingoldsby, "The Latin American Family: Familism v. Machismo," *Journal of Comparative Family Studies* (1991): 57–62. See also Raymond E. Wiest, "Male Migration, Machismo, and Conjugal Roles: Implications for Fertility Control in a Mexican Municipio," *Journal of Comparative Studies* (summer 1983): 167–181.

32. Kenneth S. Cooper et al., *Eastern Hemisphere* (Morristown, N.J.: Silver Burdett Ginn, 1995), pp. 376–383.

33. Robin Wright, *Sacred Rage: The Crusade of Modern Islam* (New York: Linden Press/Simon and Schuster, 1985), p. 55.

34. Banks et al., *United States and Its Neighbors*, p. 353.

35. Davidson, *The American Nation*, p. 200.

36. Arthur M. Schlesinger, Jr., *The Disuniting of America: Reflections on a Multicultural Society* (New York: W. W. Norton, 1991), p. 97.

37. Lewis H. Morgan, *League of Hodenosaunee or Iroquois* (Rochester, N.Y.: Sage and Brother, 1851), p. 111.

38. Banks et al., *United States and Its Neighbors*, p. 114.

39. Davidson, *The American Nation*, p. 47.

40. Lewis H. Morgan, *Ancient Society* (1877; reprint, Cambridge, Mass.: The Belknap Press of Harvard University Press, 1964), p. 68.

41. James Walls, "The International Year of the World's Indigenous People: 'First Nations' Speak Out," *Choices* (June 1993): 17.

42. Banks et al., *United States and Its Neighbors*, p. 123.

43. William Cronon, *Changes in the Land: Indians, Colonists, and the Ecology of New England* (New York: Hill and Wang, 1983), p. 50. See also H. J. Lutz, "Aboriginal Man as an Historical Cause of Fires," *School of Forestry Bulletin, No. 65,* (New Haven, Conn.: Yale University, 1959), pp. 1–22.

44. Cited in Michael Williams, *Americans and Their Forests* (Cambridge: Cambridge University Press, 1989), p. 44.

45. Omer C. Stewart, "Why the Great Plains Are Treeless," *Colorado Quarterly* (summer 1953): 48.

46. H. Maxwell, "The Use and Abuse of the Forests by the Virginia Indians," *William and Mary Quarterly* (1910): 355–380.

47. Paul S. Martin, "Prehistoric Overkill," in *Pleistocene Extinctions: The Search for a Cause* ed. Paul S. Martin and H. E. Wright, Jr. (New Haven, Conn.: Yale University Press, 1967).

48. Williams, *Americans and Their Forests,* p. 49.

49. Martin and Wright, *Pleistocene Extinctions,* p. 115.

50. Calvin Martin, *Keepers of the Game* (Berkeley: University of California Press, 1978), p. 105.

51. Jerome R. Reich and Edward L. Biller, *United States History* (New York: Holt, Rinehart and Winston, 1988), p. 65.

52. Banks et al., *Regions Far and Near,* p. 108.

53. Banks et al., *United States and Its Neighbors,* p. 597.

54. "Nice Country, Nice Mess," *The Economist,* 29 June 1991, 9.

55. Banks et al., *The World Past and Present,* p. 377.

56. Robert Lerner, Althea K. Nagai, and Stanley Rothman, "History by Quota?" *Academic Questions* (fall 1992): 79.

57. Schlesinger, *The Disuniting of America,* p. 30.

58. Lerner, "History by Quota," pp. 77–78.

59. Ibid., p. 77.

60. Robert Lerner, Althea K. Nagai, and Stanley Rothman, "Filler Feminism in High School History," *Academic Questions* (winter 1991–1992): 34.

61. Gary Nash, *American Odyssey: The United States in the Twentieth Century* (Glencoe, Ill.: Macmillan/McGraw-Hill, 1991).

62. Elbridge Henry Goss, *The Life of Colonel Paul Revere* (Boston: Joseph George Cupple, 1891), 1:118.

63. Ibid., p. 128.

64. *National Standards for United States History* (Los Angeles: National Center for History in the Schools, 1994), p. 57.

65. Ibid., p. 107.

66. Paul R. Gross and Norman Levitt, *Higher Superstitions: The Academic Left and Its Quarrels with Science* (Baltimore: Johns Hopkins University Press, 1994).

67. Ibid.

68. John Leo, "The National Museums of PC," *U.S. News and World Report,* 10 October 1994, 21.

69. John Leo, "The PC Attack on Heroism," *U.S. News and World Report,* 31 October 1994, 36.

70. Yoshiko Uchida, *The Bracelet* (New York: Philomel Books, 1993), p. 1.

71. Deborah Hopkinson, *Sweet Clara and the Freedom Quilt* (New York: Alfred A. Knopf, 1993).

Chapter 6

Diversity: A One-Way Street down Leftist Lane

Nothing in the world is more dangerous than sincere ignorance and conscientious stupidity.

Martin Luther King, Jr.

The mass media love to use the word "diversity" whenever and wherever possible, and among liberal college professors and multicultural textbook publishers—most of them missionaries of diversity—the word and the phenomenon are feverishly promoted. Educators think they are relevant when they bow to "diversity." Even many major businesses (for example, Mobile, Apple Computer, Xerox, Digital Equipment, AT&T, and Procter and Gamble) are increasingly genuflecting before the altar of diversity, constructed by multiculturalists. They believe that diversity programs in the workplace will enhance productivity and sales. Few stop to ask what the quest for diversity means and what long-term effects it might have on their nation's well-being.

Multiculturalists argue that diversity has been an American phenomenon since the Founding Fathers. Nathan Glazer shows that America's Founding Fathers indeed spoke of diversity, but it was not the diversity that multiculturalists are trying to impose on the country. To the multiculturalists it means diversity of race, ethnicity, countercultures, and varying sexual life-styles. To the Founders it referred "to the differences among the laws of the states, not to the diversity of religion, race, and ethnicity."[1]

Many institutions have ignorantly climbed aboard the bandwagon by trying to implement what they think is diversity, often not understanding what multiculturalists really mean by diversity. Note the following example. A conservative Lutheran university in suburban Chicago recently published an article titled "Focus on Diversity." Apparently, wanting to be trendy, the article notes that the institution is now diverse because it no longer has an all-Lutheran student body, as it once did. It goes on to say that its "value-centered Christian education" attracts "students of all denominations," and that it no longer prepares only Lutheran parochial school teachers but also offers a variety of other majors.[2] This university seriously thinks it is practicing diversity as multiculturalists promote it. But if one were to ask its administrators whether the school condones placing all religious beliefs on the same level of validity or truthfulness, or if it approves the existence of homosexual groups on campus, the answer would be an unequivocal no. This kind of credulity and ignorance often exists in American society today with regard to diversity. Such ignorance only helps multiculturalists become more entrenched.

THE SHAM OF DIVERSITY

Any serious observer of the so-called diversity phenomenon, particularly as it is practiced and promoted on our college campuses, immediately sees that "diversity" is not diversity at all. It is a pretense, a sham, a fraud, a one-way street down leftist lane.

Webster's Unabridged Dictionary defines diversity with the synonyms difference, dissimilitude, unlikeness. But the exponents of diversity typically contradict this meaning. As Joseph Epstein has said, the current quest for diversity is only a diversity of like-minded individuals. It is a rigid conformity to a leftist philosophy of life; it is group-think, lock-step conformity with leftist thinking, and not diversity at all. We can point to any number of illustrations showing the one-sidedness of the so-called diversity phenomenon.

• Seattle University formally invited Thomas Lauer, a Central Intelligence Agency (CIA) employee, to serve as a visiting professor in 1991, but canceled his appointment before he arrived on campus. Evidently, the administration feared protests and disruptions from the multiculturalists, who felt that permitting students to learn from a CIA agent would not fit the leftist agenda of "diversity."[3] Logically, however, this is precisely what one would expect if genuine diversity existed.

• California State University rejected scholarships from the Sons of Italy, the Italian American organization, which earmarks some of its monies for needy American students of Italian descent. The university's special assistant to the president informed the organization that the university would not accept racially or ethnically directed scholarships unless they were intended for African Americans, Native Americans, or Hispanics.[4]

• Houston University in Texas dismissed a Russian immigrant, Fabian Vaksman, from the school's graduate program because of his anti-Marxist views which angered the History Department's powerful Marxist professors. According to an Associated Press report, Vaksman has now won a court ruling to be reinstated so he can complete his doctorate. But the university said it would appeal the court's decision.[5] Here, too, diversity is a sham, not to mention the violation of the time-honored tradition of academic freedom in higher education. What would have happened had the Marxist professors been treated as they had treated the graduate student? They would have howled that they had been deprived of academic freedom and that the university was stifling diversity.

• Linda Chavez, a Hispanic-American who believes Hispanic immigrants should learn English in the United States as soon as possible, was disinvited after she was asked to give the commencement address at the University of Northern Colorado in 1990.[6] The next year Chavez received another insult from the exponents of diversity when Arizona State University canceled her speaking engagement. The person who wrote the cancellation letter said: "The Minority Coalition has requested that we cancel this engagement and bring other speakers whose views are more in line with their [sic] politics."[7]

• Similarly, Indiana University's Union Board, in 1993, refused to let Patrick Buchanan, the conservative columnist, be one of its campus speakers. His views were classified as "extremist."[8]

Indeed, the diversity that is being pushed and forced on students and administrators by multiculturalists and their apostles on virtually every university or college campus is a giant fraud. A recent (1993) survey of fifty colleges and universities by Young America's Foundation found college students were almost exclusively subjected to leftist speakers. Only three of the fifty universities had conservative or moderately conservative speakers for their commencement exercises. None had any speaker who was a free market scholar, a Reagan- or Bush-appointed judge, or a religious leader.[9]

The diversity that is promoted is diverse only in the sense that it is at odds with the traditional Western, capitalistic, or Judeo-Christian value system. Any belief or behavior that questions the leftist or neo-Marxist agenda of the diversity proponents is immediately condemned and commonly squelched, with countless university administrations condoning or carrying out such intolerant action.

Have the promoters of diversity ever asked some of the following to speak on campuses? Thomas Sowell, Shelby Steele, Billy Graham, Clarence Thomas, Rush Limbaugh, William F. Buckley, Walter Williams, or other noteworthy conservatives. Has anyone ever heard diversity proponents welcome on campus the formation of groups such as Right to Life, Rush Limbaugh clubs, the Fellowship of Christian Athletes, or the

Christian Coalition? What multiculturalists want is a diversity of like-minded individuals, with no tolerance for conservative or Euro-American norms and values. The diversity exponents are engaged in the "cloning of the American mind," as one analyst phrased it. Their talk of diversity is primarily Orwellian doublespeak.[10]

Unbelievably, such one-sided behavior is being promoted and approved on many university campuses, where we would expect genuine diversity of thought and ideas. If universities and colleges will no longer allow genuine diversity, where then might it be found? Certainly not in the classrooms or books controlled by multiculturalists. The warriors of multiculturalism in essence destroy genuine diversity in the name of diversity.

KEEPING PREJUDICES ALIVE

According to the *New York Times*, citing statistics from the American Council on Education, about 25 percent of all colleges have diversity requirements.[11] But most diversity programs keep people's prejudices alive by accenting ethnic, racial, sexual, and behavioral differences. So-called diversity-minded students on many college and university campuses have pressured the spineless administrators into giving ethnic and minority groups segregated housing, bringing back the separate-but-equal philosophy. Thus more and more campuses now have dormitories, or dormitory floors, for black students only, houses for those of Hispanic origin only, "J" houses for Jewish students, and separate housing for homosexuals and lesbians. The University of Pennsylvania, for example, has a black yearbook, even though the institution's black population totals only about six percent. At the University of California at Berkeley, blacks and Hispanics cheer for the same sports team but sit in separate (segregated) sections.

Many university administrators and professors are either unwilling or unable to see what is alarming many perceptive students. Haynes Johnson, in his recent book *Divided We Fall*, cites one such student at the University of Wisconsin, who saw the tragedy of the new prejudices countenanced by universities. "What essential social skills do we learn by practicing separatism?" she asked. She was commenting on the university's MultiCultural Center, which has primarily become a place for students of one minority group.

While racial or ethnic groups are forming separate housing and other kinds of segregated student activities, all-white groups are prohibited. The all-white group would constitute racism; the other practice signifies multicultural diversity.

Vassar College in 1991 had a separate graduation ceremony for black students, some of whom wore African "liberation" colors: red, green, and black. This special attire was paid for by general student fees. What would have been the reaction if white students had asked for a separate graduation ceremony? In the loudest shouts imaginable, many students would scream racism, and justifiably so. But when minority groups request privileges that are clearly racist, leftist officials in education, stricken with white guilt, bow to their requests in the name of diversity.

This kind of diversity, based on ethnic, sexual, and racially segregationist politics, is keeping group prejudice alive and is even spawning new forms of prejudice. It teaches people to become color conscious rather than color blind, and it resuscitates the racist separate-but-equal principle. What the diversity advocates are presently doing could hardly be done better by the Ku Klux Klan.

AFROCENTRICISM: DIVERSITY OR NEO-RACISM?

Diversity exponents are enthusiastically supporting a new ideology, Afrocentrism, which argues that "culture and civilization are racially determined."[12] Afrocentrism also degrades and despises everything that is Eurocentric. Black Americans are told to reject Western concepts and mentality and to replace them with African concepts so that people will understand "the centrality of Africans in post modern history," says Molefi Kete Asante, an Afrocentric guru.[13]

Leonard Jeffries, the controversial Afrocentrist and black professor at the City College of New York, says that Europeans (white people) are "ice people," who grew up in cold caves and gave the world the three Ds: domination, destruction, and death.[14] Black people, on the other hand, are "sun people," who are warm, humanistic, and communitarian because they grew up in the sunny part of the world and have more melanin in their skin.[15] This kind of reasoning, says Anne Wortham, a black opponent of Afrocentrism, "resembles the claims of Nazi leaders, who preached German racial superiority."[16]

Other Afrocentrists, such as Asa Hilliard, argue that "Africa is the mother of Western civilization."[17] Martin Bernal has also made this claim in his *Black Athena: The Afroasiatic Roots of Classical Civilization* (1991). This book is a warmed-over argument from Marcus Garvey, a radical black Jamaican, who in 1914 said: "To study the history of the Negro is to go back into a primitive civilization that teems with the brightest and best in art and the sciences."[18] In the guise of diversity, multiculturalists have introduced Afrocentrism into the school curricula of major cities including Portland, Pittsburgh, Milwaukee, Indianapolis, Detroit, Baltimore, Atlanta, and elsewhere by means of the *African-American Baseline Essays* (1990).[19] The *New York Times* reported on October 10, 1990, that a school system in Indianapolis, teaching Afrocentrism, tells its high school students that Africans were "the first to show genius in art and architecture." The person in charge of this school system's multiculturalist education also tells students that Africans sailed to America 2,000 years before Columbus. Neither claim can be historically verified. They are the mere fabrications of alienated black multiculturalists, who have an intense dislike for America and the cultural heritage that has made it great.

Afrocentrists want black Americans to learn only from black teachers. This is racism. Nevertheless, the exponents of multiculturalist diversity, who are quick to accuse the society at large of racism when blacks are not on a par with whites, even when there is no racism, fail to see the racist aspects of Afrocentrism which they are avidly promoting.

Afrocentrists also argue that black Americans should not be subjected to Euro-American culture but instead need to study and adopt African culture. The implication here is that there is only one African culture, never mind that Africa has hundreds of cultures and language groups, not just one. More to the point is the question that various critics of Afrocentrism have asked: Will adopting African culture, which usually means wearing some African nation's clothing styles, replacing one's European name with an African name, and imitating some African rituals make any black American a more productive, prosperous, or well-adjusted citizen? The average black American knows the answer is no, and that is probably why the vast majority of blacks have little or no interest in Afrocentrism. This racist ideology is not promoted by rank-and-file black Americans but by the radical, alienated multiculturalists.

If Afrocentrism continues to grow and gain momentum, racial relations in the United States can only regress. The progress that has been made in racial integration since *Brown v. Board of Education* (1954) and since the Civil Rights Act (1964) is being subverted.

The timidity of the media's reporters and analysts was very conspicuous in the all-black-male ("Million-Man March") gathering that assembled in Washington, D.C., in October 1995. Louis Farrakhan, who organized this massive gathering of black men, displayed behavior that paralleled some of Adolph Hitler's performances in the 1930s. Hitler was able to pack hundreds of thousands of people in open-air places; so did Farrakhan. Hitler sometimes spoke for two or more hours; so did Farrakhan. Hitler accused the Jews of exploiting the society; so did Farrakhan. Hitler pointed to his ability to attract large crowds to justify his ideology; so did Farrakhan. Hitler spoke with uniformed body guards; so did Farrakhan. But the media failed to note these parallels.

AFFIRMATIVE ACTION: PROMOTING COLOR CONSCIOUSNESS

Forever bent on having more diversity, multiculturalists are increasingly using racial and ethnic quotas (known as Affirmative Action) to achieve their goals. In the name of diversity, the University of Texas School of Law recently defended its racist policy of admitting black applicants with Texas Index scores of 190 and Hispanics of 189, whereas whites had to have a minimum of 199.[20] Similar examples can be found at virtually every major university in the country.

Merit or competitive admission to universities is now seen as racist, an impediment to "diversity." Students are increasingly admitted on the basis of skin color or ethnicity, not intellectual acumen or academic preparation. The original intent of Affirmative Action was equal opportunity, not racial preference. As Dinesh D'Souza has said: "Quotas which were intended as instruments of *inclusion* now . . . function as instruments of *exclusion* [*sic*]."[21]

The few who dare criticize Affirmative Action are quickly and effectively silenced by those who see themselves as the only true exponents of racial justice. Dissenters are socially isolated, even "purged," as Stephen L. Carter, a black professor at Harvard University, shows in his *Reflections of an Affirmative Action Baby* (1991). Speaking about quotas, Carter declares: "Few Western-style purges are more disheartening, and more threatening to freedom, than the disdainful treatment of intellectuals who dare to challenge fashionable academic orthodoxy."[22] Carter maintains that these purges are especially tragic when they exclude dissenters who are black. Here he has in mind renowned black scholars and critics of Affirmative Action such as Thomas Sowell, Walter Williams, Glenn Loury, Julius Wilson, and Shelby Steele whose black experience and thoughts cannot be shared with other blacks who stand to benefit from them. Black opponents of Affirmative Action are silenced by being called "Oreos" (black outside but white inside), while white dissenters are labeled racists. Such labels scare off large numbers of would-be public critics. These intimidated souls, often harbor their resentment within themselves, and so instead of quotas extinguishing the flames of racism, they often reignite them. When that occurs, it is never considered the fault of the quota propagators; only the critics are guilty.

Quotas are also an insult to the dignity of the minority. Because of quotas, many individuals never know whether it was their skin color or their competency that gained them admission to an elite university or an appointment to a prominent post.

The quota practices have been given a new twist in the Clinton administration. Since May 1993 this president has allowed tours of the White House to be conducted on the basis of diversity standards.[23] No longer are individuals allowed to tour on a first-come basis, which was the practice for decades before Clinton became president. Now individuals may tour the White House only when a group is adequately mixed, racially and ethnically, so that each group will be "more representative of America." Those who arrive first are often held back so that every group will be of a "diverse composition."

The Clinton administration has recently implemented yet another form of diversity quotas. In the Department of Justice, bureaucrats recently compiled a Federally Scheduled Ethnic Entities (FSEE) list that includes black Americans, Hispanics (the list calls them Latinos/Latinas), Asian Americans, Pacific Islanders, American Indians (on the list it is Native Americans), and Eskimos (the list names them People of the Northern Sun). According to Peter L. Berger, a renowned sociologist, the list of FSEEs is "intended to help employers and others to define more clearly the categories of people to be scheduled for inclusion in a properly diversified labor force."[24]

In the end, quotas are also harmful to society as a whole. For example, Thomas Sowell has shown that in Sri Lanka (formerly Ceylon) racial quotas eventually led to "race riots, atrocities, and civil war."[25] And Alexander Bickel's study shows that "a quota is a divider of society, a creator of castes."[26]

Despite such studies, the diversity mongers are unmoved. They are passionately engaged in implementing racial and ethnic quotas wherever they can, and with their minds already made up, they don't want to see contrary facts. The quest for diversity blinds them from seeing any problems with quotas. Unfortunately, the American courts, including the United States Supreme Court, have not helped matters. As Melvin Urofsky notes: "Even as political leaders tried to define what Affirmative Action meant, the courts pondered whether and how the Constitution allowed such programs."[27]

One wonders how long it will be until quotas will be extended to other areas of life. Less than one percent of the airline pilots are black. When will the advocates of the quota system demand that 12 percent of the pilots be black and 9 percent Hispanic (matching up with the current percentage of blacks and Hispanics in America)? It is doubtful that such a large percentage would be really qualified. Who would be willing to be a passenger on a plane where the qualifications are lowered to meet quotas? Would even the promoters of diversity be willing to ride on such planes? Do we want grade-point averages lowered so that quotas also can be met in medical schools? If so, are we willing to have such individuals perform highly technical medical procedures on us when they become physicians?

If taken to its logical conclusion, Affirmative Action will require that football, basketball, or baseball players also be hired on the basis of quotas. We all know that blacks are overrepresented and other minority groups extremely underrepresented; for instance, there are few Chinese or Vietnamese in varsity or professional basketball. Obviously, an across-the-board quota system would be absurd, but multiculturalists have perverted Affirmative Action's initial goal to the point that reverse discrimination is operative and "equality" is more important than quality.

By 1996, Affirmative Action had finally aroused the indignation of enough Americans, including some blacks, that some politicians openly voiced their opinions as to the injustice of this policy. Opponents of Affirmative Action argue that the practice essentially gives preference to people on the basis of race, sex, or ethnicity, and thus it is reverse discrimination. The issue has gone beyond mere debate. The opponents gathered enough signatures to get the matter, known as the California Civil Rights Initiative, on November's election ballot for people in California to vote for or against the policy.

FROM SEXUAL PERVERSION TO SEXUAL PREFERENCE

Not so long ago one could finish high school and not know that an extremely small percentage of people in society were homosexuals. Today children in kindergarten, if not earlier, hear about some individuals being called gay or homosexual. These youngsters may not understand what these terms really mean, but they do know that these individuals do something different sexually.

Multiculturalism's apostles not only promote the tolerance of homosexual behavior, but also work fervently to get schools, churches, and businesses to accept it as an alternative lifestyle. On many major university campuses, students who express objections to homosexual behavior, which is increasingly being approved and institutionalized by universities and colleges, are disciplined or even expelled. Several years ago a student at the University of Michigan was punished for writing a limerick about a well-known sports figure's alleged homosexual behavior.[28] This student's traditional views were genuinely diverse from those advocated by the diversity proponents, but they were not tolerated. He was required to write an essay for the school paper confessing his sin, and he also had to participate in homosexual rap sessions.

At another university some male students tacked a sign on their dormitory door which read: "This Room Is Straight." These students were forced to undergo twenty hours of counseling. At the counseling sessions they were asked how they could condemn homosexuality if they had never tried it. At Marietta College in Ohio, a student referred to lesbianism as "deviant" in a paper published by the student newspaper. For this he was charged with "sexual harassment." The administration intended to expel him from the college, and undoubtedly would have done so, had not the Individual Rights Foundation (California based) interceded with a litigation threat for violating the student's First Amendment rights. The Board of Trustees blocked the administration's intended action, and the student retained his good standing.[29]

Given that opposing positions and views are increasingly not allowed to be expressed in the name of diversity, homosexuality is becoming more and more legitimated, especially on America's campuses. The educated community seems to be extremely ignorant of what homosexual behavior is and seems to be unaware that homosexual behavior violates the natural physiological functions of the human body. Thus it has been condemned for thousands of years by all civilized societies until recently.

If colleges, legislators, and social institutions were not so easily swayed by homosexuals (who only represent two or three percent of the country's population), they would draw a firm line to keep homosexuality on the list of unacceptable behavior. University administrators and professors, who repeatedly tell taxpayers that universities are research institutions, should give more honor to research by examining what scientific medical studies have revealed about homosexual behavior. Instead, they commonly give support to the homosexual movement. For instance, Cornell University offers a minor in homosexual and bisexual studies. Grinnell College (in Iowa) has a resource center, a library, and a conference center for homosexual studies, and UCLA has a fraternity for male homosexuals and a sorority for lesbians.[30]

If university/college administrators and faculty would look at the research data rather than listen to homosexual propaganda that ignores the scientific findings, as well as common sense, they would find that the evidence unequivocally shows homosexual behavior to be destructive to those who engage in it. In 1984 the *Journal of the American Medical Association (JAMA)* published the results of a medical study showing that the human rectum is not made for penile intercourse. Unlike the female vagina, whose mucosa squamous multilayered epithelium protects it from abrasive effects during penile intercourse, the rectum has only a single layer of columnar epithelium. In sexual intercourse, the rectum "is not only incapable of protecting against any abrasive effect but also promotes the absorption of sperm antigens, thus enhancing their exposure to the immune apparatus in the lymphatic and blood circulation."[31] In short, the anal canal is not made for sex, no more than the ear canal is. Yet despite the scientific evidence, many college/university administrators, professors, liberal clergy, and even some physicians continue to believe the propaganda that homosexual behavior should be accepted and even promoted as a harmless, "alternative lifestyle."

As the general public knows, practicing homosexuals expose themselves to serious infections, of which AIDS is the most common and the most deadly. Thus it is no surprise to read, as the *Los Angeles Times* pointed out on June 16, 1994, that AIDS is now the number-one killer of homosexual males. In 1990 the Colorado Department of Health reported that 85 percent of 1,500 AIDS cases involved homosexual behavior.

The scientific data cited below reveal homosexual behavior so unnatural that heterosexuals often find it hard to believe. But facts are facts. Thus uncomfortable as one might be (and I am) in mentioning the following homosexual practices, for the sake of the uninformed, the following facts are cited. Not to mention them would be to withhold evidence from the public that it has a right to know, especially as homosexuality is considered to be part of multiculturalism.

One medical study of male homosexuals that included samples from Los Angeles, Atlanta, New York, and San Francisco by Harold Jaffe and associates found 62 to 78 percent had engaged in "rimming."[32] Another study found 92 percent of the male homosexuals and 53 percent of the lesbians participated in oral-anal sex.[33] Similar results have been found in Canada.[34] Oral-anal sex is dangerous. One medical report in San Francisco reveals that such behavior easily leads to the ingestion of fecal matter and thus produces a high incidence of hepatitis A.[35]

In addition to oral-anal behavior, many homosexuals engage in grotesque behavior. A study by Jaffe and his associates found 33 to 52 percent of the homosexuals engaged in "fisting."[36] Another study revealed many homosexuals use "toys," inserting foreign objects or small animals (often gerbils) into the rectum. And 29 percent said they had taken "golden showers," urinating on their partner(s).[37]

In a study of five major metropolitan areas in the United States, researchers found sado-masochistic behavior was practiced by 37 percent of male homosexuals.[38] In April 1993, the National Sado-Masochist, Leather/Fetish Conference was held in Washington, D.C. This conference had for sale leather whips, full-length body racks, hoods of chain, cattle prods, and electro-torture devices for interested homosexuals.[39] If some readers doubt that sado-masochism is practiced by many homosexuals, they might want to consider some want ads that appeared in the homosexual magazine the *Advocate*. One advertises: "Slave wanted by doctor. Not pretend fantasy. Must surrender totally." A second says: "Enemas: Lean young (18+) white men call . . ." Another offers: "Spankings, All Kinds."[40]

If most university/college administrators, professors, and business leaders really knew that extreme sexual behavior was widespread among homosexuals, they, as rational and educated leaders, would no longer support homosexuality. But as we know, it is supported under the rubric of "diversity."

The present permissive, and perhaps ignorant, posture toward homosexuality is reminiscent of the Greco-Roman culture that St. Paul condemned in his letter to the early Christians in Rome:

Claiming to be wise, they became fools. . . . For this reason God gave them up
to dishonorable passions. Their women exchanged natural relations for unnatural, and their men likewise gave up natural relations with women and were
consumed with passion for one another, men committing shameful acts with men
and receiving in their own persons the due penalty for their error (Romans 1:22,
26–27).

But Paul's words are widely ignored. For example, the administration
at Stanford University even advertised for homosexual resident advisers,
and at Cornell University applicants for the job of resident counselors
had to watch movies showing homosexuals engaging in sex with one
another.[41] Given the research findings on homosexual behavior, which
reveal the unnatural and biologically harmful effects, it is not hard to
see why Paul wrote the above words.

A large percentage of male homosexuals also engage in sex with young
boys. To note this is not engaging in fear-mongering, homophobic, or
insensitive behavior, as some may say. But it is done to inform the public
regarding the man-boy "love" issue. For some time there has been an
organization advocating pederasty. One member of the North American
Man Boy Love Association (NAMBLA) recently said that although man/
boy love represents a minority "within the gay subculture, it [is] far from
unusual."[42] In support of this claim, he cites a 1978 study by Bell and
Weinberg which revealed that 25 percent of white homosexual males and
14 percent of black homosexual men had sex with boys 16 years or
younger.[43] Another study found 23 percent of a sample of 4,329 male
homosexuals had sex with boys under 16 years of age.[44]

These findings are supported by additional studies—notably by Kinsey's research showing that 37 percent of homosexuals had engaged in
sexual relations with boys under 17 years of age and 28 percent with
boys under 16 years;[45] and by another study revealing that 35 percent of
boys between 15 and 19 years of age had been approached to have sex
by adult homosexuals.[46]

The *Journal of Homosexuality* in 1991 devoted an entire issue to man/
boy homosexuality, and not one article condemned the behavior. One
essay questioned the nationwide assumption that sexual contact with an
adult is harmful and traumatic to the child. It also tried to distinguish
between child sexual abuse and pedophilia, implying that the two should
not be equated.[47]

Given our society's increasing acceptance of homosexuality, it is easy
to see why the advocates of man/boy relationships are becoming more
assertive. Consenting-adult homosexuals have made tremendous inroads
in recent years. Some organizations, for example, give hiring preferences
to homosexuals, as Northeastern University in Boston has recently
done.[48] The National Education Association (NEA) now supports efforts

to teach first graders about the acceptability of homosexuality.[49] And in 1993 a curriculum committee in New York City almost succeeded in subjecting first graders to books that pictured homosexuality and lesbianism as acceptable ways of living. The following pro-homosexual books were on the committee's proposed list: *Heather Has Two Mommies; Jennifer Has Two Daddies; Gloria Goes to Gay Pride,* and *Jennifer Lives with Eric and Martin.* Another, *Daddy's Roommate,* shows two men sleeping together as would a husband and wife.[50] Finally, the mayor of San Francisco pronounced and blessed the "virtual marriages" of 200 gay and lesbian couples in March 1996.[51]

Conceivably, legislators, educators, businesses, and many religious leaders could be persuaded that it is bigoted not to allow sexual contact of any variety. As Don Feder says: "If homosexuality is legitimized [which has already occurred] no perversion (sadomasochism, incest, sex with children) can logically be opposed."[52] In a society in which moral relativity already reigns, it does not seem far fetched that NAMBLA's objectives will also be given legitimacy someday. This group has already made serious advances toward legitimacy. Since 1993, it has indirectly, received approval from at least twenty-one member countries of the United Nations' Economic and Social Council by granting consultative status to the International Lesbian and Gay Association (ILGA) of which NAMBLA is a member. In 1990 ILGA recognized pedophiles as a "sexual minority."[53] The "minority" designation is the first step in getting government someday to protect pedophiles under civil rights laws.

When the day comes that pedophilia becomes acceptable in America, the Trojan horse and its multicultural warriors will have essentially conquered the nation, and America the beautiful will have become America the decadent.

FROM TOLERATING TO "CELEBRATING" DIVERSITY

In the fall of 1993, *Time* magazine published a special issue titled "Celebrating Diversity." This expression is heard quite frequently in the propaganda of multiculturalism. When it is uttered, the impression is given that we have something new and great in America. So we must celebrate it.

Multiculturalists who think ethnic and cultural diversity is a new phenomenon in the United States are simply ignoring the nation's immigration history, especially the period of 1880 to 1915. During this era a huge influx of immigrants from Germany, Russia, Greece, Poland, Romania, Serbia, Croatia, Armenia, Turkey, and other countries arrived. Given their large numbers and different cultures, it was not uncommon to see people wearing all sorts of foreign dress on the streets of our large cities. Most of the immigrants were too poor to buy American-style clothing.

And in factories, coal mines, and meat-packing houses, it was common to hear the workers speak half a dozen, or more, foreign languages.[54]

According to the 1900 census, 13.6 percent of the U.S. population was foreign born, representing over forty countries.[55] In contrast, the 1990 census revealed a total of only 7.9 percent foreign-born.[56] Indeed, as Louis Menand writes, "we are far more 'American' now than we were 60 years ago. . . . And in many ways, we're becoming a more integrated people every day."[57] Yet the multiculturalists are forever telling Americans that the United States today has more diversity than at any time in history. So yet another multiculturalist refrain has proven false.

There was a great deal of diversity in the American past, but unlike the situation today diversity was tolerated, not celebrated. Americans in the past saw no need to celebrate something they did not see as beneficial or advantageous to their nation's welfare. Even the immigrants—and certainly their children—soon gave up their diversity. They wanted to become Americans, not retain foreign differences. There were no hardcore multiculturalists, as we have today on college or university faculties and in the halls of government, lamenting the meltdown of immigrant cultures in the great American melting pot. There were no multiculturalist ideologues telling immigrants to resist assimilation. Nor did anyone accuse the United States of committing cultural genocide as immigrants were expected to become assimilated Americans.

In the name of diversity, since 1980, election ballots have been issued, especially in California, in Spanish, Chinese, and some American Indian languages. This is quite different from the 1790s, 1840s, and 1860s when the Congress had enough wisdom to reject requests to print government documents in German.[58] By refusing to publish documents in German, the Congress showed it was willing to tolerate the German presence but not to celebrate it. The Congress would do well to repeat its actions of 200 years ago. But alas, many of its members also appear to be infected with the virus of multiculturalism, and thus it appeases multiculturalists and their anti-assimilationist bedfellows.

There are two kinds of diversity promoters. One type is simplistic, believing they can encourage and advance diversity without planting the seeds of ethnic or racial enmity or conflict. These activists do not seem to believe that decades of multicultural diversity in the former Yugoslavia produced the present civil war in which the Serbs, Croats, and Bosnians are now slaughtering each other. It is rather ironical that while the Clinton administration is part of the United Nations' efforts to stop the ethnic warfare in the Balkans, it is at the same time expending considerable energy to implement multiculturalist practices at home.

The simplistic types often utter the clichés of diversity in ignorance. Here is an example. On Thanksgiving Day 1995, the CNN television channel asked school children in the primary grades what Thanksgiving meant to them. One young boy, apparently mouthing the propaganda that his teachers had fed him, said that he was "thankful for diversity." If diversity continues to grow, and with it the inevitable arrival of schisms, divisions, and multi-morality, this young lad will have been thankful for the wrong thing—for the future destruction of his present culture.

George Santayana's now well-worn words are not being heeded: "Those who cannot remember the past," he warned, "are condemned to repeat it."[59] History has no impact on these credulous promoters. They are interested only in keeping all ethnic and racial differences alive, even encouraging the formation of new separate groups on the basis of race and ethnicity. They fail to see the logical outcome of diversity programs, namely, group conflict and strife. As Andrew Hacker has recently said: "A multicultural America may seem benign in a classroom syllabus, but we shouldn't be surprised if the result is conflict in the streets."[60]

The other kind of diversity promoters are the hardcore multiculturalists who are influenced by Marxism. They seem to follow a script, notably Lenin's, which stated that "Guaranteeing the rights of a national minority is inseparably linked with the principle of complete equality [communism]."[61] In the same way, multiculturalists are trying to use the power of government to preserve the culture of every ethnic and minority group. They scorn assimilation, and potential conflict does not seem to bother them. Nothing is more important for them than multiculturalist diversity.

AWAY WITH THE "CANON"

Multiculturalists have given the word "canon" a negative connotation by contending that the works (the "canon") of prose, poetry, and philosophy that were for decades, and even for centuries, considered essential in a curriculum that provided a good liberal-arts education, are today racist, sexist, and culturally bigoted. This conclusion, as we have stated, stems largely from multiculturalism's neo-Marxian ideology which sees everything as political. Thus they seek to remove or at least minimize use of the works of Homer, Plato, Aristotle, Virgil, Augustine, Dante, Shakespeare, Milton, Locke, and others like them. The works of these dead white European males (DWEMs), as they call them, must give way to current writings that revolve around the sociopolitical problems of race, class, and gender.

Debate over the canon, specifically over the required courses in Western civilization, at Stanford University resulted in the university dropping the required courses in Western civilization, replacing them with a group of nonrequired courses known as "Culture, Ideas, Values." These new courses are devoted to multiculturalism's trinity: race, ethnicity, and sex. With this new direction, the university has capitulated to multiculturalism's anti-Western and Euro-American prejudices. Much irony is inherent in this incident. Stanford University, as Roger Kimball says, is "a glittering product of Western culture,"[62] but by this action it accepted the multiculturalist propaganda that Western culture is evil and oppressive.

Whether or not the faculty at Stanford (or other institutions) realizes it, by succumbing to the demands of the radical multiculturalists, it helped those who say that all education is political. The multiculturalists' neo-Marxist cry that everything is political is becoming a self-fulfilling prophecy. By requiring courses that revolve around race, ethnicity, and sex—all political topics—curriculum changes are showing that education is becoming political in colleges and universities. But more than that, education is no longer true to the process of intellectual discovery. Instead, it is becoming political browbeating.

The argument over the so-called canon has occurred at numerous other institutions of higher learning as well as Stanford. Wherever multiculturalists are getting their way, the consequences have been tragic; chief among the casualties is the longstanding Western belief that truth and ideas transcend race, class, and sex, and that the truths taught by the classical authors are true and relevant for all people. It was Karl Marx who first argued that the ideas of truth were class-bound: "It is not the consciousness of men that determines their existence, but on the contrary, their social existence determines their consciousness."[63]

Social existence and conditions sometimes do help shape ideas and affect the understanding of truth, but it is quite another thing to argue that this is the only way to truth or ideas. The multiculturalist Marxist view of truth asserts that no truth exists outside of people's social experience. In other words, truth is not universal, and it must serve the group from which it comes. That is why the new courses offered by multiculturalists focus on minority or "oppressed" groups.

As Erik von Kuehnelt-Leddihn has shown, the Marxists (communists) and the Nazis (fascists) are both leftists, politically. In putting both groups left of center, he is going against today's common understanding of the former being leftist and the latter rightist, a faulty perception that apparently arose as a result of the Nazis having fought against the communists in World War II.

Kuehnelt-Leddihn correctly argues that communists and Nazis are more alike than different, ideologically. For instance, both groups are socialists, opposed to capitalism. Indeed, the official name of the Nazi party used the word "socialism" as in the *Nationalsozialistische Deutsche Arbeiter Partei* (NDASP). Hitler's followers referred to themselves as NSDAP, as dedicated socialists. Kuehnelt-Leddihn rightly argues that neither communists nor Nazis believe in democracy; both see the government as the people's savior; both dislike religion, especially Christianity; both dislike and distrust individualism; both are materialistic; neither likes private property; both outlaw opposing political parties; both promote central control of government; both see the end justifying the means; and both see truth as relative and political.[64] As Hitler's propaganda spokesman, Joseph Goebbels, declared: "Truth is that which serves the German people." This leftist understanding of truth relativizes truth, a position diametrically opposed to the Judeo-Christian concept of truth which has always held that truth is transcendent and universal, independent of people's social experience, be it ethnic, sexual, or racial. The assumption that truth is universal and transcendent is especially pertinent to Western universities which have always justified their existence in terms of searching for universal truth, not "truths" that are bound to race, class, or sex.

As noted in Chapter 3, what old-line Marxism was unable to achieve with its sociopolitical propaganda and its militaristic muscle until 1990— namely, to destroy the basic institutions of the capitalist culture—neo-Marxist-oriented multiculturalism is beginning to accomplish by destroying the belief in objective, transcendent truth, on which American institutions are built. As Stanley Fish, the radical multiculturalist at Duke University, has said in connection with demolishing the so-called canon: "The whole idea of 'Americanness' has been thrown in question."[65]

The dismantling of the "canon" has other consequences as well. First, as William Reeves observes: "It is a cruel hoax to eliminate Western civilization [courses] from the education of America's most recent immigrants." He argues that they "deserve to know the best that has been known and thought."[66] Indeed, they come to this country because it is, as Lincoln said, "the world's last best hope." The last thing these people want is alienated multiculturalists telling them that the country they have entered to achieve the American Dream has a culture that is not worth studying. Second, a lopsided bias is at work on many campuses. For instance, at Cornell University students are required to take at least one course in a non-Western culture, but they can graduate without taking a single course in Western culture or civilization.

The canonoclasts are making at least three statements here: (1) Western culture is not worth studying; (2) even if it is worth studying, it is not important whether or not students are exposed to it; and (3) if students do not study Western culture, they will hopefully have no future interest in defending it from the onslaughts of future multiculturalists' attacks. People will not defend something they no longer understand.

DIVERSITY AS SELF-FULFILLING PROPHECY

As all sociologists know, a false definition seen and treated as true eventually creates what the false definition asserts. This phenomenon is called a self-fulfilling prophecy, and it fits the current hype regarding diversity. Even though there is less diversity in America today than in the past, in time people could begin to join or identify with ethnic/subcultural groups or deviant cultural practices previously seen as detrimental to national unity and personal well-being. Not to be left out of the diversity phenomenon, they will conform and play the part. Then the promoters of diversity will say: "You see, we told you ours was a diverse society." The false prophecy will have been fulfilled, and America will have become Balkanized.

NOTES

1. Nathan Glazer, "The Constitution and American Diversity," *The Public Interest* (winter 1987): 11.

2. "Focus on Diversity," *The Forester* (summer 1994): 1.

3. "University Cancels C.I.A. Officer's Appointment," *The Chronicle of Higher Education*, 2 October 1991, A4.

4. Peter Collier and David Horowitz, eds., "Italians Need Not Apply," *Surviving the PC University* (Studio City, Calif.: Center for the Study of Popular Culture, 1993), p. 326.

5. Ibid., p. 30.

6. Denise K. Magner, "Reagan Appointee's Speech Canceled After Students at Arizona State Object to Her Conservative Views," *The Chronicle of Higher Education*, 11 September 1991, A19.

7. Ibid.

8. Nick Felten, "Good, Bad, and Ugly at IU," *Campus* (fall 1994): 12.

9. Tony Mecia, "Leftist Speakers," *Campus* (winter 1994): 13.

10. David Thibodaux, *Political Correctness: The Cloning of the American Mind* (Lafayette, La.: Huntington House Publishers, 1992).

11. Michael Winerip, "Faculty Angst over Diversity Courses Meets the Student Zeitgeist at U Mass," *New York Times*, 4 May 1994, A13.

12. Anne Wortham, "Errors of the Afrocentrists," *Academic Questions* (fall 1992): p. 40.

13. Molefi Kete Asante, *Afrocentricity* (Trenton, N.J.: Africa World Press, 1989), p. 6.

14. Cited in Arthur M. Schlesinger, Jr., *The Disuniting of America: Reflections on a Multicultural Society* (New York: W. W. Norton, 1992), p. 67.

15. Robert Hughes, "The Fraying of America," *Time*, 3 February 1992, 49.

16. Worthman, "Errors of Afrocentrists," p. 45.

17. Cited in Schlesinger, *The Disuniting of America*, p. 69.

18. Marcus Garvey, "A Talk with Afro-West Indians: The Negro Race and Its Problems," in *The Marcus Garvey and Universal Negro Improvement Association* (Berkeley: University of California Press, 1983), p. 57.

19. Schlesinger, *The Disuniting of America*, p. 70.

20. Jeffrey Burk, "Texas Law School Sets a New, Racist Standard," *Campus Report* (December 1993): 1.

21. Dinesh D'Souza, *Illiberal Education* (New York: Free Press, 1991), p. 29.

22. Stephen L. Carter, *Reflections of an Affirmative Action Baby* (New York: Basic Books, 1991), p. 103.

23. Thomas Roeser, "Enough of This Diversity Nonsense," *Jacksonville (Illinois) Journal-Courier,* 30 June 1993, 8.

24. Peter L. Berger, "Sorting Us Out," *First Things* (February 1994): 12.

25. Thomas Sowell, *Preferential Policies: An International Perspective* (New York: William Morrow, 1990), p. 181.

26. Alexander Bickel, *The Morality of Consent* (New Haven, Conn.: Yale University Press, 1975), p. 133.

27. Melvin I. Urofsky, *A Conflict of Rights: The Supreme Court and Affirmative Action* (New York: Charles Scribner's Sons, 1991), p. 38.

28. John Leo, "The Academy's New Ayatollahs," *U.S. News and World Report,* 10 December 1990, 22.

29. See "Individual Rights Foundation Case Docket," *The Defender* (March 1994): 9.

30. DKL, "Squeaky Chalk," *Campus Report* (February 1994): 2.

31. Giora M. Mavligit et al., "Chronic Immune Stimulation by Sperm Alloantigens: Support for the Hypothesis That Spermatozoa Induce Immune Dysregulation in Homosexual Males," *Journal of the American Medical Association,* 13 January 1984, 240–241.

32. Harold Jaffe et al., "National Case-Control Study of Kaposi's Sarcoma and Pneumocystis Carinii Pneumonia in Homosexual Men, Part 1, Epidemiologic Results," *Annals of Internal Medicine* 99 (August 1983): 148.

33. Paul Cameron and Kay Proctor, "Effect of Homosexuality upon Public Health and Social Order," *Psychological Reports* (June 1989): 1172.

34. M. T. Schechter et al., "Changes in Sexual Behavior," *Lancet,* 9 June 1984, 1293.

35. Lawrence Corey and King K. Holmes, "Sexual Transmission of Hepatitis A in Homosexual Men: Incidence and Mechanism," *New England Journal of Medicine,* 22 February 1980, 435–438.

36. Jaffe, "National Case-Control Study," p. 148.

37. Cameron and Proctor, "Effect of Homosexuality," p. 1171.

38. Ibid.

39. Joyce Price, "Sadomasochistic Display Held in Federal Building," *Washington Times,* 14 May 1993, A3.

40. *Advocate,* 13 August 1991, 10 and 30 July 1991, 16.

41. Thomas Sowell, "Boomerang," *Forbes,* 12 October 1992, 63.

42. David Thorstad, "Man/Boy Love and the American Gay Movement," *Journal of Homosexuality* 20 (1991): 253.

43. Ibid., p. 269.

44. Karla Jay and Allen Young, *The Gay Report* (New York: Summit Books, 1979), p. 275.

45. P. H. Gebhard and A. B. Johnson, *The Kinsey Data: Marginal Tabulations Conducted by the Institute for Sex Research* (New York: Saunders, 1979).

46. M. Schofield, *The Sexual Behavior of Young People* (Boston: Little, Brown, 1965).

47. Gerald P. Jones, "The Study of Intergenerational Intimacy in North America: Beyond Politics and Pedophilia," *Journal of Homosexuality* 20 (1991): 275–295.

48. See Mary Crystal Cage, "Diversity or Quotas?" *The Chronicle of Higher Education*, 8 June 1994, A13.

49. "Gay and Lesbian Caucus Targets Youth: First Graders Must Be Taught Tolerance," *Education Reporter* (August 1994): 1.

50. For a detailed account of this "diversity" attempt, see Stephanie Gutmann, "The Curriculum That Ate New York," *Insight*, 15 March 1993, 6–11.

51. Cary Goldberg, "Virtual Marriages for Same-Sex Couples," *New York Times*, 26 March 1996, p. A8.

52. Don Feder, *A Jewish Conservative Looks at Pagan America* (Lafayette, La.: Huntington House Publishers, 1993), p. 69.

53. "U.N. Grants Voice to Gay Group with Pedophile Ties," *Lambda Report* (September 1993): 1.

54. See "Journey to America," a video produced by Public Broadcasting System, 1991.

55. *Abstract of the Twelfth Census of the United States, 1900* (Washington, D.C.: Government Printing Office, 1904), p. 13.

56. *Statistical Abstract of the United States, 1993* (Washington, D.C.: United States Department of Commerce, 1993), p. 50.

57. Louis Menand, "School Daze," *Harper's Bazaar* (September 1992): 381.

58. William A. Henry III, "Against a Confusion of Tongues," *Time*, 13 June 1983, 30.

59. George Santayana, *The Life of Reason* (New York: Scribner, 1905), 1:284.

60. Andrew Hacker, " 'Diversity' and Its Dangers," *New York Review of Books*, 7 October 1993, 22.

61. Vladimir Ilyich Lenin, *Collected Works* (Moscow: Progress Publishers, 1972), 20:42.

62. Roger Kimball, *Tenured Radicals* (New York: Harper and Row, 1990), p. 28.

63. Karl Marx, *A Contribution to the Critique of Political-Economy* (1859; reprint, New York: International Publishers 1970), p. 21.

64. Erik von Kuehnelt-Leddihn, *Leftism Revisited: From de Sade and Marx to Hitler and Pol Pot* (Washington, D.C.: Regenery Gateway, 1990).

65. Cited in James Atlas, *Battle of the Books: The Curriculum Debate in America* (New York: W. W. Norton, 1990), p. 59.

66. William J. Reeves, "Who Wants a Color-Coordinated Cross-Cultural Core Curriculum?" *U.S.A. Periodical* (March 1993): 56.

Chapter 7

Political Correctness: Multiculturalism's Police

The modern world is full of old Christian virtues gone mad.
                                        G. K. Chesterton

In order to achieve the goals of multiculturalism, its promoters try to bar and even punish speech or behavior that criticizes or deters the values or practices of non-Western or minority cultures. They believe such a stance is necessary because they see those cultures as culturally disadvantaged and oppressed as a result of the Western or Euro-American culture's racism, sexism, classism, and cultural imperialism. To agree with the aims and methods of minority cultures, as well as implement them, is said to be "politically correct" (PC) and to act contrary is "politically incorrect." Although they do not purportedly use these terms, their behavior indicates otherwise, especially when they deem a statement or an act to be politically incorrect. Generally, it is the critics of multiculturalism who use the term when they are criticizing its advocates for advancing their radical causes.

The expression "politically correct" appears to have originated in a speech that Karen de Crow made in 1975 while she was president of the National Organization for Women (NOW). In that speech, according to William Safire, she said that NOW was moving in a "politically correct" direction.[1]

During the last several years, most Americans have gained a fairly good idea of what being "politically correct" means—namely, getting people to conform to the thoughts, names, and actions that are promoted and advanced by the zealous advocates of multiculturalism. When individuals, for instance, college or university students, do not conform, they are sometimes disciplined or even expelled. Actually, it constitutes reverse bigotry practiced in the guise of eliminating bigotry. In the words of Rush Limbaugh, PC is political cleansing, excising people's thoughts and ideas that are contrary to your own.[2]

Safire may be correct in dating the expression's literal origin, but its meaning goes back much farther. The communists of the former Soviet Union and the fascists of Hitler's Germany practiced their version of political correctness long before the current multiculturalists came on the scene. Speech or behavior that was not in line with communist or fascist values was not "politically correct," and as such was sternly and severely punished.

Multiculturalism's obsession with getting people to be PC often is reminiscent of communist and fascist tactics. Its advocates may not send the politically incorrect to Siberia or to concentration camps—they do not have that much power—but they are increasingly imposing various punishments, some of them quite severe, on those who do not conform to their rigid norms. The PC enforcers are even coercing students on many college and university campuses into participating in specially designed "sensitivity sessions" that amount to brainwashing. They are also suspending and expelling students for ignoring their newly devised speech codes. While they are telling the public they support diversity, they want everyone to conform in goosestep-like fashion to their ideology, their reverse bigotry. Many colleges and universities have special administrators whose primary duties are to enforce the PC agenda. At the University of Pennsylvania that person is called the judicial inquiry officer.

POLITICALLY CORRECT GOALS

The PC promoters may seem to have numerous goals, but in reality they amount to only two: (1) to impose multiculturalist values that relativize all knowledge and standards of truth, except their own; and (2) to dismantle the Euro-American culture.

In order to accomplish their goals, the PC advocates, like genuine radicals, accept no middle ground: One either is for them or against them. As one observer put it: "Either you are pro-gay rights or homophobic. Either you are fighting for feminist causes or you are a chauvinist."[3]

POLITICALLY CORRECT NAMES AND LABELS

Many of the multiculturalists' efforts are ridiculous when they try to make Americans use the "politically correct" term for some trait or behavior. But to the PC promoters none of their efforts is humorous. PCers see nothing funny about anything they consider important, and what they see as important is political in nature. Every concern of theirs is somber and gravely serious. Like the communists and Nazis, they see nothing amusing about any of their beliefs or policies.

Recently, one wag at Harvard Divinity School came upon two outdoor recycling bins; one marked "White Paper Only" and the other "Colored Paper." He changed the second bin to read "Paper of Color," humorously conforming to the PC term "people of color," which today includes people who are black, brown, red, and yellow, but not white. The school's recycling coordinator did not find the changed sign humorous. "If this is meant to be a joke," he pompously stated, "I don't think it's funny."[4] Nor, one might add, do the PCers think it humorous when people laugh at their insistence that fat people be called the "laterally challenged" or short and tall people the "vertically challenged."

The push for PC names or labels commonly takes two directions. The first is to make a minority or ethnic group or disadvantaged person look good, and the second is to minimize or eliminate certain symbols or time-honored heroes of the nation's dominant culture. The second approach is illustrated by what occurred at the University of Massachusetts at Amherst in 1993. Students and the cooperative chancellor tried to ban the historic Minuteman, the school's official mascot. This symbol, used since 1972, was too white, too male, and too macho, they insisted. The PC efforts, however, were stymied by an outraged public.

In order to make certain groups or individuals look good, the following PC names have been advocated, and even forced on people and institutions. Many PC terms are humorous at best. Here are some examples.

POLITICALLY INCORRECT	POLITICALLY CORRECT
Physically handicapped	Physically challenged[5]
Tall or short people	Vertically challenged
Fat people	Laterally challenged
Prostitutes	Sex workers
Bums or hobos	Homeless people
Nonwhite minorities	People of color
Illegitimate children	Children of single mothers
Homosexual	Gay/Lesbian
Sodomy	Same sex
Hispanics	Latinos
Freshman	First year or freshperson
Pets	Animal companions

Blackboard	Chalkboard
Illegal aliens	Undocumented workers

Along with PC attempts to make certain groups look good, serious efforts have been made to make certain culturally accepted groups or practices look bad. Again, here are some illustrations

POLITICALLY INCORRECT	POLITICALLY CORRECT
Hunters	Animal rights violators
Heterosexuals	Straights
Heterosexual values	Heterosexism
Not pro-homosexuality	Homophobia
Admiring a beautiful woman	Looksism
Columbus Day	Indigenous People's Day
Logical thinking	Logocentrism
Classical books	The Canon
Biblical Christians	Religious right
Patriotism	Chauvinism

The PC disciples leave no stones unturned. They have even invaded computer software. The word processing program of WordPerfect 6.0 comes with built-in style checker, called Grammatik. It gives the user a hefty dose of PC. Should one happen to type the word "girl," it tells the writer to avoid using this term, as well as "girlish," when referring to an adult woman. It also informs the user that "colored" is offensive to blacks and that "African-American" is to be used. The program further says that one is not to use words like "chairman" or "stewardess." Such words are inappropriate; they are too gender specific.[6]

In the 1960s it became unacceptable to use the term "colored people" when referring to American Negroes. We were all urged to call them "black people." In reality, we are back to the 1960s when we are urged to use the term "people of color," which is the PC term for all nonwhite minorities. What is the difference between colored people and people of color? It is like saying that colored paper is different than paper of color.

Another PC promotion is the term "Native American." But this term is both incorrect and an insult to every native-born American, for it implies that only American Indians are natives and that all other Americans are foreigners. Furthermore, it ignores the historical fact that American Indians once were immigrants too. The only difference is that they arrived much earlier than the Europeans. Yet multiculturalists try at every opportunity to institutionalize the term "Native American"—perhaps to assuage the white guilt that plagues so many multiculturalists.

ATHLETIC NICKNAMES AND MASCOTS

The PC patrol has also entered the sports arenas accusing the nick-names of given teams of being "politically incorrect," especially those that employ names or symbols of American Indians. Thus concerted, but so far unsuccessful, attempts have been made to have a number of professional baseball and football teams drop their Indian nicknames or mascots. The Atlanta Braves have recently been assailed for not dropping their nickname. The tomahawk chop, done regularly by the Atlanta fans during the games, has also come under attack. It is said to be offensive to the nation's first inhabitants. Similarly, the names Washington Redskins and Cleveland Indians are considered "politically incorrect."

The PC crowd has not been very successful in the area of professional, commercial sports, but it is a different story on college/university campuses. No where has there been a faster knee-jerk compliance to the PC demands than on the campuses. Marquette University (Milwaukee) recently dropped the name "Warriors." In October 1993, at the University of Iowa student supporters from the University of Illinois, prior to a Big Ten game, were forbidden to use any symbols or images of American Indians, including "Chief Illiniwek," the University of Illinois mascot, in the parade at Iowa City. The University of Southern Colorado dropped the nickname "Indians" and did away with its mascot, "Warrior Willie." Fort Lewis College (Colorado) changed its logo the third time in as many years. Initially, its logo was a mounted, charging U.S. cavalry soldier holding an extended sword. The PCers saw this image as offensive to American Indians. In 1992 the sword was replaced with a pennant displaying the school's initials, FLC. Then in 1993 the school dropped the cavalry man and adopted a golden eagle.[7]

Numerous other colleges and universities have acquiesced to the PC crusade of not "offending" American Indians. But the fact is that not all Indians are offended. For instance, the PCers were rebuffed at the College of William and Mary (Virginia) when they wanted to eliminate the school's athletic nickname, The Tribe. Before they were able to mobilize their forces to have the school ban its Indian nickname, an astute conservative reporter of the campus newspaper *The Remnant* interviewed the chiefs of Virginia's resident Indian communities and found that every one of them liked the nickname and wanted the college to keep it.[8]

Nor did the Indians in Florida object to Florida State University's using the nickname "Seminoles." Neither did Indians in Kansas go along with the PCers, where Chief Dawes gave his approval to the Indian mascot, Giego, for use by Ottawa University. Chief Dawes said opposition to Indian mascots and nicknames comes from "the fringe militants who make their living by making this fuss, not legitimate Indian leaders."[9]

To Marxist-oriented multiculturalists, these Indians are in a state of

false consciousness. They need to be enlightened by the PC correct elite
so that they will stop the insensitive Euro-Americans from insulting the
"native Americans" and their culture.

Although numerous other schools could be cited using Indian names
or symbols, it is not only Indian names and mascots that are under PC
attack. The Minuteman controversy at the University of Massachusetts
has already been noted. Dixie College (Utah) no longer flies the Confederate flag that once symbolized the college's Southern name.[10] At the
University of Alabama (Birmingham) the newly unveiled mascot,
"Blaze," a Nordic-looking character, lasted only one day. Reportedly, it
did not represent women or minorities. It looked too much like a "dominant," white male.[11]

Any mascot that might possibly suggest white-male dominance must
go. The so-called tolerant, diverse multiculturalists are especially intolerant with regard to anything that might hint, ever so vaguely, of white-
male prominence. So whenever athletic logos might lend credence to
white-male dominance, they are expurgated. The University of South
Carolina's mascot is a gamecock, and its athletic yell is "Go Cocks, go."
This was an enormous PC taboo, so it had to be eliminated. Kennesaw
State College in Georgia, whose athletic teams call themselves the "Hooters" and whose basketball arena is called "Hooterdome," dropped the
nickname in 1993 upon complaints from radical feminists. The term allegedly demeans women because "hooters" is also a coarse term for
women's breasts.[12]

When one reads or hears about the furor that the PCers are creating
relative to the use of nicknames and mascots by athletic teams, a couple
of questions come to mind: First, are these people really serious?
Astoundingly, they are. Second, don't they know that nicknames are
selected to bestow honor on the teams who use them? Nicknames or
mascots are not used to demean or insult, for instance, the American
Indians, from whose cultures many are derived. Mature Indians know
this, and accordingly a number of them and their leaders have recently
approved the use of nicknames for various sports teams.

DOWN WITH TRADITIONAL, EURO-AMERICAN VALUES

"Political correctness" is not confined to changing names or terminology. It frequently attacks the existing values and standards of the Euro-
American culture. Thus it is PC to

burn the American flag

place condoms in campus dormitories

accept women into the military

despise fur coats

promote and defend Affirmative Action

support animal rights groups

bash WASPs

force the Boy Scouts to accept atheists

remove Christian symbols from public buildings

permit women reporters in men's locker rooms

scorn IQ tests

let boys play with dolls

call American blacks "African-Americans," not blacks

call American Indians "Native Americans"

support abortion on demand

not criticize illegitimate births

accept homosexual ("same-sex") marriages

condemn Christopher Columbus

see AIDS as a heterosexual disease as much as it is a homosexual one

ban prayer in public schools

allow homosexuals in the military

bash white males

have only women teach women's studies

have only blacks teach black history

depict capitalism as evil

portray Judeo-Christian values as stifling diversity

Changing names so they are PC has also invaded religious terminology. In 1994 *The New Testament of the Inclusive Language Bible* was published by Cross Cultural Publications. This "translation" neuters "God the Father," a common biblical expression, by rendering it as "Parent" or "heavenly Parent." The opening words of the Lord's Prayer say: "Our heavenly Parent." Where Jesus says: "I and the Father are one" (John 10:30), this volume has: "I and My heavenly Parent are one." Even more recently, the United Church of Christ (UCC) issued a new hymnal, and of course, it conforms to "political correctness." The phrase "Son of God" in the familiar Christmas carol *Silent Night* was replaced by "Child of God,"[13] an example of neutering Christ. In the quest for the politically correct, by striving for "inclusive language" in religious publications some glaring inconsistencies have resulted. As Warren Farrell has said, the PCers, together with their feminist cohorts, only want inclusive language when it stands them in good stead. Thus the feminine pronoun, she or her, is only appropriated to God, never to the devil.[14]

In pursuit of being religiously PC, as Kenneth L. Woodward has observed, at least one thing has been forgotten. That is, "good hymns are works of art, not ideology. Their integrity deserves respect, and so do the traditions from which they spring."[15]

FREE SPEECH FOR ME BUT NOT FOR THEE

In order to enforce political correctness, its proponents have constructed speech codes that spell out what may or may not be spoken. Such codes have been largely produced on college and university campuses, where liberal administrators (see Chapter 12) have succumbed to the disciples of multiculturalism. As of May 1992, more than 300 institutions of higher learning punished "speech either in specific speech codes or as part of their overall rules of conduct."[16]

Rutgers University's (New Jersey) speech code says it will punish "students whose words offend on the basis of race, religion, color, ancestry, sex, handicap, marital status, or sexual orientation."[17] Most university speech codes are remarkably similar to the one at Rutgers. Whether the codes violate the First Amendment is, of course, not a concern of multiculturalists. That would matter only if *they* were not able to express their radical views. What counts is free speech for me, not for thee. As James Hunter correctly says, the PC position "is so 'obviously superior,' so 'obviously correct,' and its opposite so 'obviously out of bounds' that [opposing views] are beyond serious discussion and debate."[18]

Speech restrictions at universities are not plaguing just professors and students. A senior manager at the Duke University Medical Center was suspended without pay for four weeks because he "apparently referred to a job applicant as a homosexual after observing his mannerisms during the application process."[19]

Frequently, the PCers seem to care more about who says what rather than what is said. If professors or students are white males, they are particularly vulnerable to being accused of "offensive" or "insensitive" speech and ideas. At Tufts University a black student alleged she was humiliated by a professor's "racism and callousness." He had recommended *Tally's Corner* (a frequently used urban sociology book), and he also had had some questions about Affirmative Action.[20] At the University of Missouri, Professor Frederick Spiegel decided to retire rather than fight the charge of being a "racist" because he criticized Supreme Court Justice Thurgood Marshall."[21]

In 1991 Judge Robert W. Warren ruled against the University of Wisconsin's speech code that barred what it considered slurs or epithets pertaining to a person's race, sex, religion, sexual orientation, and ethnic origin. The judge declared that the "fighting words" doctrine of the *Chaplinsky v. New Hampshire* case (1942), which universities have tried to hide behind, did not apply to the university's code. In a unanimous decision, the U.S. Supreme Court ruled in *R.A.V. v. St. Paul* (1992) that free speech cannot be barred even if it includes racial epithets and the burning of crosses. This ruling led some journals, for example, *The New Republic* (July 13 and 20, 1992) to declare that this ruling would make campus speech codes impermissible. Indeed, this was a logical conclusion but not necessarily true to fact. As of summer 1996, the *R.A.V. v. St. Paul* decision had not really led colleges to annul speech codes, nor had it stopped the harassment of students who express themselves contrary to PC dogma.

As noted in Chapter 6, at Marietta College (in Ohio) a student referred to lesbianism as "deviant" in a campus newspaper. He was charged with "sexual harassment," and the college intended to expel him. What would have happened had the situation been reversed? That is, what if a lesbian student had called this same student "homophobic," and he had charged her with sexual harassment? Does anyone who is familiar with what is happening on many campuses today believe this college or any other institution would have threatened the lesbian with expulsion? No, because multiculturalists commonly practice reverse bigotry.

The University of Minnesota recently confiscated literature of the Young Republicans and other conservative groups under the ruse that these groups did not receive prior approval to distribute it. Here, as in other instances, the Individual Rights Foundation came to the rescue, and the case was settled without litigation.[22] At Occidental College (California) a sexual harassment code, written in conformity with the requirements of the federal Department of Education, prohibited "unwelcome jokes, invitations, comments, and looks." This code even allowed third-party members to file charges. The Leonard Law (California), which bars all institutions of higher learning from writing rules that are contrary to the First Amendment, was invoked by the Individual Rights Foundation and the college had to rescind its code.[23]

There are dozens of other tragic examples of PC–fascist-like tactics directed against free speech, too numerous to list or discuss in this chapter. Nonetheless, one more case merits mention. The Phi Kappa Sigma fraternity, a racial and ethnically mixed group, at the University of California at Riverside (UCR) used rush t-shirts depicting a *sombrero*-clad mascot. The t-shirt aroused the PCers' ire and of course the university administration. As is quite common, it sided with the accusers who branded the fraternity as "racist." Even the fraternity's national headquarters capitulated to the PC hysteria on campus. It demanded that the members formally apologize, perform sixteen hours of community service, and attend two sensitivity seminars on multiculturalism. But even this was not enough: The university's assistant vice chancellor revoked the fraternity's charter. Soon the fraternity heard from John Howard, the founder of the Individual Rights Foundation. Howard and the fraternity filed a suit against UCR accusing them of violating the Leonard Law and the country's First Amendment. The university soon realized that it stood on precarious ground and dropped all charges. But Howard and his organization did not let the university merely drop the charges. They took the PC practice of sensitivity training and turned it on its head by demanding that the university send its high-level administrators to sensitivity training for five hours—not in racism, sexism, or homophobia, but in respect for the nation's First Amendment. The sensitivity trainer was a constitutional lawyer.[24] What a felicitous turn of events for freedom lovers!

After reading these examples, which are only a small sample of the total, we might well wonder whether we are in America or in a totalitarian country. Camille Paglia is right when she describes the PC movement as "fascism of the left."

PC radicals are not just attacking free speech. They have also engaged in stealing and destroying campus newspapers that do not suit their political tastes. Protesters at the University of Massachusetts (Amherst) in 1992 stole 10,000 copies of the *Daily Collegian* because the paper did not publish "a large editorial condemning the first Rodney King verdicts."[25] In 1993 over 8,000 copies of a conservative paper, *The Lionhearted*, were seized on another campus by student protesters who objected to the paper's "caricature of a bikini-clad woman carrying a sign which read 'Feminist at Work.' "[26] At the University of Pennsylvania, some black students destroyed 14,000 copies of a student newspaper in April 1993 because they did not like its coverage of blacks. The university's administration—in its typically timid manner—decided not to punish the thieves.[27] What would have happened had a group of white males destroyed 14,000 copies of a PC newspaper?

The late columnist Walter Lippmann once wrote: "If there is a dividing line between liberty and license, it is where freedom of speech is no longer respected as a procedure of the truth and it becomes the unrestricted right to exploit the ignorance, and to incite the passions of the people."[28] Inciting the passions of the people—namely, credulous students and equally credulous and spineless university administrators—so that they no longer respect freedom of speech, has recently been an alarmingly successful PC tactic. One might excuse students for succumbing to the PC crowd, but how does one excuse their professors? Do they no longer have anything to profess when it comes to understanding and defending basic American rights such as the First Amendment? How will today's students as tomorrow's leaders retain and preserve our nation's freedoms at which multiculturalism has been gnawing away for a number of years with bigger and bigger bites? If students repeatedly see their mentors conform and knuckle under to the "politically correct" rather than uphold what is morally and constitutionally correct, how will they hold on to the liberties that their forefathers fashioned out of the Euro-American culture? How will they ever know it was not just any culture, but the Euro-American culture, that produced realistic visionaries who formulated the greatest principles and practices of liberty ever devised in human history? This will especially be true if multiculturalism's PC police succeed in outlawing critical examination of other cultures whom they want to have equal status vis-à-vis the American culture at large.

As noted in the previous chapters, the Trojan horse of multiculturalism has enabled its warriors to make significant and tragic inroads into American society. The recent PC attempts to outlaw the nation's longstanding, Constitutional tenets and practice of free speech are but one example of multiculturalism's powerful and tragic effects. As noted in chapters 1 and 2, multiculturalism is not some harmless phenomenon that merely acquaints us with other cultures, but rather it is a concerted social movement that seeks to undermine, dismantle, and replace basic American values, including the right of free speech.

HATE CRIMES, ANOTHER LEFTIST CONCEPT

In recent years the PCers have created the concept of hate crimes, building this concept into speech and conduct codes on many university campuses. They have now moved off the campuses to the state legislatures and have persuaded uninformed, credulous state and federal legislators to pass anti-hate crime laws that threaten people's private thoughts. As Rush Limbaugh says, the concept of hate crimes is an invention of political leftists to help them get "power over our *private thoughts*."[29]

In trying to sell the idea of hate crimes to the public, the PCers argue that such crimes are more harmful than nonhate crimes. Ask a zealous PC fan whether a white male, who once publicly voiced his dislike of minorities and who later killed a minority person in a bar brawl should receive the same sentence as, say, a white male who plans and proceeds to kill his wife's extramarital lover, also white. The answer will be no because the PCer will invariably consider the first crime more serious, because it occurred as a result of hate, whereas the second case was motivated by cold, calculated premeditation, as well as hate. In the first instance there was no premeditation, so why would PC advocates see it as more serious? Because no one should be permitted to think or say anything "insensitive" about any individual of a nonmajority or "less privileged" group. If any harmful behavior follows a previously "insensitive" remark, such a person is then guilty of a hate crime.

Whether or not a crime is committed out of hatred is of no consequence to either the victim or to society, for the effect is the same. If there is any difference, it is a purely political one, and that is why so-called hate crimes are held to be more serious than most other crimes.

Hate crimes rest on what an accused individual *said* or *expressed* before an incident or during it. Such "crimes" invariably clash with the First Amendment's guarantees of freedom of thought and expression. In a free society even bigoted speech—unfortunate as that might be—must be permitted. Once verbal expressions are criminalized on the basis of hate, there is no limit to what can be outlawed in the realm of speech. The ultimate political tyranny for people in a free society is to have authorities invade and investigate their private thoughts or verbal expressions. Given the present bent toward political correctness, how long will it be before the government will pass laws against so-called hate crimes, such as speaking against Affirmative Action, radical feminism, abortion on demand, illegitimate births, homosexuality, or multiculturalism? We have already seen how campus codes have been formulated to regulate speech and conduct—and sternly enforced—by numerous college and university administrations. When will the leftist PCers get the state and federal governments to pass laws making it a hate crime for anyone who speaks out against what they define as "politically correct"? If what has occurred on the campuses is a harbinger, that day might not be far off.

SEXUAL HARASSMENT LAWS

The politically correct movement has made tremendous inroads in the area of sexual harassment laws. These laws are redefining, often destroying, age-old relationships between men and women. Increasingly, men are afraid or unsure of what they may or may not say to a woman at work or elsewhere. "May I still look at a beautiful woman in a swimming suit on the beach without being taken to court?" "May I compliment a female acquaintance regarding her appearance without having her accuse me of sexual harassment?" "Shall I critically probe a female professor's comments in the classroom?" "Might she then charge me with sexual harassment?" Questions like these are on the minds of many men, and they are not indicative of paranoia.

With regard to the first question, people would do well to remember that in 1989 authorities in Canada forced a University of Toronto professor, Richard Hummel, to undergo extensive counseling for allegedly staring at a woman in the university's swimming pool. With regard to the third question, in 1988 the University of Washington at Seattle, expelled a male student for sexual harassment because he asked polite but probing questions of a female instructor in a course devoted to women's issues. And given the second question, the National Organization of Women says that sexual harassment exists whenever a man's behavior is "offensive or objectionable to the recipient." In other words, sexual harassment is whatever some possibly disgruntled woman thinks it is, regardless of how subjective and groundless her thinking might be. The irony here is colossal, especially since these kinds of definitions are coming from individuals who earn their livelihood in universities that were founded to promote objective, scientific reasoning.

That this kind of subjectivity is accepted and introduced by many educated individuals, in a scientific age, is ironic, and it reveals a rebellion against science and its logical methods. In true multiculturalist fashion, the bent toward subjectivity—a basic premise underlying sexual harassment laws—is another way by which multiculturalists show contempt for what they dub "logocentrism."

Sexual harassment laws are tragic in other ways as well. They violate one of the fundamental principles of the sexual equality argument, namely, that women are to be treated equally vis-à-vis men. Women, so the radical feminists argue, are not dainty little creatures who need to be protected and put on a pedestal. They must have all the rights and opportunities men have, and even be allowed to serve in the military. If that is so, then why is it necessary to protect them with anti-sexual harassment laws? Sexual harassment laws are saying, in effect, that women cannot take care of themselves; that they need laws to protect their weaker nature.

Warren Farrell has said it best. He notes that in one decade women have received "more protection against offensive jokes in the workplace than men [have received] in centuries against being killed in the workplace."[30] Farrell also observes that the present-day sexual harassment laws make all men unequal to all women. Moreover, what once was gossip expressed to a girlfriend now is often used as evidence in a court of law.[31]

Sexual harassment laws are also contrary to nature. Katie Roiphe has it right when she says that these laws fail to recognize that "unwanted sexual attention is part of nature."[32] Indeed, what would the world be like if nature did not move men to notice and pursue women? There would likely be no human populace. It appears that the radical feminist push for sexual harassment laws reveals a disguised anger against nature, or worse, against God who created two different sexes.

Sexual harassment laws are not the only example illustrating that multiculturalism's move toward PC behavior is bent on ignoring and rejecting nature. It also does so by trying to legitimate and institutionalize homosexuality, behavior that is unequivocally contrary to nature (see Chapter 6). The PCers need to be told (although it would probably make little or no difference) that those who defy nature eventually reap its curses, for example, environmental pollution.

Similar to the speech codes, sexual harassment laws often violate First

Amendment rights and perhaps the Fourteenth Amendment as well, as shown in the following incident. At the University of Nebraska (my alma mater), a male graduate student in psychology had a picture on his desk of his wife wearing a bikini at the beach. One day his two female office mates told him that the picture "created a hostile work environment."[33] At first he thought his female office partners were joking, but they soon let him know they were serious. The department chair sided with the two women and had him remove the picture, trampling on his constitutional right to free expression.

Some colleges and universities have self-appointed gender monitors— reminiscent of tactics in a totalitarian society—who go around the campus to see whether they can find "offensive" art and then demand that the administration take it down. Most administrators quickly comply, caring little or nothing about freedom of expression. At the University of North Carolina, a sculpture depicted a male student reading a book and holding his arm around a female eating an apple. This statue was "politically incorrect" because it reinforced traditional male-female roles. Soon a radical student group, the Committee Against Offensive Statues, had the chancellor relegate it to an inconspicuous place on campus where few would see it.[34] In another incident, PC students and some faculty members at Colgate University barred the exhibition of nude photographs by the renowned photographer, Lee Friedlander.[35] Examples like these can be multiplied across the nation—all of them occurring because of so-called sexual harassment concerns and all of them in violation of our nation's First Amendment.

Given the current state of sexual harassment laws and their accompanying policies, an additional observation merits mentioning. It pertains to an old saying: "The weakness of men is their facade of strength, and the strength of women is their facade of weakness." This saying once again has proven itself to be true in a way that many men or women have not yet realized. A few radical women, who unknowingly feigned sexual weakness have been able to get men (who overwhelmingly make up most legislating groups) to enact sexual harassment laws that made men unequal to women. By establishing these laws, men showed their weakness by thinking they were strong, even magnanimous. They thought they had no reason to fear such laws. The women showed their strength by asking for protection (unadmitted weakness) from unwanted sexual comments or gestures.

SOME HUMANS ARE VERY FRAGILE: HANDLE WITH CARE!

In order to achieve the PC agenda, whether it is adopting its language terminology, sexual harassment laws, or outlawing of free speech, proponents have learned an effective way of getting people to comply: Accuse them of "insensitivity." This tactic has helped the PCers get growing numbers of people to use and accept names, labels, and concepts, even when they are laughable or ridiculous. No one wants to be accused of being insensitive. This ploy has also enabled PC ideologues to get university and college administrators, an increasing number of businessmen, and even legislators to conform to their repressive ideology, the First Amendment notwithstanding.

At the University of Pennsylvania in 1993, Eden Jacobowitz, a Jewish student, tried to quiet a group of black women who were partying outside his dormitory. He told them they were acting like a bunch of "water buffaloes," a friendly term that has no racial connotation among Jews. Several female students, however, charged Jacobowitz with racial harassment (insensitivity). After the absurd charge received nationwide publicity, mostly negative, the university and the accusers dropped the charges.

Students may no longer object to having a homosexual roommate, for example, at Pennsylvania State University. If they do, they are labeled as insensitive, or worse, bigoted. At numerous universities, dormitory personnel conduct sensitivity workshops intended to "sensitize" students to everything that is deemed PC. These workshops are reminiscent of the brainwashing many American prisoners were subjected to by the North Korean communists during the Korean War in the 1950s.

Ironically, these sensitivity sessions are totally insensitive to those whom the PCers seek to sensitize. In one such session at the University of Cincinnati, the sensitivity "facilitator" harangued the white-male participants, telling them they were all racists and that blacks were not racist because they lacked power. She further ranted that white men, because they hold all the power, oppress all minorities, women, homosexuals, and the handicapped.[36] At San Bernardino Valley College (California), a professor of writing asked his students to write on pornography and to discuss Jonathan Swift's "A Modest Proposal." The professor was accused of sexual harassment. The college officials reprimanded him and required him to undergo sensitivity training.[37] Instances similar to these have been occurring on campuses across the nation in the name of promoting multiculturalist sensitivity.

A Harvard University professor had to cancel showing a film because it included a black maid. To show such a film would have been insensitive.[38] And John Leo reports that at Sarah Lawrence College in New York a student was charged with discriminatory harassment, another term for insensitivity. He also had to watch a video on homophobia and write a paper on it. Why? The poor fellow laughed when one of his friends shouted "faggot" during a campus argument.[39] At Southern

Methodist University (Texas), a student was punished for calling his roommate a "Mexican."

The PC efforts to establish sensitivity, of course, are all based on a double standard. Only white heterosexual males are capable of committing insensitive acts. Racial minority groups, homosexuals, or women are apparently not capable of being insensitive. For instance, at Cornell University homosexuals removed the American flag from a university building and replaced it with a pink triangle. If the situation had been reversed, the perpetrators would have been charged with insensitivity and probably expelled. Or consider the incident at Swarthmore College in Pennsylvania, where it was "politically incorrect" to fly the American flag. A socialist group on campus called the flag a "symbol of oppression and exploitation." In September 1994, when the Swarthmore students finally were able to vote on the matter, they overwhelmingly decided to restore the flag to the campus.[40] Who would ever have imagined that a vote would have to be taken to determine whether the American flag might be flown on an American campus!

Lest readers think the PC crusade is only happening on campuses, it is appropriate to some note off-campus incidents as well. According to one report, in October 1993 the state of California tried to confiscate a car license plate that displayed the letters PUSSY on it. The owner explained that she loved her cat. But the PC purists thought this license plate demeaned women, and they saw it as a form of sexual harassment.

Recently, the Federal Aviation Administration conducted a sensitivity session that "forced men to walk through a gauntlet of women, who fondled the men's genitals and ridiculed their sexual prowess."[41] As noted earlier, the sensitivity trainers are insensitive to those whom they accuse of being insensitive. One recalls Christ's words here: "Physician heal thyself."

In addition to not tolerating any comment or action that could possibly be construed as offending a member of a minority group, the PC movement also condemns any statement or negative evaluation of American subcultures or ethnic groups. If cultures are not to be critically evaluated, then logically the Allies in World War II were in error to destroy the Nazi culture; then the Christian missionaries must be condemned for eventually getting the Chinese to abandon the footbinding of young girls, a cultural custom that lasted a thousand years and did not end until the early twentieth century;[42] then the outlawing of slavery, at one time found in most societies, has also been a grievous, ethnocentric error.

These and many other cultural changes were in large measure brought about by individuals, who not only criticized given cultural practices, but also often brought force to bear in order to effect the desired changes. As noted earlier in the book, the American civil rights laws of the 1960s most likely would never have been enacted had there been no criticism of the racist and segregated practices in American culture.

One writer critical of the current sensitivity frenzy that is so prevalent in today's American culture said it eloquently: "A world in which only the inoffensive would be expressed would not merely be bland; it would be sterile."[43] Indeed! If one is not permitted to criticize culture(s) or subcultures, then what may be criticized? It is one thing not to criticize skin color, race, or innate characteristics over which people have no control, but it is quite another matter not to criticize culture over which people do have control. Culture, being man-made can and often should be changed. Skin color, racial features, and people's sex are ascribed characteristics made by God; they cannot be changed.

To prohibit scholars, students, or citizens from criticizing or evaluating other cultures or some ethnic group is an unmitigated tragedy. If one may not criticize the culture of societies or ethnic groups, then how will any of them improve? To this question, the relativistic multiculturalists respond that it is ethnocentric to assume that another society's culture needs improving. They should all be equally valued (an argument noted in Chapter 4). This line is fed to the public, and sad to say, it is often accepted. It is especially accepted by individuals in education.

In pursuit of cultural sensitivity, the PC crusaders have also launched an attack on ethnic humor. It is "politically incorrect" to tell or laugh at an ethnic joke. To multiculturalists, every minority or ethnic group is apparently so fragile and sensitive that one may not say anything humorous about any of them. Universities and colleges have, of course, been the first to outlaw ethnic jokes or laughter. For example, in 1989 the president of Stanford University was outraged by an ethnic joke file in the computers and ordered them destroyed. The Computer Science Department ignored the order, saying that would be tantamount to burning undesirable library books.[44] Newspapers and magazines have also joined the chorus in condemning ethnic jokes.

"Political correctness" has killed the old Latin proverb that says: "*Ridentibus arride*" (Laugh with those who laugh.) In the past, many ethnic groups in the United States who interacted with one another were no strangers to interethnic jokes. In Minnesota, for example, ethnic jokes were tossed back and forth among the Germans, Norwegians, Swedes, and Finns. In other parts of the country, jokes were told about the Irish, Scots, and English. There was a lot of give and take. These people had a sense of humor; they knew the difference between humor and an ethnic pejorative. Ethnic jokes did not divide these people. Many of them even intermarried.

The entire matter of PC is absurd, and like so much of multiculturalism, it has detrimental implications for the nation as a whole. Americans do not need thought or speech control, determined by "politically correct" enforcers, who tell them what to believe, think, or say.

NOTES

1. William Safire, "Linguistically Correct," *New York Times*, 5 May 1991, 18.
2. Rush Limbaugh, *See, I Told You So* (New York: Pocket Books, 1993), p. 227.
3. Tim Stafford, "Campus Christians and the New Thought Police," *Christianity Today*, 10 February 1992, 17.
4. John Hinton, "Ivy League Theology," *Academic Questions* (spring 1993): 42.
5. Recently (1994), a book discussing the problems of the physically handicapped was published carrying this term as its title. See Dale C. Garell, *Physically Challenged* (New York: Chelsea House, 1994).
6. "The Week," *National Review*, 11 July 1994, 10.
7. "College Changes Mascot Again, Again, and Again," *The Chronicle of Higher Education*, 13 April 1994, A4.
8. John Leo, "Indians Just Don't Get It," *U.S. News and World Report*, 27 January 1992, 22.
9. " 'Giego' to Return to Ottawa University," *The Chronicle of Higher Education*, 8 December 1993, A6.
10. "Dixie College Lowers Confederate Flag," *The Chronicle of Higher Education*, 9 February 1994, A4.
11. "Mascot Laid to Rest at University of Alabama," *The Chronicle of Higher Education*, 6 October 1993, A4.
12. Christopher Shea, "A Cloud over Symbols," *The Chronicle of Higher Education*, 10 November 1993, A33. See also John Leo, "Looking Back at a PC Extravaganza," *U.S. News and World Report*, 31 January 1994, 20.
13. Kenneth L. Woodward, "Hymns, Hers and Theirs," *Newsweek*, 12 February 1996, 75.
14. Warren Farrell, *The Myth of Male Power: Why Men Are the Disposable Sex* (New York: Simon and Schuster, 1993).
15. Woodward, "Hymns," p. 75.
16. Nat Hentoff, "Students Quickly Losing Their Freedom of Speech," *Campus Report* (May 1992): 7.
17. Ibid.
18. James Davison Hunter, *Before the Shooting Starts* (New York: Free Press, 1994), p. 5.
19. "Duke Administrator Sensitized," *Campus* (spring 1991): 13.
20. "Take Care," *The Economist*, 10 February 1990, 23.
21. "Thurgood Marshall Beyond Reproof," *Campus* (spring 1991): 13.
22. See "Individual Rights Foundation Docket," *The Defender* (March 1994): 9.
23. Ibid., p. 1.
24. Bill Cerveny, "Counter Coup: Rolling Back the Attack on Free Speech," *The Defender* (March 1994): 4.
25. Robert Bullock, "Race Riders Strike Another Paper," *Campus Report* (December 1993): 1.
26. Ibid.

27. Christopher Shea, "Won't Punish Black Students Who Threw Away Campus Papers," *The Chronicle of Higher Education,* 22 September 1993, A35.

28. Walter Lippmann, *The Public Philosophy* (Boston: Little, Brown, 1955), p. 126.

29. Limbaugh, *See, I Told You So,* p. 230.

30. Farrell, *The Myth of Male Power,* pp. 288–299.

31. Ibid., 288.

32. Katie Roiphe, *The Morning After: Sex, Fear, and Feminism on Campus* (Boston: Little, Brown 1993), p. 87.

33. Nat Hentoff, "A 'Pinup' of His Wife," *Washington Post,* 5 June 1993, A21, cited in Christina Hoff Sommers, *Who Stole Feminism?* (New York: Simon and Schuster, 1994), p. 271.

34. Sommers, *Who Stole Feminism,* p. 272.

35. Ibid.

36. Nicholas A. Damask and Craig Cohone, "Inside the Sensitivity Laboratory: Mind Control, Multicultural Style," *Campus* (winter 1994): 3.

37. "The Docket," *The Defender* (July 1994): 9.

38. George F. Will, "Curdled Politics on Campus," *Newsweek,* 6 May 1991, 72.

39. John Leo, "Looking Back at a PC Extravaganza," *U.S. News and World Report,* 31 January 1994, 19.

40. "On College Campuses, Old Glory Is Center of Controversy," *Education Reporter* (October 1994): 4.

41. Deborah Lambert, "Office Oppression Comes of Age," *Campus Report* (October 1994): 2.

42. Lin Yutang, *My Country and My People* (New York: Halcyon House, 1935), p. 168.

43. "In Praise of Secularism," *The Economist,* 11 March 1989, 17.

44. Patty de Llosa, "The View from Palo Alto," *Fortune,* 24 April 1989, 339, 342.

Chapter 8

From Melting Pot to Boiling Pot

> It is possible to lead astray an entire generation, to strike it blind, to drive it insane, to direct it toward a false stupidity.
>
> Alexander Herzen

Multiculturalists have been working hard to introduce bilingualism into America's institutions. Grade schoolers of Hispanic background in many parts of the United States are being taught in Spanish rather than in English; election ballots are printed in Spanish and often in other languages too; and information pertaining to governmental services is increasingly being published in Spanish. Not being familiar with the havoc bilingualism has wreaked in Canada, for instance, some Americans naively do not see anything wrong with these bilingual practices, and, of course, the loyal multiculturalists are adamant in having it no other way. Thus America is presently being pressured to initiate and publicly fund bilingualism which threatens the nation's longstanding assimilation process, its melting pot.

Goethe once said: *"America, du hast es besser"* (America, you have it better). He, like many others, envied America, in part because of its success in assimilating millions and millions of immigrants. For more than three centuries immigrants came from all parts of the world representing a wide variety of languages and cultures. No other country, encompassing so much geography, has ever achieved such comprehensive and sustained assimilation of so many millions of immigrants. Historians have called it the American exception. This exception is now being threatened by the politics of multiculturalism's bilingual agenda.

AMERICA, A MELTING POT

The earliest reference to the American melting pot image is found in Hector St. John de Crevecoeur's *Letters from An American Farmer*, published in London in 1782, but written about ten years earlier. In this monograph de Crevecoeur, himself a naturalized American from France, described Americans and their culture to his friends overseas in the following words: "[T]hey are a mixture of English, Scotch, Irish, Dutch, Germans, and Swedes. From this promiscuous breed, that race now called Americans have arisen. . . . Here [in the United States] individuals of all nations are melted into a new race."[1]

One century later, Theodore Roosevelt echoed de Crevecoeur's observation, even employing some of his imagery: "We Americans are the children of the crucible."[2] A decade after Roosevelt's remark, the great historian Frederick Jackson Turner reinforced the words of de Crevecoeur and Roosevelt. He wrote that the United States "fused" immigrants "into a mixed race."[3]

Lord James Bryce, the British observer of American life and a one-time ambassador to the United States, in the 1890s also saw the melting pot's assimilating power. He stated: "What the traveller, and what the Americans themselves delight to point out to him, is the amazing solvent power which American institutions, habits, and ideas exercise upon newcomers of all races."[4]

Then in 1909, Israel Zangwill, the son of Jewish immigrants, wrote a play, *The Melting Pot*, which played before audiences of several American cities. Everywhere it received high praise. It showed the melting pot as an American reality by portraying the life of a Jewish immigrant family in New York absorbing the American culture, its English language, and its *Weltanschaaung.* Zangwill declared:

Here you stand, good folk, think I, when you stand in your fifty groups, with your fifty languages and histories, and your fifty blood hatreds and rivalries. But you won't be long like that, brothers, for these are the fires of God. A fig for your feuds and vendettas! Germans and Frenchmen, Irishmen and Englishmen, Jews and Russians—into the Crucible with you all! God is making the American.[5]

The melting-pot phenomenon made Americans out of millions of immigrants and their children, and in countless instances it produced outstanding Americans. Many of them became national figures and heroes. General John Pershing (*Pfoersching* in German), whose ancestors came from Germany in the 1740s, was a true melting-pot product. He led the American military against Germany in World War I. In World War II, the Allies had General Dwight D. Eisenhower (Eisenhauer in German) lead their forces to defeat Nazi Germany. There is no doubt that Pershing and Eisenhower, both of whose German ancestors came to Pennsylvania in the 1740s, were thoroughly assimilated Americans, products of the melting pot.

Would Pershing and Eisenhower, and the thousands upon thousands of American soldiers of German descent, have fought the Germans overseas had America not been a melting pot? What would have been the result had the Germans in the United States remained unassimilated, the course that multiculturalists presently encourage immigrants to take? America would undoubtedly have lost World War II. Ironically, and tragically, that outcome would have enabled the Nazis to implement some of multiculturalism's present goals such as speech codes, political correctness (although of a different kind), and anti-assimilationist policies long before the multiculturalists arrived on the scene with their agenda.

One need not compose lists of countless Americans, well-known or not, to document the point that the United States has had a melting pot like no other nation. The rosters of students in any American college or university overwhelmingly demonstrate how effective the nation's melting pot has been. These rosters reveal the names of individuals whose ancestors came from Portugal, Poland, Scotland, Russia, China, Japan, Germany, Greece, and many other countries. Moreover, the majority of these students no longer speak a single word of their grandparents' or great-grandparents' language. Nor does this bother them. Often they no longer know what ethnic origin their name reflects. They are, after all, Americans, people of the melting pot.

DESPISING AND REJECTING AMERICA'S MELTING POT

The first serious opponent of America's great melting pot, its crucible, was Horace Kallen, an early twentieth-century multiculturalist. He advocated, and coined the term, *cultural pluralism*, meaning: damn the melting pot. Many of today's multiculturalists, who detest America's cultural assimilation, sound like they tore a page out of Kallen's writings. Similar to multiculturalists of today, Kallen harbored a strong dislike for the assimilated culture of the United States. He believed the immigrant left one type of oppression behind only to be subjected to another, American expectation to assimilate. Contemptuously, he called this expectation "the Americanization hysteria," or the "Americanization psychosis."[6] Fortunately, there were saner voices at the time. Robert Park and Herbert Miller, two renowned sociologists at the University of Chicago, wrote: "Assimilation is as inevitable as it is desirable."[7] Theirs was a pragmatic assessment rather than one prompted by alienation, as in the case of Kallen.

Kallen scorned the assimilation of immigrants, and he also tried to

argue that the melting pot did not exist, an argument that multiculturalists are trying to resuscitate in spite of overwhelming evidence to the
contrary. In support of his argument, Kallen pointed to the existence of
some forty languages and dialects that were spoken in the United States
in the 1920s, and observed that more foreign newspapers were published
and read in the United States per capita than in all of Europe.[8] This was
certainly true of the immigrants who came in the early 1900s, but Kallen
failed to note that the Germans, Swedes, Dutch, and others who came
to the United States in the 1700s or mid-1800s no longer spoke in their
mother tongues in the 1920s, nor did they still read non-English newspapers. In three generations they had assimilated. For instance, Dwight
D. Eisenhower and his siblings, born in the late 1800s, no longer learned
how to speak German, nor did the Pershing children, whose ancestors,
like the Eisenhowers, came to America in the 1740s.

Even those who held on to their foreign language and culture the
longest, of which the Germans were quite prominent, by the time descendants of the immigrants entered the third generation—and certainly
by the fourth—the American melting pot, that powerful crucible, assimilated them. Nor did Kallen ever note that the children of the immigrants
in the 1920s were no longer unassimilated ethnics twenty-five years later.
Thousands upon thousands of the first- and second-generation children
of German, Italian, and Japanese immigrants—born in the 1920s—two
decades later willingly and bravely fought for America in World War II
against the countries from which their ancestors emigrated. The melting
pot had definitely done its job.

Confusing Assimilation with Amalgamation

In their attempt to deny the American melting pot, anti-assimilationists
commonly equate cultural assimilation with biological amalgamation,
the intermarrying of people from different races. Informed writers of
assimilation always distinguished between assimilation and amalgamation, but that is no longer true. A few years ago, *Time* magazine (April
9, 1990) published a cover story titled "Beyond the Melting Pot," which
argued that because the United States now had a larger percentage of
blacks, Hispanics, and Asians than in the past, it had moved beyond the
melting pot. That is, there was less intermarriage between these groups
and whites than there was between the different white groups who came
from Europe. There now is less assimilation than in the past. This is
equating cultural assimilation with biological amalgamation, which is an
example of muddying the conceptual waters.

To be sure, biological amalgamation is often part of the cultural assimilation process, but it is not a necessary one. When we examine actual
statistics on interracial marriages (amalgamation), we see that the per-

centages of such marriages are increasing, not declining. Although the number of interracial marriages is not large, the percentage increases in recent years have been noteworthy. In 1970 the United States had 310,000 interracial couples; by 1993 the figure had grown to 1,195,000, an increase of 385 percent in twenty-three years.[9] In a study that gathered data from thirty-three states, Matthijs Kalmijn found that 10 percent of black men outside of the South married white women in 1986. In 1968, one year after the United States Supreme Court declared antimiscegenation laws unconstitutional, the figure was only 3.9 percent.[10]

Promoting Afrocentrism

The opponents of the melting pot have recently taken another tack, namely, to promote Afrocentrism, which tells American blacks that they cannot meaningfully identify with American culture, and that they must look to Africa for their values and rituals. In this way, the Afrocentrists overlook the undeniable fact that American blacks have melted into American culture more so than any other immigrant group.

Some of the ideas that the Afrocentrists promote lack authenticity. For instance, the current "African" holiday of Kwanzaa, which takes place from December 26 through January 1, is not African. It is an American invention, first proposed and designed by Maulana (Ron) Karenga in 1966, a professor of Pan-African studies at the State University of California at Long Beach.

The idea of Kwanzaa (sometimes dubbed the "black Christmas") lay dormant throughout the 1970s and 1980s. But recently multiculturalists, good friends of the Afrocentrists, together with the help of the liberal media, have been trying to give this event national prominence. Aside from its inauthenticity, the promotion of Kwanzaa tends to segregate, not integrate, blacks from the mainstream American culture and has the potential of making Americans more rather than less race or color conscious. Because of Kwanzaa's non-African origin, it is doubtful whether this holiday can provide what Herbert Gans calls "symbolic ethnicity,"[11] a state whereby American ethnic groups participate in occasional, nostalgic-cultural activities or customs that their ancestors once actually lived and practiced in their homeland.

Afrocentrists seem to have lost sight of the fact that blacks in the United States are Americans, not Africans. Black Americans have thoroughly absorbed the American culture, more so than other ethnic groups. Gunnar Myrdal, the Swedish sociologist, who wrote *An American Dilemma* (1947), called blacks in the United States "exaggerated Americans," meaning they were more assimilated to American culture than many whites. The black scholar, Thomas Sowell, states: "little or no African culture survives among American negroes."[12] He is quite correct, and it is for that reason that Kwanzaa had to be contrived.

Martin Luther King, Jr., also recognized the complete assimilation of American blacks. Said he: "The Negro is an American. We know nothing of Africa. He's got to face the fact that he is an American."[13] This is a very different message from the one being spread by today's Afrocentrists.

Denying America's Ongoing Assimilation

In 1995 Richard Alba, the sociological expert on American assimilation, using 1990 census data, showed that the melting pot is still viable. In his article, "Assimilation's Quiet Tide," he states: "assimilation was, and is, a reality for the majority of the descendants of earlier waves of immigration from Europe."[14] In spite of this evidence, multiculturalists continue to deny the reality of the melting pot. Only if we focus on some rare exceptions, a few isolated ethnic pockets, can it be argued that the assimilation of immigrants in the United States has not worked. But that would be specious generalizing from a small proportion of the population to the nation as a whole.

For some time many critics of the melting pot thought they had indeed found a genuine exception to the American melting pot: the Basques of northern Nevada, eastern Oregon, and western Idaho, often known as the Basque Triangle. Numerous articles were published on the "unmeltable" Basques. The Basques first came to the United States during the California Gold Rush in the late 1840s, and another small wave came in the 1890s. They live mostly in the rural Northwest, engaged primarily in raising sheep. Over the years, they have strongly resisted assimilation by getting only a little education and by practicing endogamy, in-group marriage. Yet even they were able to escape the American melting pot for only a couple of generations. A 1975 study of Basques in northeastern Oregon shows that less and less of them practice endogamy and that the Basque language is no longer widely used. The majority speak English quite well, and their children are attending colleges and universities in Oregon.[15]

In short, the Basques simply delayed their assimilation a little longer than most other ethnic-immigrant groups. And they were able to do so only because of their rural isolation. Had most of the Basques resided in urban areas, their evasion of the melting pot would have ended even sooner.

Some disclaimers of the melting pot apparently see the presence of symbolic ethnicity—which is only tangential to ethnic groups in America—as proof that there never was an American melting of ethnics and their cultures. In using this approach, the multiculturalists fail to recognize that even the cynical Sinclair Lewis admitted in his *Main Street* (1920) that the melting pot was the instrument by which "sound American customs absorbed without one trace of pollution another alien invasion."[16] Those who deny the melting pot also fail to see, as Benjamin Schwarz notes, that the melting pot did not cleanse America so much of its ethnic minorities as it "cleansed its minorities of their ethnicity."[17] Schwarz states that America never was "a little of Russia, a little of Italy, and a little of Poland all mixed together. Instead the various nationalities were made into Americans as ore is refined into gold. Americanization purified them, eliminating the dross."[18] Assimilation was, and still is, says Alba:

[A] phenomenon not imposed upon resistant individuals seeking to protect their cultural identities—a common image of assimilation in recent, largely negative, discourse. . . . [Instead it is the] unintended, cumulative byproduct of choices made by individuals seeking to take advantage of opportunities to improve their social situations.[19]

Forcing Bilingual Education on Children

The greatest hindrance to a nation's assimilation process is, of course, the implementation of nationwide bilingualism. It has never failed to divide a country. When the Roman empire gave the Greek language status equal to its native Latin, the empire poured into its midst the acid of dissolution. The presence of multilingualism in Yugoslavia, among other multiculturalist practices, helped pave the way for the current (1990s) civil wars between its various ethnic groups. And for the last decade Canada has been tearing itself apart by forcing its English-speaking citizenry (75 percent of the country's population) to accept French as a language equal to English, with official legal status. Canada's politicians and bureaucrats—most of whom have capitulated to multiculturalism—have for some time naively thought that they can make bilingualism work, even though no nation of any significance in history has ever been able to do so. Canada's bilingual advocates are either too ignorant or too ethnocentric to learn from history. If readers doubt this, they ought to live in Canada for a few months, not merely visit it. They will come back seeing that bilingualism only produces the curse of Babel with its bitter fruits of national divisiveness.

The early multiculturalists of the 1960s cleverly capitalized on white guilt spawned by the civil rights movement, and also took advantage of the ignorance and credulity of many legislators. Under the guise of a "pilot program," which would putatively help disadvantaged children of Mexican immigrants, white legislators in the U.S. Congress—ignorant of bilingualism's effects in history and apparently moved by white guilt—passed the Bilingual Education Act of 1968. This law was an amendment to Title VII of the Elementary and Secondary Education Act of 1965. Initially, the act of 1968 did not specifically refer to bilingual instruction but rather to "special educational needs." The act's promoters, however, knew what their decision meant. As Abigail Thernstrom writes, the congressmen were "close to unanimous in rejecting assimilation as an ideal. . . . Congressman James H. Scheuer of New York echoed the sentiment: 'I think we have discarded the philosophy of the melting pot. . . . We have a new concept of the value of enhancing, fortifying, and protecting [people's] differences.' "[20]

In 1974, and again in 1978, this legislation was renewed and given expanded power. Now the act was no longer an experimental pilot program. It stipulated that schools were "to encourage the establishment and operation, where appropriate, of educational programs using bilingual practices."[21] Thernstrom notes "bilingual education now meant instruction using the native language, with perhaps a bit of English thrown in sometime during the day. And it meant the native culture as well."[22] Also in 1974, the Supreme Court injected itself into the bilingual issue by ruling that Chinese-American children in San Francisco were entitled to federal help equal to what Hispanic children with limited English ability were receiving. This decision, known as the *Lau v. Nichols* case, went beyond confining bilingual education to Hispanic school children. Now bilingual education had become a basic right for any ethnic group whose children had "a limited ability to understand English."[23]

Proponents of bilingual education often argue that it helps ease the transition of children whose first language is not English to the English language. But anyone who has closely studied the issue of bilingual education knows this was never the intent of the self-appointed radical lobbyists, who falsely claimed to represent most Hispanics. They lobbied for the Bilingual Education Act of 1968 and its revisions in 1974 and in 1978 with the idea of getting government to help preserve the Spanish language and culture in the United States under the auspices of civil rights. Thus they hoped the government would strike a blow to the nation's 300-year-old melting pot. The lobbyists' efforts have succeeded beyond their expectations primarily because federal lawmakers in Washington were too guilt-ridden, too ignorant, or too unwilling to learn from history how their votes for bilingual education would plant the seeds of national disunity. Nor did the national politicians seem to care that when they succumbed to the Hispanic lobbyists, there was "No other ethnic group," says Linda Chavez, "including 250,000 immigrants who come here from Asia each year, . . . clamoring for the right to have its language and culture maintained in this country at public expense."[24]

The nation has forgotten Theodore Roosevelt's views on national bilingualism. He stated: "We believe that English and no other language is that in which all the school exercises should be conducted."[25] Similarly, John Dewey saw the public school as the avenue by which a child could "escape from the limitations of the social group in which he was born."[26] Promoters of bilingual education in effect are saying: "In your face, Roosevelt and Dewey." Their goal is to keep children in their group's social or cultural setting, regardless of how adversely that might affect their future in America. To multiculturalists, of course, who see all cultures in an equal light, immigrant-cultural groups impose no social or economic limitations on their children; there is nothing from which immigrant children need to escape.

Earlier in the book, I stated that English was not my first language, and I firmly believe that people ought to learn more than one language. But if an ethnic group wants its children to learn their ancestors' foreign language, it is the family's responsibility, not the government's or the school district's. Nor ought governmental resources and power be used to undermine the nation's existing culture and unity by requiring schools with twenty students of a given ethnic group to teach those pupils the Three Rs in a foreign language, as present bilingual programs demand.

Present bilingual programs in our nation's elementary schools have at least three negative effects. First, they deter children from learning English as well as they might were they not engaged in studying their basic school subjects in Spanish, or whatever the other language might be. For instance, Rosalie Porter, an expert on bilingualism, reports a number of empirical studies in her book, *Forked Tongue,* showing that teaching children first in their native (foreign) language in grade school makes them "less proficient in the second [English] language."[27] These students will be handicapped later when they compete for jobs and positions that require facility in English. In 1988 only 4,000 out of 7,000 applicants from New York City schools passed an entry-level jobs test in English ability. The data showed that not one of the test takers who was in the city's bilingual-education program passed the test.[28]

A second harmful effect pertains to academic performance. Research shows that students of bilingual programs perform considerably below those who never were in such programs. Christine Rossell, a leading expert on bilingual education, found that 93 percent of the studies she reviewed showed that bilingual teaching had either negative or no effects at all in math achievement. With regard to social studies, children in bilingual classes were all too often not even exposed to these subjects.[29] Corroborating these findings, Nathan Glazer observes: "One will never do as well in the United States living in Spanish, or French, or Yiddish, or Chinese, as one will do living, learning, and working in English.[30]

That the recipients of bilingual teaching will someday be occupationally and economically handicapped does not disturb the bilingual, multiculturalist promoters. But once the consequences will become widely prevalent, it is quite likely that the blame then will be laid somewhere else rather than where it belongs, namely, on the multiculturalist practice of bilingualism.

A third negative effect is its role in destroying the American assimilation process, the melting pot, and thereby tribalizing the country, similar to present-day Canada. When that happens, America will no longer be a melting but a boiling pot and will be producing the bitter fruits of multiculturalism.

Bilingual Education: Immigrants Don't Want It

Like other items on the multiculturalist agenda, bilingual education has been pushed primarily by alienated, leftist multiculturalists who despise America and its melting pot. The people whom multiculturalists ostensibly are trying to serve, namely, the Hispanics in the United States, overwhelmingly do not want bilingual programs. The small number of self-appointed, radical Hispanic lobbyists think they know better than the immigrants who see America as the land of promise and opportunity, best realized by having command of the English language.

Recent surveys show that the vast majority of Spanish-speaking immigrants want and expect their children to learn English in American schools. One national survey, published in the *New York Times* in 1992 revealed that over 90 percent of Hispanics (both citizens and noncitizens) agreed or strongly agreed that their children should learn English.[31] In 1989 a Florida study found that "98.1 percent of Hispanic parents thought it was important for their children to read and write 'perfect' English."[32] Nonetheless, the anti-assimilationist, leftist lobbyists in Washington, D.C., and the state capitols continue to beguile legislators, persuading them to foist bilingual education on the children of unwilling Hispanic parents. In the early 1990s, "two-thirds of first-grade students from Spanish-speaking homes [were] taught to read in Spanish, and three-quarters [were] taught grammar and vocabulary in Spanish as well."[33] These bilingual efforts deprive countless Hispanic children of adequate time to learn their subjects in English, but this does not bother the leftist advocates. Nor does it bother them that these students will not be prepared to enter college or obtain competitive jobs if they are not competent in the English language. Their agenda is to destroy the melting pot, not heed the wishes of the majority of Hispanic parents.

In 1968, the total cost of the Bilingual Education Act was $7.5 million; in 1994, that amount had risen to the stupendous figure of over $10 billion. The cost is only part of a tragic story. According to Rosalie Porter, the results of bilingual educational legislation reveal unmitigated failure. In New York City, for instance, the data show that students who began school with their parents' foreign language lagged behind in academic performance on all grade levels, compared to those who took their classes in English from their first day in school. Those from nonbilingual classes entered into mainstream classes significantly earlier. In El Paso, Texas, "English immersion students were also mainstreamed into regular rooms in 3–4 years, compared to 6–7 years for the bilingual students."[34] Similar results have been obtained in Washington, Florida, California, and other states.[35]

With the introduction of the Bilingual Education Act in 1968, the United States unwittingly expressed a death wish. For two centuries the nation Americanized its immigrant children through the public school by immersing them in the English language, which enabled them to become citizens literate in their country's cultural, political, and economic processes. In short, the public school was the nation's principal melting pot. With multiculturalism and bilingual education, it is now slowly becoming a potential boiling pot.

Bilingual Ballots

The anti-assimilationists have now moved to other fronts and invaded the electoral process by getting uninformed legislators to enact a federal law (Voting Rights Act, 1975) that prints election ballots for certain groups. Here is but a sampling: Aleut (Eskimo), Yup'ik, Navajo, Pima, Mohawk, Lakota, Cree, Plaute, Yiddish, Chinese, Japanese, and of course, Spanish.

Bilingual ballots strike a sharp blow to the American melting pot, and they also undercut an informed democracy. The United States has always operated under the assumption that its citizens must be informed in order to vote intelligently. This assumption was premised on the notion that people are able to read, write, and understand the English language in which political issues are debated. Now with the advent of bilingual or multilingual ballots, this 200–year-old assumption is eroding.

Granting U.S. Citizenship in Spanish

Multiculturalists, like soldiers seeking to conquer, recently launched an attack on granting U.S. citizenship only in the English language. In July 1993 an Arizona judge conducted the United States citizenship ceremony in which a considerable part of the proceedings was in Spanish for a group of Hispanics taking the oath of citizenship. This is the clearest signal ever given to immigrants that they need not learn the English language and thus can avoid the melting-pot process. Moreover, this anti-assimilationist practice came from one of the nation's judges. Through this practice, the United States is beginning to destroy cultural assimilation, and to set the stage for ethnic conflict. Rather than blending together immigrants from numerous countries by requiring them to learn the English language—the primary ingredient of the American melting pot—multiculturalists in many guises, often even as judges in the legal system, are trying to destroy the melting pot at every opportunity.

CANADA'S BILINGUALISM: A BASKET CASE

In 1759 the British conquered French Canada (Quebec). Four years later England issued a Royal Proclamation that, among other things, kept intact the French language in Canada, giving it essentially equal status with English. Eleven years later (1774), the British passed the Quebec Act, a law that provoked the American colonists and fanned the embers of the American Revolution, and also set the stage for an unassimilated, divided Canada. Unlike the United States to its south, which at this time was assimilating and uniting people through its melting pot philosophy, as de Crevecoeur's earlier words make clear, the British Parliament unwittingly handed Canada a key ingredient for its future boiling pot. That ingredient was bilingualism as it tried to appease Quebec.

By 1837 the lid blew off Canada's boiling pot. Louis Joseph Papineau, an unassimilated Frenchman, ignited an ugly, bloody rebellion, which ultimately failed. Alarmed at the uprising, the British asked Lord Durham, the governor-general, to investigate. A key recommendation of the Durham Report of 1839 was to assimilate the French by having only one language, English, for all of Canada. "The difference of language," said he, "aggravates the national animosities."[36] He saw that with two languages the country would never be united. In 1839, the British Parliament, lacking Durham's wisdom, saw nothing amiss in having Quebec retain the French language, as well as other cultural customs. Nor was the Parliament wiser in 1848 when it repealed Section 41 of the Union Bill of 1840, which required English to be the language of legislative records. Nor did the British North America Act of 1867, which formed the confederation of four provinces called the Dominion of Canada, reveal any more sagacity. This act accepted English and French as the country's two languages, and stipulated that both were to be employed in the federal Parliament's debates and deliberations.

By the mid-1960s Canada was experiencing serious problems with its bilingualism. Analysts were wondering whether the country would survive long enough to celebrate its centennial in 1967. In the 1970s, 1980s, and 1990s French-speaking Quebec continually agitated and even taunted the English-speaking population (the Anglophones, as they are called in Canada; French-speaking Canadians are known as Francophones).

In 1982 Canada finally managed to get its own constitution, but that document revealed no more wisdom than any of the previous laws the British Parliament had approved. The writers of the new constitution apparently were infected by utopianism: their dream was to make the country truly bilingual—English and French-speaking. The new constitution stated: "English and French are the official languages of Canada and have equality of status and equal rights and privileges as to their use in all institutions of the Parliament and government of Canada." Quebec, however, did not accept the constitution; it continues to reject it, desiring to be recognized as a "distinct society."

In October 1992 Canada held a national referendum to determine whether its citizens would agree to Quebec as a "distinct society." This unrealistic request, a fruit of bilingualism, was rejected. But Canada still has no peace on this issue. On October 30, 1995, Quebec held a provincial referendum to decide whether it would remain part of Canada or become a sovereign, independent country. A bitter campaign raged throughout the month of October. Many federalists (opponents of Quebec independence), both inside and outside of Quebec, virtually panicked. Two days before the election, politicians rallied thousands of antiseparatist supporters from various parts of Canada who converged upon Montreal. They pleaded for Quebec to remain part of Canada. Finally, the people voted on October 30, and the separatists lost by a whisker, with 49.6 percent of the vote versus 50.4 percent for the antiseparatists. So intense was the political drama that 90 percent of the eligible voters turned out to cast their ballots.

The antiseparatists' narrow victory has by no means resolved Canada's problem with Quebec. With the province literally split down the middle, inevitably Quebec will secede, especially since the majority of the separatist vote was cast by young voters. In a few years the number of older voters will decrease, giving the young separatists even more clout. Moreover, reports indicate that many of the antiseparatists, especially the Anglophones, intend to leave Quebec. They fear the Quebec government will exclude them from getting and retaining jobs because they cannot speak French or because they do not have a French surname. Government paper work is conducted only in French, and bilingual French physicians will not speak to Anglophones in English in a French-designated hospital.[37] Thus it appears that secession is only a question of *when*.

In the debate prior to the 1995 vote, the Canadian media failed to address the matter of how Quebec's secession might benefit the rest of the country. First, it would end Canada's bilingual nightmare which has cost billions of dollars—for example, compelling libraries to translate public archives and governmental records into French in the English-speaking provinces—and has shattered the little unity the country had prior to the present turbulence. Second, it might also help some of the country's leaders regain some common sense. For instance, in 1993 a food inspector removed food items imported from England from store shelves because their wrappers were printed in English only.[38] Finally, it might even have the good fortune of getting the country to realize that its bilingualism problems with Quebec were exacerbated when it adopted a pro-multiculturalist posture in 1971. That was the year the federal Parliament passed its Multicultural Act. Ten years later, this policy was enshrined in Section 27 in the Charter of Rights and Freedom portion of the country's first nationally produced constitution.

STORM CLOUDS ON AMERICA'S HORIZON

Some American immigration analysts minimize the bilingual appeasements and concessions that have been made to radical Hispanic lobbyists. They argue that ultimately Hispanics will assimilate like all other immigrants have in the past. Although surveys show that the majority of Hispanics want to learn English, the actual picture appears less promising. Here is why.

In 1968 and in the 1970s, the liberal majority in Congress voted to mollify the leaders of radical Hispanic groups such as the National Council of La Raza and the United Latin American Citizens. These groups and their leaders, as Linda Chavez shows, neither represent the majority of Hispanics in the United States nor do they "promote English—or civics—classes for Latin immigrants."[39] These self-appointed radicals "place greater emphasis on retaining Spanish, and thus encourage Hispanics to remain separate from the culture in which they preside."[40] The Bilingual Education Act of 1968 and its amendments in 1974 and 1978 are helping the radical Hispanic leaders to achieve their anti-assimilationist goals and thereby widen the cracks in the nation's unity.

Some radical Hispanic groups publicly defy the American assimilation process. Many people of Mexican origin in California now openly brag that they will make California into the "State of Aztlan" once they become the majority ethnic group in that state. The Aztlan (Chicano) segment of Mexican Americans is an irredentist group whose goal is to repossess the states of California, Arizona, New Mexico, and other parts of the Southwest. This radical contingent does not recognize what it calls the "foreign borders" of California, Arizona, New Mexico, and other parts of the southwestern United States. They liken the acquisition of these states in 1848 (ceded to the United States in the Treaty of Guadalupe Hidalgo) to a Hitlerian conquest.

The Aztlan irredentists are waiting for a more favorable demographic composition—a larger unassimilated Mexican population—in the Southwest to realize their goals.[41] The federal government's support of bilingual education, treasured and valued by the multiculturalists, of course, aids and abets the nefarious goals of the Aztlan irredentists, for it helps increase the unassimilated Mexican population in the United States.

The situation is not much brighter in Miami, Florida, where a random, door-to-door poll of 4,500 people in 1989 found that 80 percent of those interviewed (Hispanics) saw themselves as Hispanics first and Americans second.[42] In 1982, Miami's mayor, Maurice Ferre, bragged: " 'Within ten years there will not be a word of English spoken in [Miami] . . . one day residents will have to learn Spanish or leave.' "[43]

The storm clouds of bilingualism are becoming more ominous. A few years ago, Lauro F. Cavazos, President Bush's secretary of education, speaking about the education of immigrant children, said: "[W]e must do all we can to help maintain their native language and culture."[44] Thus, at least some governmental leaders are beginning to accept multiculturalism's agenda, of which bilingualism is a major component. It also reveals that the government, in a socialistic fashion, is seen as responsible for maintaining and preserving the foreign language of a given ethnic group. Informed Americans will ask: Since when is it the function of government to perpetuate an ethnic group's language and thereby its culture as well?

Richard Rodriquez, a Hispanic and a pro-assimilationist, reminds us that bilingual advocates fail to recognize that the immigrant child has "the right—and the obligation—to speak the public language of *los gringos*."[45] But the United States has ignored this right, and the American taxpayer is paying dearly for it. In 1994 $10 billion were spent on "not teaching English to immigrants, but teaching course work in native languages."[46] Certainly, this is a misdirected use of the taxpayer's money.

CREATING ELITISM

Sociologists make much of the concepts of manifest and latent functions. Manifest functions are those that are planned, intended, and recognized, whereas latent functions are neither planned nor intended, and often are not recognized. One noteworthy latent function of bilingualism is elitism. Those who fluently speak a bilingual country's two languages, as in Canada, get "the top jobs in politics, government and foreign service, the judiciary, and several of the professions, including economics and public relations."[47]

Although elitism is contradictory to a democracy, it becomes inevitable in a bilingual nation. In order for a bilingual country to implement and impose its language policies, it must employ individuals (essentially bureaucrats), who are conversant in both languages. These employees, says Linda Diebel, become the elite.[48]

BILINGUAL EDUCATION HANDICAPS IMMIGRANT CHILDREN

To the uninformed, exposing immigrant children, most commonly children of Hispanic parents, to bilingual education in American grade schools will aid and enhance their learning process and help them advance. But the opposite is the case. This should come as no surprise, for in order to advance economically in the United States, where English is the only language, command of the English language is absolutely necessary. Without immersion in English, children of immigrants will only rarely be able to attain better paying, or self-fulfilling, jobs; nor will they be able to enter any of the professions. Research shows that use of the English language in the United States is directly related to occupational and income attainments.[49] Wise Hispanic parents in the United States know this and so don't want their children in bilingual education programs. As they state, "we want them to be able to become doctors or lawyers, not janitors or floor sweepers." Richard Rodriguez is the son of an immigrant Mexican family, and English was his second language. He observes: "Those who have the most to lose in bilingual America are the foreign-speaking poor, who are being lured into a linguistic nursery."[50]

Foisting bilingual education on children whose parents do not want it is unmitigated paternalism. Multiculturalists and their bilingual promoters reject the melting pot to such a degree that the wishes of informed parents are of no consequence to them.

BILINGUALISM STIFLES CIVIC DISCOURSE

One of the United States' great strengths has been its common language, its people, made up of millions of immigrants and their offspring, who have learned and spoken just one language, English, for more than three centuries. It enabled Americans to engage in productive, civic discourse, a discourse that helped America's republican form of government thrive, whereas in times past republican governments of other nations always failed.

A country can have civic discourse only in the presence of a high degree of national unity and social intimacy among its people, fostered and held together by a common language. In the words of the columnist, George Will: "To be sociable [people] must share a language."[51] If a common language is lacking, prejudice and divisions invariably follow.

Once bilingualism enters the scene, the context of civic discourse becomes fractured. Bilingualism or multilingualism erects a Tower of Babel, and with it comes national disunity and civic conflict. One need only look to Canada, Sri Lanka, India, Belgium, and to the former Yugoslavia.

INVOKING THE "R" WORD

Multicultural proponents of bilingualism have no qualms about play-ing dirty politics. To attain their goal they often make scurrilous charges; for example, they portray the opponents of bilingualism as racists.[52] Such an accusation intimidates all too many people and thus allows the ac-cusers to get their way. It also redefines racism, a concept that social scientists have commonly defined as an attitude, belief, or practice that discriminates against or for groups or persons on the basis of race.

Race is a biological quality, an ascribed characteristic. One cannot learn to become a member of a given race, whether black, white, red, or yel-low. Language, on the other hand, is a cultural quality, an achieved characteristic. Thus to call opponents of bilingualism racists is pure dem-agoguery. Yet the advocates of bilingualism often employ this tactic as they try to silence the defenders of America's 300–year-old English-speaking culture.

U.S. ENGLISH

In 1983 Senator S. I. Hayakawa (D-Calif.), seeing the disaster that Can-ada's bilingualism had created and the newly legislated bilingual edu-cation efforts in the United States, founded the organization U.S. English. Its primary goal is to help the nation pass a constitutional amendment that will make English the official language of the United States. Haya-kawa, born of Japanese parents in Canada, a naturalized American citi-zen, and a one-time professor of semantics, more than most knew the value of a common language. The proposed amendment reads: "Section 1. The English language shall be the official language of the United States. Section 2. The Congress shall have the power to enforce this article by appropriate legislation." Given the predominantly liberal composition of the U.S. Congress in the 1980s and early 1990s, this proposed amend-ment never made it out of committee and thus neither the House nor the Senate could vote on it.

Determined multiculturalist opponents of U.S. English frequently and falsely accuse the movement of trying to legislate an "English only" law, meaning that the organization's members want to outlaw all languages except English in the United States. U.S. English has no such intent, as the proposed amendment clearly indicates. Its supporters only want to preserve the country's national unity through the use and retention of one common language. They also do not believe it is government's func-tion to provide funds for bilingual education. If individuals want to learn a foreign language, they may certainly do so, but at their own financial cost. Neither U.S. English nor the proposed amendment has the slightest objection to any one learning more than one language. If the United

States were to pass a constitutional amendment making English the official language, it would not be a strange, eccentric act, for many national constitutions state their country's official language.

The official English proposal expects immigrants—as millions did previously—to learn to speak English for their own and the nation's benefit. Immigrants entering Sweden are expected to learn Swedish; those entering France learn French; and so on. There is nothing unusual about the United States wanting its immigrants to learn to speak English, its national language.

When well-mannered guests go to a host's house, they abide by the rules of the host. They do not impose their own rules. Supporters of one official language (English) for the United States expect the same of its immigrants. When immigrants to the United States, or any other country for that matter, seek to engage in official, public business, they need to learn and speak the language of the nation that now gives them sustenance, not to mention political and economic freedom. They have no moral right, nor ought they have a legal right, in spite of what radical groups tell Hispanic immigrants, namely, that government agencies and businesses are obligated to communicate with them in their foreign language.

As of March 1996, twenty-three states had made English the official language. But also in March the United States Supreme Court agreed to hear a case from the state of Arizona that challenges the constitutionality of official English laws. In 1988 Arizona voters passed such a law for its state, but it has never gone into effect because of court challenges.[53] If the Supreme Court nullifies the existing official English laws in the various states, it will widen the crack in the nation's melting pot.

U.S. English and groups similar to it are necessary instruments for preserving America's unity, which is unequivocally linked to one language: American English. This organization is necessary not only because of governmental efforts that have been made in supporting bilingualism in schools, but also because of Mexico's recent actions. For example, Mexico has started "cultural institutes" that teach Spanish to illiterate Hispanics from California to New York. It has even donated Spanish textbooks in the Los Angeles school system.[54]

ENGLISH: THE LANGUAGE OF FREEDOM

English is in many ways a hodgepodge language consisting of hundreds of words derived from Greek, Latin, French, and German. Exceptions to its grammatical rules are almost as numerous as the basic rules themselves. Pronunciation patterns are extremely inconsistent and often lack good logic. This is especially obvious to any one who has studied Latin, Greek, or German. Yet, despite these flaws, English, like no other language, has been the medium by which the British and their descendants, the Americans, fashioned a culture of freedom and liberty that other societies with different languages have not even come close to equaling. Many countries, now interested in human rights and liberties, have in recent decades only been able to copy or imitate the United States. For instance, a few years ago, when Poland freed itself from the totalitarian clutches of Soviet communism, it looked for inspiration and guidance to the American Declaration of Independence, that exemplary document of freedom, first written in English. As J. R. Joelson has observed: "English is the language of liberty."[55]

Joelson shows that the world's greatest articles and documents of human rights and freedom were first written in the English language. He lists nine of these documents: the Magna Carta, Habeas Corpus, the American Declaration of Independence, Virginia's Bill of Religious Freedom, the Constitution of the United States, the American Bill of Rights, Lincoln's Emancipation Proclamation, the Fourteenth Amendment, and the 1964 Civil Rights Act. In addition, for centuries the English language has conveyed the *spirit* of freedom that gave rise to these documents.

Without being a linguistic determinist, one is nevertheless moved to ask: Why has no other language inspired such monumental hallmarks of freedom? This question is all the more significant when one considers that these documents did not arise in just one culture or in one century. Instead, they occurred over a span of seven centuries and in two countries. Moreover, in one instance the country (England) was a monarchy and the other (the United States) a republic.

Ancient Athens may have had some semblance of a democracy, but it never left a single document of human freedom or individual rights to posterity. For centuries, Rome spread its tentacles over Europe, Northern Africa, and the Fertile Crescent, but its universal language (Latin) inspired no articles of democratic freedoms. German, the language of philosophy and science, bequeathed to the world precision and military efficiency but left no legacy of human liberty. Spanish, the language of the Conquistadors, spread to Central and South America and molded a culture for millions in a vast expanse of land with more natural resources than North America. But it inspired no democratic freedoms or human rights in Latin America. Most countries in Latin America are just beginning the process of democratic freedoms and human rights.

Language is not just a significant part of a culture; it embodies culture. It shapes the conceptions and perceptions of a culture's practices—for example, its views on democracy and human rights, or the lack of them. Obviously, this is not a popular position to take today when more and more people have accepted multiculturalism and its contrary-to-fact propaganda that argues all cultures are equal or of equal value.

To be sure, the Sapir-Whorf hypothesis, which argues that language shapes people's view of reality, has some weaknesses.[56] All theories do. Nevertheless, this theory sheds some light on why the world's greatest documents of human freedom and liberty were first enshrined in the English language. It is of no small consequence that democracy and freedom of expression are only in their embryonic stages in Latin America, especially when one remembers that the Spanish language has no words for compromise or dissent. It is all but impossible to have freedom of discussion, political compromise, or dissent when a country's language is devoid of these concepts. Thus it should not be surprising that Mexico, for instance, has no institutionalized two-party system. Nor is it very surprising to see opposition leaders in Mexico get assassinated, as happened in 1994. The country's culture has no tolerance for serious dissent. Mexico is far from a full-fledged democracy, a fact that the "politically correct" American media fail to make clear.

Democracy has long been absent in countries other than Mexico, too. For example, El Salvador and Nicaragua are just beginning to implement some freedoms that Britain and the United States have enjoyed for centuries. If the notion of human rights and other liberties succeeds in Latin America and Africa, it will in no small measure be due to the legacy that the English language has left for other nations to imitate.

Making the United States a bilingual country with Spanish the second language and status equal to English would rupture the nation's social and political stability, similar to Canada's present state of affairs. It would have disastrous effects on the existing American institutions of liberty and human rights. Along with accepting the Spanish language, the United States would receive huge loads of cultural baggage that would greatly deteriorate American culture.

Will multiculturalists, who are also zealous promoters of pro-feminist values, like to have *machismo* (see Chapter 4) become part of the new bilingual culture? National bilingualism of necessity always results in more than the mere speaking of another language. It also connotes the introduction of another (foreign) culture, together with its beliefs and practices. Many of these practices—as in the case of Spanish from Latin America—are in direct conflict with many components of the traditional American culture.

AMERICA'S IMMIGRATION PROBLEM

In 1965 the U.S. Congress drastically rewrote the nation's immigration laws. This in some ways was the beginning of multiculturalism. Prior to 1965, immigrants were allowed into the United States on the basis of quotas assigned to given nations. European countries were permitted to send a higher percentage of emigrants to the United States than non-European nations. The 1965 law changed all that. The old system was seen as "racist," and now the gates were opened to immigrants from Latin American countries and other Third World nations with cultures extremely different from the mainstream U.S. Culture. President Lyndon Johnson and the Congress apparently were given to both white guilt and ignorance. Both thought the United States could receive immigrants from non-Western societies, with very different cultures, and still remain unaffected. Thus, unbeknown to the president and the Congress, the 1965 immigration law set the stage for the possible unraveling of America's culture. The cultures and values of these new immigrants are sometimes even diametrically opposed to the Euro-American culture. As a result, it is much more difficult assimilating these newcomers than immigrants from Europe in the 1800s and early 1900s. This problem is exacerbated by the multiculturalists, who are also encouraging immigrants not to assimilate.

Legal immigration has also encouraged large-scale illegal immigration, especially from Latin America, enlarging the American Hispanic population so vastly that assimilating these newcomers has become difficult. Thousands of these immigrant children are being sent to bilingual schools, where they not only learn little or no English, but also gain little knowledge about American institutional values and practices, so necessary for proper assimilation and wholesome civic discourse.

Studies show that Hispanic immigrants to the United States take longer than most other newcomers to assimilate.[57] Given the 1965 immigration law, governmental support of bilingualism, along with runaway-illegal immigration, the assimilation of Hispanic immigrants will slow down significantly. If the present trend continues, the assimilation of Hispanics eventually may come to a virtual standstill.

Assimilating Hispanics is also made more difficult by geographic propinquity. European immigrants, who arrived in the 1800s and early 1900s, rarely returned to the land of their birth to renew their foreign language and customs. The ocean made that too difficult. So they were compelled to abandon their language and culture, and to assimilate, becoming part of the melting pot. With Hispanic immigrants, especially since the 1960s and their easy access to the automobile, it is a different story. No ocean or great distance separates them from their friends and relatives back home, and so they go back to Mexico, for example, to renew their language, culture, and prejudices.

The currently large influx of immigrants, many of them illegal, is severely handicapping America's longstanding assimilation process. Illegal immigrants avoid the melting pot more than those who enter the country legally. And then there are the "bilingualists [who] simplistically scorn the value and necessity of assimilation."[58] Like so many multiculturalists, they are alienated from the American culture. It matters little that the nation has given them more economic and political comforts and free-doms than any other culture in history.

Nearly two decades ago (1981), one observer, Anthony Smith, warned Americans that bilingual education was bringing about reverse assimi-lation and renewed ethnicity. He also cautioned that this kind of edu-cation could lead to divisiveness as well as to irredentism—specifically, attempts by radicals of Mexican origin (e.g., the Aztlan cited earlier) trying to recover the "lost" territories of 1848, the American Southwest.[59]

If the present bilingual policies and politics continue, Mauro Mujica, an immigrant from Peru and current chairman of U.S. English, foresees numerous problems in America's future. Referring to countries like Can-ada, Belgium, and the Balkans, he warns: "All you have to do is look at all these other places to see what can happen. Our national unity and national prosperity is dependent on a shared language."[60] Mujica is right, but multiculturalists, who are the main supporters of bilingual programs, prefer separate cultural identities to national unity. They prefer a "salad bowl" to a melting pot.

America's past immigrant groups are often simplistically compared to the immigrants of today. Those unconcerned about current bilingual or multilingual problems, feverishly encouraged by multiculturalists, point to immigrants of the past—the Germans, Italians, Greeks, Russians, and so on—all of whom eventually assimilated, dropping their ancestral lan-guages. To be sure, these groups assimilated, but there was, however, a significant reason to do so. The federal government kept its nose out of the matter. When the German immigrants spoke their native language in Milwaukee, Cincinnati, Indianapolis, and St. Louis, the Italians in Bos-ton, and the Poles in Chicago and Buffalo, the government in the late 1800s and early 1900s did not fund those languages with billions of tax dollars; it did not pander to any ethnic group; there were no government mandates for bilingual education programs in grade schools. Today, however, the government is using taxpayer money to keep alive the for-eign language and customs of immigrants. This clearly discourages im-migrants and their children from assimilating.

What would America look like today had the federal government in the 1800s and early 1900s supported and funded bilingual education and thereby discouraged assimilation? To whom would the millions of German and Italian descendants have been loyal during World War II had they not been assimilated? These are not idle questions; every ad-vocate of national bilingualism needs to ponder them with the utmost seriousness.

"AMERICANS NEED TO BECOME BILINGUAL"

Some advocates of bilingualism often complain that most Americans, even those with a college degree, cannot speak more than one language, whereas their European counterparts can speak more than one foreign language. Bilingual advocates often ask: Would it not be good if Americans, like so many Europeans, were also able to speak more than one language? Indeed, individuals have a definite advantage, and reason to be proud, if they are bilingual, or better yet, trilingual. The European–American comparison is flawed, however. The many Europeans who speak more than their native language do not live in bilingual countries. Nor do their countries encourage immigrants to keep their foreign language, much less fund such efforts, as is presently done in the United States. Individuals in these countries learn to speak another language primarily as well-educated persons. Often they learn English because it has become today's universal language. It is not their country's policy or legislation that produces bilingual or multilingual citizens in Germany, France, Italy, or Sweden. Immigrants who enter any of these European countries must learn the respective nation's official language. In contrast, the multiculturalists contend that immigrants need not learn English in order to become patriotic, productive American citizens.

If the multiculturalists succeed in chipping away at America's 300–year-old melting pot, by implementing greater proliferation of Spanish in public grade schools, they will eventually replace it with an overheated boiling pot. It will make the United States the Quebec of the South.

NOTES

1. Hector St. John de Crevecoeur, *Letters from an American Farmer* (1782; reprint, New York: E. P. Dutton, 1951), pp. 54–55.

2. Theodore Roosevelt, "American People," in *Theodore Roosevelt Encyclopedia,* ed. Albert Bushnell Hart and Herbert Ferleger (New York: Roosevelt Memorial Association, 1941), p. 10.

3. Frederick Jackson Turner, *The Frontier in American History* (New York: Henry Holt, 1921), p. 23. Turner's observation was first made in a paper, "The Significance of the Frontier in American History," which he presented to the American Historical Association in July 1893.

4. James Bryce, *The American Commonwealth* (London: Macmillan, 1891), 2: 725.

5. Israel Zangwill, *The Melting Pot* (1909; reprint, New York: Macmillan, 1911), p. 37.

6. Horace Kallen, *Culture and Democracy in the United States* (1924; reprint, New York: Arno Press and New York Times, 1970), pp. 165, 167.

7. Robert E. Park and Herbert A. Miller, *Old World Traits Transplanted* (Chicago: Society for Social Research, 1925), p. 307.

8. Kallen, *Culture and Democracy,* p. 162.

9. *Statistical Abstract of the United States* (Washington, D.C.: U.S. Department of Commerce, 1994), p. 56.

10. Matthijs Kalmjin, "Trends in Black/White Intermarriage," *Social Forces* (September 1993): 124.

11. Herbert Gans, "Symbolic Ethnicity: The Future of Ethnic Groups and Culture in America," *Ethnic and Racial Studies* (January 1979).

12. Thomas Sowell, *Ethnic America* (New York: Basic Books, 1981), p. 184.

13. Martin Luther King, Jr., cited in Robert Warren, *Who Speaks for the Negro?* (New York: Random House, 1965), p. 216.

14. Richard D. Alba, "Assimilation's Quiet Tide," *The Public Interest* (spring 1995): 3.

15. Donald G. Burns, "Ethnicity Among the Basques of Northeast Oregon," in *Basques of the Pacific Northwest* ed. Richard W. Etulain (Pocatello: Idaho State University Press, 1991), pp. 33–38.

16. Sinclair Lewis, *Main Street*, cited by Benjamin Schwarz, "The Diversity Myth: America's Leading Export," *The Atlantic Monthly* (May 1995): 62.

17. Ibid.

18. Ibid.

19. Alba, "Assimilation's Quiet Tide," p. 4.

20. Cited in Abigail M. Thernstrom, "Bilingual Miseducation," *Commentary* (February 1990): 45.

21. Ibid.

22. Ibid.

23. Ibid.

24. Linda Chavez, *Out of the Barrio* (New York: Basic Books, 1991), p. 38.

25. Theodore Roosevelt, "True Americanism," *American Ideals and Other Essays: Social and Political* (New York: G. P. Putnam's Sons, 1898), p. 26.

26. Cited in Stephen Steinberg, *The Ethnic Myth: Race, Ethnicity and Class in America* (New York: Atheneum, 1981), p. 128.

27. Rosalie P. Porter, *Forked Tongue* (New York: Basic Books, 1990), p. 116.

28. Thernstrom, "Bilingual Miseducation," p. 47.

29. Ibid.

30. Nathan Glazer, "Pluralism and the New Immigrants," *Society* (November/December 1991): 33.

31. Roberto Suro, "Poll Finds Hispanics Desire to Assimilate," *New York Times*, 15 December 1992, A1, A18.

32. Eloise Salholz et al., "Say It in English," *Newsweek*, 20 February 1989, 23.

33. Linda Chavez, "Let's Move Beyond Bilingual Education," *USA Today*, 30 December 1991, 11A.

34. Rosalie P. Porter, "Bilingual Education Flunks Out," *The American Experiment* (spring 1995): 5.

35. Ibid.

36. Sir Charles Lucas, ed., *Lord Durham's Report on the Affairs of British North America* (Oxford: Clarendon Press, 1912), 2: 41.

37. Gail Russell Chaddock, "Quebec Separatists Keep Up Pressure for Independence," *Christian Science Monitor*, 9 November 1995, 6.

38. Mordecai Richler, *Oh Canada! Oh Canada!* (New York: Alfred A. Knopf, 1992), p. 7.

39. Linda Chavez, "Hispanics vs. Their Leaders," *Commentary* (October 1991): 49.

40. Ibid.

41. Brent Nelson, *America Balkanized* (Monterey, Va.: American Immigration Control Foundation, 1994), p. 32.

42. Ibid., 15.

43. Cited in Chavez, "Hispanics vs. Their Leaders," p. 48.

44. Lauro F. Cavazos cited in Brent Nelson, *America Balkanized* (Monterey, Va.: American Immigration Control Foundation, 1994), p. 23.

45. Richard Rodriquez, *Hunger of Memory* (Boston: David R. Godine, 1982), p. 19.

46. Jerry Mosier, "Equal but Separate," *National Review,* 19 December 1994, 22.

47. Linda Diebel, "The Rise of a Bilingual Canadian Elite," *Maclean's,* 4 July 1983, 22.

48. Ibid.

49. P. Garcia, "Dual Language Characteristics and Language: Male Mexican Workers in the United States," *Social Science Research* (1984): 221–235.

50. Richard Rodriguez cited in George Will, "In Defense of the Mother Tongue," *Newsweek,* 8 July 1985, 78.

51. Ibid.

52. Margaret Carlson, "Only English Spoken Here," *Time,* 5 December 1988, 29.

53. Tony Mauro, "English-Only to Face Test in High Court," *USA Today,* 26 March 1996, 1A, 7A.

54. Peter Brimelow, *Alien Nation* (New York: Random House, 1995), p. 194.

55. J. R. Joelson, "English: The Language of Liberty," *The Humanist* (July/ August 1989): 35.

56. Benjamin L. Whorf, *Language, Thought and Reality* (Cambridge, Mass.: MIT Press, 1956).

57. Richard Alba, "Social Assimilation Among American Catholic National-Origin Groups," *American Sociological Review* (December 1976): 1040.

58. Rodriquez, *Hunger of Memory,* p. 26.

59. Anthony Smith, *Ethnic Revival* (New York: Cambridge University Press, 1981), p. 17.

60. An Interview with Mauro Maujica, "U.S. English," *Human Events,* 21 April 1995, 15.

Chapter 9

Multiculturalism's Threat to the Family

The security and elevation of the family and family life are the prime objects of civilization.

Charles Eliot

REDEFINING THE FAMILY

For decades sociologists have presented traditional, noncontroversial definitions of the family. Those definitions reflected the daily experiences of the average person. The family was seen as a social group consisting of a man and woman who formed a sexual and economic union intended to be life-long. The majority of them had children whom they raised to adulthood from the time of birth or legal adoption.

Then came the radical 1960s and 1970s, the period during which so many long-established customs and institutional practices began to unravel. Divorce rates, for example, climbed higher each year causing broken homes, and along with it, childhood and adolescent insecurity. Illegitimate birth rates rose dramatically. American crime rates spiraled upward. The period was shadowed by the ever-present threat of nuclear war between the two superpowers: the United States and the Soviet Union. There was also the lingering fear of the past Great Depression. The parents who were reared in the 1930s were now determined that their offspring would "have it better." So their children, born in the late 1940s and early 1950s, grew up pampered, coddled, and underdisciplined. Having never had any economic worries and able to acquire almost anything they desired, they became alienated from their parents and society, whom they called "the Establishment." Their alienation was intensified by a conterminous event, the Vietnam War. For many of them, life lacked all meaning and purpose. Judeo-Christian values and beliefs that served their parents, grandparents, and great-grandparents exceptionally well now were questioned and rejected as "bourgeois," a term borrowed from Marx and his followers.

Although the parents of the 1960s children still honored traditional values, many were hypocritical and inconsistent regarding those values. They saw nothing wrong, or at least they did not think about the implications, for instance, in having their children taught cultural and moral relativism in schools. Their children were graduated from high schools, colleges, and universities accepting, unwittingly, the oft-repeated statement: "Everything [even truth] is relative." Quite naturally, then, they rejected the values for which the traditional family had stood, and the traditional concept of the family as well.

Soon the family had to be redefined. If everything is relative, who is to say that any kind of sexual relation between consenting adults is not just as good or right as that between husband and wife. Thus by the time the White House Conference on the Family convened in 1980, a major impasse had occurred. The participants—many of whom had absorbed the relativistic, radical philosophy as students—could not agree on the nature of the family and its relationship to marriage. One reporter described the conference saying: "Pluralism and tolerance were the passwords."[1]

The radicals at this conference, similar to the present-day multiculturalists, who see homosexuality as an alternative lifestyle, wanted a broad definition of family—one that would include any domicile relationship between a child and adult. They considered the traditional definition that saw the family as consisting of two heterosexual adults—husband and wife or mother and father—engaged in rearing one or more children as too restrictive. In spite of efforts to impose a leftist agenda, the conference finally adopted a definition that did not include homosexual unions.[2]

Three years prior to the White House Conference on the Family, President Jimmy Carter evoked laughter when he told the Department of Urban Development: "So those of you who are living in sin, I hope you'll get married. Those of you who have left your spouses, go back home. And those of you who don't remember your children's names, get acquainted."[3] Carter's admonition was ignored, marking one of the early manifestations of cultural and moral relativism that a decade later would become a rather widespread attitude—namely, marriage was no longer the only acceptable context for sexual relations.

The cultural relativism of multiculturalism and its multi-morality has affected the definition of the family in yet another way. For instance, go to a furniture store where double-bed mattresses are sold. It is common to see promotional signs saying: "This mattress provides comfort for you and your partner." The politically correct word is "partner," not "spouse." The word "spouse" puts too much emphasis on husband and wife, and also implies that the sexual cohabitation of an unmarried man and woman is deviant or wrong. To multiculturalists that is moral bigotry. Finally, "spouse" also says that double beds are not made for two homosexuals.

FROM WHITE HOUSE CONFERENCE TO SCHOOL TEXTBOOKS

The leftist, politically oriented values and beliefs that surfaced during the White House Conference on the Family did not disappear when the conference ended. Their promoters now moved into school textbooks. They systematically began portraying the family in nontraditional ways. In the mid-1980s Paul Vitz, a psychologist, surveyed forty contemporary social studies texts used for grades 1 through 4 and found that the family was commonly defined as "the people you live with." The texts avoided objective, traditional definitions of the family. When pictures were shown of children in a household, it was common to see them with a mother only; fathers were rarely present. Vitz further notes: "There [was] not one text reference to marriage as the foundation of the family. Indeed not even the word marriage or wedding occur[red] once in the forty books!"[4] The message sent to young, malleable students here is obvious. Being married must not be seen as a cultural prerequisite to bearing and rearing children, forming a family.

Vitz also found no text featuring a mother or woman as homemaker; the words "housewife" and "homemaker" were never used. Such terms are seen as Euro-centric, a mark of Western imperialism. On the other hand, there were "countless references to mothers and other women working outside of the home in occupations such as medicine, transportation, and politics."[5] He could not find "one portrayal of a contemporary American family that clearly feature[d] traditional sex roles."[6]

Clearly, the traditional family is an anachronism to the disciples of multiculturalism; it does not fit their radical, leftist ideology. It is too much of a product of the "imperialistic" Euro-American culture.

THE NEVER-MARRIED-PARENT FAMILY AS A BONA FIDE CULTURE

As mentioned in Chapter 2, the multiculturalist ideology sees all kinds of group behavior as bona-fide cultures. Thus they consider never-married-parent families merely to be another kind of "culture" and since all cultures and subcultures are equal, there is no reason to criticize or find unacceptable the phenomenon of never-married parents as an alter-

native way of life, a bona fide culture. Television and newspapers—
striving to be politically correct and supportive of multiculturalism—are
by no means averse to depicting 15–year-old, never-married mothers
with their child(ren) in much the same way as they show adult married
mothers with their children. The media also show unmarried fathers,
often only a year or two older than the underage girls they impregnated,
interacting with mother and child(ren). The reporters may even lament
that these kinds of "families" are not receiving enough public welfare,
but there is never any insinuation that never-married mothers and fathers with their children are not families like others where marriage was
the necessary first step to begin a family. The social and moral stigma
surrounding illegitimacy, once so strong, is suddenly gone.

This kind of thinking has undermined the traditional family and the
values it has for centuries sought to inculcate in its children and to be-
queath to posterity. Presenting single-parent families as just another acceptable "culture" makes it increasingly difficult for children to accept
and internalize traditional family values even in two-parent homes. Accepting never-married families without shame or stigma, however, is not
without consequences. David Popenoe, a sociologist, says: "there is a
strong likelihood that the increase in the number of fatherless children
over the past 30 years has been a prominent factor in the growth of
violence and juvenile delinquency."[7] One survey of 14,000 prison in-
mates in 1991 found that over 50 percent of the prisoners did not live
with two parents while they grew up.[8] The multiculturalists and their
media supporters commonly ignore these facts.

AWAY WITH TRANSRACIAL ADOPTIONS

Multiculturalism also wants to end interracial or transracial adoptions.
The first major condemnation of such adoptions came from the National
Association of Black Social Workers (NABSW) which in 1972 proclaimed
that the adoption of black children was "racial genocide." This radical
group has been joined by the North American Council on Adoptable
Children, and in June 1994, by the National Association for the Advance-
ment of Colored People (NAACP).

Not long after the NABSW action, multiculturalists labeled black children in white homes "Oreo cookies"—black outside but white inside.
Soon, American Indian children raised by white families were dubbed
"Mackintosh apples"—red outside but white inside. Children of Japanese, Chinese, Korean, or Vietnamese origin were tagged as "bananas,"
and adopted children of Mexican background were called "coconuts."
Implicit in all of these labels or transracial adoptions is the specious
argument that the color or race of people determines their culture. As
noted earlier, this is simply a new form of racism. But because some

non-Western or nonwhite group(s), seen as "cultures," advance this argument, it is not called what it really is—racism.

As one might expect, conforming bureaucrats and legislators are quick to say "me too" with regard to accepting some radical or leftist propaganda. Liberals want to be multiculturally correct. They want to show that they care and that they are not cultural imperialists. They also believe such actions will lessen some of their white guilt. Thus by the end of 1993 three states (Arizona, Minnesota, California) passed legislation explicitly giving preference to same-race child placement.[9] Whether empirical evidence warranted this kind of legislative action did not seem to matter. Moreover, studies show that anti-transracial laws are not needed.

Rita Simon's study is one such study. In her sample of 240 white families who adopted children of different racial origins, she found that the majority of the children had no problem with race.[10] Noting Simon's study, one editorial writer wrote: "In college many [interracial] children have found it an advantage to have inroads into both black and white communities. About one-half called race an 'unimportant factor' in their lives, an attitude the NABSW labeled 'inappropriate.' "[11]

Throughout 1993 and 1994, newspapers across the nation published dozens of articles and editorials on transracial adoptions. *The Houston Chronicle* titled one report "Tribe Intervenes in Adoption." This was a case in which the Yovapi Apache tribe in Arizona tried to bar the adoption of three Indian brothers by a white couple.

The basis of the opposition to transracial adoptions is multiculturalism, of course! Its values have been touted to minority groups in particular for nearly two decades, and they have begun to have their effects. Moreover, transracial adoption also provides a convenient way to play the role of victim vis-à-vis the Euro-American culture.

APPLE PIE BUT NOT MOTHERHOOD

The arms of multiculturalism stretch widely. Its advocates are also attacking the heart and core of the traditional nuclear family by picturing motherhood as an epiphenomenon of the Euro-American, white-male-dominated culture. As Christina Hoff Sommers, no friend of the radical (gender) feminists and their multiculturalist companions, notes, this "bourgeois" culture "is prosecuted under the banners of 'cultural pluralism,' 'inclusiveness,' and 'diversity.' "[12]

Typically, the attack on motherhood is launched by radical, gender feminists, who are close bedfellows with the disciples of multiculturalism. Both are not only highly supportive of each other, but they also have ideological assumptions in common. Multiculturalism (as shown in Chapter 3) works with neo-Marxist premises, and so does radical feminism. Thus the traditional nuclear family, with motherhood at the epicenter, is considered "bourgeois" and "patriarchal." And anything that is bourgeois or patriarchal is obviously anachronistic. The traditional family, along with motherhood, are not, therefore, worthy of the honor and respect they have elicited for centuries or even for millennia.

In keeping with this Marxist posture, Mardy Ireland, a radical feminist, for example, authored a book, *Reconceiving Women: Separating Motherhood from Female Identity*, in which she argues that the "culture" of the family must be changed so that a mother plays only a biological role.[13] Her identity must be derived solely from the economic realm outside of the family. For a mother to acquire an identity from having borne and raised children is the unpardonable sin, for in this way she perpetuates the Eurocentric, patriarchal culture.

The multiculturalist/feminist attack on motherhood, and thus on the family as well, has taken yet another tack. In Mount Holyoke, Massachusetts, the Gorse Child Studies Center, under the direction of Patricia Ramsey, is replacing the traditional Mother's Day holiday with what is called "Family Day." To Ramsey and her organization, Mother's Day is a regressive symbol of sexism.[14] The attack on this holiday and others has led educators in Ohio and Wisconsin school districts to stop teaching anything about any holidays.[15]

How much longer will America be able to honor its mothers? How much longer will the well-known, oft-quoted sentence attributed to Abraham Lincoln be heard? Said he: "All that I am or hope to be, I owe to my angel mother." If the Trojan Horse of multiculturalism is taken farther and farther into the nation, how much longer will we hear the words of Alice Hawthorne: "What is home without a mother?"

According to multiculturalism, too many women have derived their identity from being mothers, and in this way help perpetuate the white-male power structure by raising great men. If women did not anchor their identity in motherhood, there would be fewer great men, or perhaps no great men at all. Instead there would be more great women who were not held back by the identity of motherhood.

According to radical feminism, a woman whose identity is tied to motherhood lives in the Marxist state of false consciousness. She needs to become aware of this false consciousness and get rid of it. She must instead derive her identity from a nonmotherhood "culture," as multiculturalists call it. Multiculturalists are more than eager to help in the process.

HOMOSEXUAL "MARRIAGES"

In 1993 New York City made it possible for homosexual partners to register legally as "domestic partners," granting homosexuals many rights and privileges that were once available only to heterosexual married couples. Since New York City's action, at least one university, the University of Chicago, has extended employee benefits to "domestic partners."

Granting homosexuals the status of "domestic partners" clearly undermines the institution of the family, conflicting with the societal and legal understanding of what constitutes a family. For instance, in 1965 the U.S. Supreme Court's decision in *Griswold v. Connecticut,* which struck down Connecticut's anti-contraception law, spoke about the rights of husband and wife, not domestic partners.

When city councils, or other lawmaking groups, grant homosexual partners the rights and status of heterosexual marriages, they declare themselves to have unlimited power. The laws of nature and God mean little or nothing to them. The Canadian columnist, Barbara Amiel, described that kind of arrogant power in the province of Ontario, Canada. She compared the legalization of homosexual "families" (same-sex marriages) in Ontario to the behavior of Caligula, the Roman emperor, who in the first century A.D. decreed that one of his consuls would be a horse because he wanted to show he had unlimited power. "Ontario," said Amiel, "has declared two spouses can be of the same gender and by so doing they [*sic*] have imitated Caligula."[16]

Ontario is not the only place that considers homosexual "marriages" valid. In the spring of 1994, the *St. Louis Post Dispatch* reported that the British Broadcasting Corporation (BBC) would give homosexual workers who take part in "a formal ceremony of commitment" one week's paid vacation to go on a honeymoon. The report also said that the BBC would give gift vouchers as wedding presents to such couples.[17]

As a result, Amiel observes, "The incidental result of this is that the legitimacy of the family will be diminished. Homosexual unions can be called 'families,' but they cannot create children."[18] In short, it is difficult not to see such unions, promoted by multiculturalists, as a threat to the traditional family that has existed for millennia, and not just in the Western world.

The potential threat to the traditional family was increased in March 1996 when in San Francisco 200 homosexual and lesbian couples were publicly united in "virtual marriages." Although these "marriages" (noted in Chapter 6) have no legal status in the United States, they may well help pave the way for the future possible legalization of such unions.

The National Education Association has been a key promoter of homosexuality. In Fairfax County, Virginia, a manual produced for the NEA by homosexual activists recommends avoiding use of the word "marriage" in favor of "permanent relationship" and using the term "partner" in place of "boyfriend or girlfriend."[19] Concerned about legalizing homosexual unions, as the province of Ontario recently did,

some American states have enacted laws that do not recognize homosexual "marriages" even if they are legal elsewhere. In March 1995,
Utah's legislature voted overwhelmingly not to recognize the homosexual "marriages" of other states should that become a reality. In the same
month the senate of South Dakota voted to make null and void all homosexual "marriages." This state's House of Representatives had already
approved the same bill earlier. Also in March, the Alaska legislature
received a bill that explicitly stated: "Marriage is a civil contract entered
into by one man and one woman."[20]

As these states realize, efforts to legitimate homosexual "marriages"
threaten the foundation of the nation's morality. Their preemptive actions bring to mind the dire warning of Don Feder, who has argued:
"The homosexual threat to the family is more subtle than that posed by
divorce. Once this particular vice is accepted, no other can rationally be
rejected."[21]

Whether the recent (May 1996) U.S. Supreme Court decision of *Romer
v. Evans,* which nullified Colorado's 1992 constitutional amendment that
declined special protection for homosexuals with reference to certain
types of discrimination, will have any effect on the "domestic partners"
relationship, is not known. It is also unclear whether this decision of the
Court will have a bearing on the legality of "same-sex" marriages, currently pushed by homosexuals and their multiculturalist allies. *Romer v.
Evans* did not deal with marriage rights and privileges.

UNITED NATIONS' CONVENTION ON THE RIGHTS OF THE CHILD

On the face of it, this lengthy U.N. document (actually a treaty) that
portrays itself as intending to protect children's rights does not appear
to be the brainchild of multiculturalists. How much multiculturalist
thinking was present among the formulators of this treaty may never be
known. As one studies this document, however, one sees a number of
elements that are quite congruent with multiculturalism's ideology.

Many observers regard this treaty as a threat to the traditional family,
similar to multiculturalism's other threats to the family already discussed
above. Article 20 states that "due regard shall be paid to the desirability
of continuity in a child's upbringing and to the child's ethnic, religious,
cultural and linguistic background." As stated above, with reference to
anti-transracial adoption efforts currently in vogue, this would seem to
permit anyone to bring suit against parents who adopted a child of a
different ethnic or cultural background. Hence opponents of transracial
adoption of children could have an extra weapon in this document to
prevent such adoptions, as they seek to keep racial and ethnic separatism
alive.

Article 43 of the treaty calls for a committee of "ten experts" from signatory countries who will see to it that the treaty is followed by all member countries of the United Nations. This, of course, applies to "violations" of Article 2, which states that a "child is protected against all forms of discrimination or punishment." Would this committee have the right to "take all appropriate measures" (Article 2) to punish parents who, say, physically or otherwise disciplined ("punished") their child? What about Article 12? It states: "The child shall have the right to freedom of expression; this right shall include freedom to seek, receive and impart *information and ideas of all kinds* [emphasis added], regardless of frontiers." If a 14–year-old child, for instance, were to bring home pornographic or pro-homosexual materials, and the parents were to disallow it, would they be taken to task by a bureaucratic committee of the United Nations?

Article 16 gives a child the "right to privacy," which has the potential of excluding parents from having any voice in a fifteen-year-old daughter's decision, for instance, to seek an abortion. This would delight pro-abortion groups such as Planned Parenthood.

This children's rights document was first adopted by the General Assembly of the United Nations in November 1989. As of April 1995, the treaty had been signed by 176 countries. President Clinton, the avid promoter of multiculturalism, and in the spirit of multiculturalism, has already signed it. The United States Senate, however, has thus far not ratified it, and, with Senator Jesse Helms as chairman of the Senate Foreign Relations Committee, it does not appear that it will even get out of the committee to the floor of the Senate for a vote.

Multiculturalism's far-reaching tentacles are not just affecting the nation's schools, universities, churches, and businesses. Its ongoing efforts to redefine the family, oppose transracial adoptions, give marital status to homosexual unions, and promote children's rights create the potential of punishing the traditional nuclear family. These efforts demonstrate that multiculturalism is more than merely learning about other cultures.

THE UNITED NATIONS' CONFERENCE ON WOMEN

For two weeks in September 1995, the Fourth United Nations Conference on Women met in Beijing, China, to promote a gender feminist agenda. Gender feminists argue that the differences between men and women are the result of culture, not biology. The conference had a number of antifamily accents. Its platform studiously avoided using the words *mother, father, wife,* or *husband.* It also avoided using the words *brother* or *sister.* For the latter it advocated *sibling,* and the word *household* replaced *family.* Eliminating these traditional terms for family members, and even dropping the word *family,* is a definite threat to the family. It's an attempt to legitimate and institutionalize any kind of relationship between adults and the children who are under their care and supervision. Whether adults with children are (or ever were) married is irrelevant. Thus the conference's platform, at least indirectly, promoted "alternative sexual relationships outside of marriage."[22]

NOTES

1. J. Francis Stafford, "The Year of the Family Revisited," *America*, 16 May 1981, 399.

2. "Family Conference Rejects Antiabortion Amendment," *New York Times*, 22 June 1980, 24.

3. Cited by Wesley G. Pippert, "Viewing the Family from the Oval Office," *Christianity Today*, 9 September 1977, 60–61.

4. Paul Vitz, *Censorship: Evidence of Bias in Our Children's Textbooks* (Ann Arbor, Mich.: Servant Books, 1986), p. 38.

5. Ibid.

6. Ibid., p. 39.

7. David Popenoe cited in Lee Smith, "The New Wave of Illegitimacy," *Fortune*, 18 April 1994, 82.

8. Ibid.

9. Editorial, "All in the Family," *The New Republic*, 24 January 1994, 7.

10. Rita Simon, *Adopting, Race, and Identity* (New York: Praeger, 1992).

11. Editorial, "All in the Family," p. 7.

12. Christina Hoff Sommers, *Who Stole Feminism?* (New York: Simon and Schuster, 1993), p. 84.

13. Mardy S. Ireland, *Reconceiving Women: Separating Motherhood from Female Identity* (New York: Guilford Press, 1993).

14. Kay Sunstein Hymowitz, "Barar the Racist," *The New Republic*, 19 and 26 August 1991, 12–13.

15. Ibid., 13.

16. Barbara Amiel, "Ontario and Gays: A New Frontier?" *Maclean's*, 6 June 1994, 9.

17. "Homosexuals at BBC Get Time Off for Honeymoon," *St. Louis Post Dispatch*, 22 May 1994, 9D.

18. Amiel, "Ontario and Gays," p. 9.

19. Peter LaBarbera, "NEA Pushes Homosexual Agenda," *Christian American* (May/June 1995): 8.

20. "Some States Trying to Stop Gay Marriages Before They Start," *New York Times*, 15 March 1995, A18.

21. Don Feder, "Acceptance of Homosexuality Opens Floodgates to All Vices," *Human Events*, 27 January 1995, 19.

22. Rush Limbaugh, "Who Are These Gals?" *The Limbaugh Letter* (September 1995): 5.

Chapter 10

The Multiculturalist Purges

If the danger seems slight, then truly it is not slight.

Francis Bacon

The preceding chapters noted that multiculturalists favor "multi" cultural practices only so long as they are not Western or Euro-American. The "big tent" that multiculturalists talk about evidently has no room for norms or values that have a biblical basis. The behavior of zealous multiculturalists frequently resembles that of a political purge as they seek to eradicate the natural/moral law that underlies Euro-American (Western) morality. They also do their utmost to bar or expunge from the public square all biblical symbols, especially those identified with Christianity. They are even beginning to harass Christians.

DOWN WITH THE NATURAL/MORAL LAW

Removing the Ten Commandments

The mere presence of any laws found in the Bible, even though these natural/moral laws (as opposed to positive or man-made laws) existed prior to the Bible, is reason enough for multiculturalists to reject them. The age-old acceptance of natural/moral law by the ancient Greeks and Romans is lost on these zealots.

Sophocles, the Greek poet of the fifth century B.C., in his tragedy, *Antigone*, shows that the Greeks operated with the concept of natural law. Similarly, the ancient Romans accepted the natural law of morality, which they believed was apprehended through sound human reason. Thus Cicero wrote: "True law is right reason in agreement with nature; it is of universal application, unchanging and everlasting; it summons to duty by its commands, and averts from wrongdoing by its prohibitions" (*The Republic*, Book III, 32:33).

In the first century A.D., St. Paul equated the natural law with the Bible's Ten Commandments. He argued that the Gentiles (pagans or non-Jews) who did not have the biblically written Ten Commandments nevertheless heeded them. According to Paul, they had the natural law "written in their hearts" (Romans 2:15). In a similar manner, Martin Luther in the 1500s declared that the Ten Commandments were the natural law stated more clearly and concisely. He asked: "Why does one then keep and teach the Ten Commandments? Answer: Because the natural laws were never so orderly and well written as by Moses."[1]

Luther, like Cicero, contended that it was through sound human reason that people apprehended the natural/moral law and that it was a universal phenomenon. He said that "all [human] reason is filled" with natural law,"[2] and "Experience itself shows all nations share this common ordinary knowledge."[3]

In short, as multiculturalists remove the Ten Commandments from America's public square, they are unwittingly doing more than expurgating biblical norms. They are also eliminating the age-old natural/moral law, a universal reality. And, strange as it may seem, the very institution—the United States Supreme Court—that exists to protect the nation's Constitution, derived in large measure from the natural/moral law, has provided legal sophistry, compatible with multiculturalism's ideology, to eradicate this age-old, universal law. This occurred in the Supreme Court's decision of *Stone v. Graham* in 1980 which banned the posting of the Ten Commandments in American public schools.

Banning the Ten Commandments from public schools prevents students from reading them, and also means that teachers may not legally teach students that many of their nation's major criminal laws, and many civil laws, are derived from the Ten Commandments. Even if some teachers may technically tell students that many of their country's laws are derived from the Ten Commandments, how can they effectively do so when these Commandments may not be taught or be visible on school premises?

For example, students must now draw their own conclusions concerning the basis of their country's antitheft laws rather than have teachers teach them that these laws have their roots in the Commandment "You shall not steal." The same is true of the laws outlawing murder which are based on the Commandment "You shall not kill (murder)." Even if some students might vaguely be able to associate the laws against murder and theft with the Ten Commandments, because these two Commandments are the most familiar ones, it is probably safe to assume that almost none are able to conclude that the laws against slander, libel, and perjury come from the Commandment "You shall not bear false witness against your neighbor." Given the declining standardized test scores that show more and more of today's students know less and less about history, literature, geography, and so on, this is not an unreasonable conclusion.

The Supreme Court's barring of the Ten Commandments from public schools made it much easier for multiculturalists to achieve their multi-morality agenda. Students are now exposed to "multi-moral systems." One example introduces students to the seven principles of Kwanzaa, a holiday recently invented for black Americans by an Afrocentrist in 1966 (see Chapter 8). Kwanzaa is a multiculturalist's delight. Although its promoters say that Kwanzaa is not a moral or religious holiday, three of its principles ("collective work," "responsibility," and "faith") have strong moral, even religious, connotations, especially the principle of faith. This does not bother multiculturalists, for they are concerned only when norms and values reflect a biblical foundation.

Several years ago, Ted Koppel of television's "Nightline" spoke at a university commencement and stated that the Ten Commandments were not merely ten suggestions as he referred to some of the nation's moral problems. In taking this stance, Koppel was not multiculturally or politically correct; in the language of multiculturalists, he was "insensitive" to the moral norms of other cultures.

Once a nation's moral foundation is significantly scuttled, serious social problems inevitably arise and multiply. That is what is happening in America today and multiculturalism's "multi-morality" will produce more social and moral deterioration. Witness the following: The crime rate in the United States has risen significantly during the past three decades, even though a slight decrease for a given year or two has sometimes occurred, as is presently true. The current slight decline, if the past is any indication, may very well be just another small dip in a generally upward trend. In 1960 the American murder and nonnegligent manslaughter rate was 5.0 per 100,000 population and in 1993 it stood at 10.0 (the rate for 1996 will likely be about 9.5, not a tremendous improvement). "The United States has the highest murder rate of any industrialized country."[4] The rate for aggravated assault was 73.0 in 1960 and 440 in 1993; the rate for forcible rape was 8.9 in 1960 and by 1993 it had increased four-fold to 41.0; the burglary rate was 456.5 in 1960 and in 1993 it rose to 1,099; the motor vehicle theft rate in 1960 was 177.6 but in 1993 it had climbed to 605.[5]

In 1960 there were 2.2 marital divorces per 100,000 Americans and in 1993 the rate was 4.6, more than double the rate of three decades ago.[6]

Out-of-wedlock births in 1960 amounted to 5 percent of all live births in America; by 1992 they had soared to 30.1 percent.[7]

Given this bleak picture of America's deteriorating cultural life, William Bennett, former secretary of education, has noted that in the 1950s the teachers' biggest problems with students were chewing gum, tardiness, and talking during class. Today it is the presence of drugs, guns, knives, assault, and teenage pregnancies.[8]

Without the natural/moral law, as reflected by the Ten Commandments, more and more Americans will undoubtedly begin to resemble the people in the days of the biblical judges (ca. 1400–1100 B.C.) when "every person [did] what is right in his own eyes" (Judges 17:6). These words are descriptive of the beliefs of multiculturalists, who have persuaded many Americans with their relativistic statement: "No group or culture has the right to impose its morality on others."

It must be noted that the removal of the Ten Commandments amounts to the removal of the natural/moral law. That law is *not* the sole possession of Jews and Christians. To argue, as multiculturalists do, that the posting of the Ten Commandments in public schools violates the separation of church and state is to ignore the intent of the Founding Fathers in formulating the Bill of Rights and the Declaration of Independence. The Founders believed in the natural law, which was often expressed in their phrase "the natural rights of man."

To outlaw the public posting of the Ten Commandments also ignores the eventual consequences of such a national policy. The words of William F. Albright, the renowned archaeologist of the Near East, come to mind. Shortly after World War II, he declared: "The Ten Commandments cannot be violated with impunity by any people or philosophical sect. The latest attempts of the Nazis and Communists to set them aside and to replace the Ten Commandments by their party lines have resulted in orgies of slaughter almost unparalleled in history."[9]

Spurning Moral Objections to Homosexuality

Multiculturalists, with the help of many state legislatures, are eradicating laws that for centuries outlawed and condemned homosexual behavior. Again, multiculturalists erroneously think these prohibitions are religious or sectarian because the prohibitions against homosexuality are stated in the Bible. They fail to recognize that homosexuality has been universally condemned because the behavior has been seen as violating the natural law.

Plato was himself a homosexual and spoke approvingly of homosexuality in his *Symposium*. Nevertheless, in his *Laws* (Book I, 636:c) he said that homosexual behavior was "contrary to nature" (*para physin*). Similarly, the ancient Hebrews heard Moses' command: "You shall not lie with a male as with a woman; it is an abomination" (Leviticus 18:22). This is simply a formal declaration of what numerous societies and cultures, from time immemorial, have known to be behavior contrary to natural law. This formal condemnation, along with the proscription of other kinds of deviant sexual behavior, says Dennis Prager, "made the creation of Western civilization possible." (Prager is a talk-show host and a conservative Jew.) He adds: "Societies that did not place boundaries around sexuality were stymied in their development."[10] He also notes that the low status of women has been directly correlated with a society's acceptance of homoeroticism, and that "the emancipation of women has been a function of Western civilization, the civilization least tolerant of homosexuality."[11]

The condemnation of homosexuality in the Old Testament is reaffirmed in the New Testament. St. Paul, as noted in Chapter 6, in writing to the Roman Christians, made it very clear that homosexual sex was a violation of nature.

Modern-day homosexuals and the multiculturalists actively promote homosexual behavior as a bona fide "culture." Both are utilizing every available means to discredit and reject the natural/moral law's condemnation of homosexuality. They try to legitimate it by calling it an alternative lifestyle. Any laws to the contrary are labeled "homophobic."

Because radical homosexuals and multiculturalists believe that the prohibition of homosexuality has only a Judeo-Christian or biblical foundation—which is totally false—they have gone on the attack against Christianity and individuals in the church. In January 1992, homosexuals verbally attacked Cardinal John O'Connor using scatological expressions because, as a Roman Catholic prelate, he condemned homosexual behavior as sinful. Earlier, in December 1989, homosexuals of the ACT UP (AIDS Coalition to Unleash Power) group invaded St. Patrick's Cathedral in New York during a Mass, screaming "bigot" and "murderer" at Cardinal O'Connor while he was preaching.[12] These harassers also mocked the church's Eucharist rite by handing out condoms as communion wafers; the press failed to report this part of the incident.[13]

On September 19, 1993, a large crowd of angry homosexuals invaded Hamilton Square Baptist Church in San Francisco before and during the church service. The congregation had invited a guest speaker from the Traditional Values Coalition to address the topic of homosexuality. The homosexuals screamed, cursed, physically roughed a woman, hurled rocks and eggs, terrorized children, and even vandalized the church grounds. They forcibly removed the Christian flag from the church's flagpole and replaced it with a "Gay Pride" flag. In addition, they tacked anti-Christian slogans to the church building, and insulted and threatened many church members. Upon seeing young children in one of the rooms, some homosexuals banged on the door and shouted: "We want your children." As outlandish as this uprising was, the police stood by and took no action, and the city refused to pursue any redress.[14]

These are not isolated incidents. In April 1991, John Leo wrote: "In the past 18 months or so, many churches across the country (six in Los Angeles alone) have been vandalized and broken into, with gay activists claiming responsibility." Leo also notes that "Masses and other religious ceremonies have been repeatedly disrupted, parishioners harassed and showered with condoms, and venomously anti-Catholic demonstrations conducted regularly outside churches."[15]

Besides physically disrupting church services and engaging in vandalism, homosexuals have resorted to mockery in their attempts to discredit and eventually to nullify the biblical norms they detest. "Savage mockery of Christianity is now a conventional part of the public gay culture. A ridiculous-looking Jesus figure carrying a cross is always featured in the gay Halloween parade in New York, along with the usual throng of hairy guys dressed as nuns."[16]

The February/March 1995 issue of the *Lambda Report* revealed that a sacrilegious picture of Jesus had appeared on the front cover of *The Advocate* (December 13, 1994), a homosexual magazine. The picture portrayed Christ in a crucified mode wearing a homosexual necklace with "cock" rings. These rings, says Judith Reisman, are "worn tightly at the base of a man's penis during [homosexual] sex to prolong his erection."[17] Above Christ's left shoulder are the words: "IS GOD GAY?" which also form the title of the magazine's cover article. The picture also has phallic-like fingers, rather grotesque in appearance, under Christ's shoulders, apparently holding him up. This portrayal shows that many homosexuals are engaged in a campaign to ridicule orthodox Christianity (a charge the editor of *The Advocate* denies).[18] Whatever the intent, depicting Christ as a crucified homosexual reveals total disrespect for Him.

The multiculturalists have greatly aided homosexuals' attempts to persuade elementary schools to adopt pro-homosexual materials. The most spectacular of such attempts was the Rainbow Curriculum in New York City in 1993 (see Chapter 4), which ended in failure. Undeterred, in January 1995, the Des Moines, Iowa, school board was asked to approve a curriculum similar to the New York plan. It was called the Multicultural Nonsexist Education Plan. It sought to have children avoid "heterosexual bias in the language" and also, "To substantially increase accurate gay/lesbian/bisexual materials in school libraries and multimedia centers."[19]

The multiculturalist goal to erase biblical norms such as the Ten Commandments and prohibitions against homosexuality shows that multiculturalists seem to believe a society can function and endure without adhering to the natural/moral law. They are campaigning for a "multimorality" divorced from the natural law. Their view of "morality" is often based on selfish lusts and moral relativism, contrary to sound human reason. As history shows, such morality invariably results in a moral meltdown, followed by social and political anarchy. Human laws cannot ignore the natural/moral law without eventually experiencing the wrath of nature.

EXPUNGING CHRISTIAN SYMBOLS

Multiculturalists are engaged in purging tactics aimed at Christianity and its adherents, who in 1994 represented at least 81 percent of the American population.[20]

Christianity is more widely and more viciously attacked than is Judaism, for several reasons. First, most people are more cautious about attacking Judaism, mindful of the Nazi atrocities. Second, Judaism is a significantly smaller religion than Christianity and so it is less threatening to multiculturalists. Third, the American culture has been shaped predominantly by Christian beliefs and values, and that is highly repugnant to ardent multiculturalists. Moreover, attacking Christianity incurs no stigma or penalty.

De-Christianizing Christmas

As with the efforts to eradicate biblical norms, the Supreme Court has unwittingly given a huge boost to multiculturalists by expunging Christian symbols from America's social fabric, especially at Christmas. In *Lynch v. Donnelly* (1984), the Court ruled that a Christmas creche could be displayed if its sole purpose was not religious and that it had to be accompanied by secular displays such as a Christmas tree, Santa Claus, colored lights, a snowman, and so on. In a more recent case, *Allegheny v. ACLU* (1989), the Court declared a Christmas creche in Pittsburgh, Pennsylvania, to be unconstitutional even though it was accompanied by nonreligious displays, because its symbolism was predominantly religious. In other words, the symbolism of Christ's birth not only must be intermixed with secular objects, but it must also have a nonreligious purpose. In short, Christian symbols may not communicate what they are designed to communicate; if they do, they must be removed. Moreover, to ban Christian symbols in Christmas displays ironically overlooks the fact that this nationwide calendar event—the Christmas season— would not exist had there been no Jesus Christ.

The anti-creche mania sometimes reveals a double standard. For example, the city of San Jose, California, ordered the traditional creche removed from its park display because it was "insensitive" to the non-Christian population. "But," as Linda Chavez writes, "city officials showed no similar sensitivity to religious scruples two weeks earlier when a group of Christians protested the unveiling of a permanent exhibit in the public park of an eight-foot statue honoring the [Aztec] god Quetzalcoatl."[21] The creche was paid for by private funds, whereas the Aztec statue was financed by $500,000 of public monies.

This incident reveals the anti-Christian biases of multiculturalists, and it also shows their apparent ignorance regarding the Latinos. As Chavez observes, if the San Jose officials really wanted to erect a "universally recognized symbol of Latino culture, it might have erected a statue of Our Lady of Guadalupe, whose picture certainly adorns more Mexican-American homes than Quetzalcoatl's does."[22]

The anti-Christian crusade is moving full speed ahead. Beginning with the Christmas season of 1995, the United States Post Office no longer allows signs on its premises that say "Merry Christmas."[23] Nor will the Post Office print any more stamps such as the Virgin Mary and the Christ Child, as it did in December of 1994. But in true multiculturalist, anti-Christian fashion, the Post Office will allow Kwanzaa displays.

The multiculturalist campaign to remove all Christian symbols of Christmas is not confined to creches in the public square or to the U.S. Post Office. Public schools have also been invaded. Sarah McCarthy reports that in some suburban Pittsburgh classrooms "teachers and students have been told not to wear Christmas sweaters and children's homemade Christmas calendars were removed from the bulletin boards due to their religious content."[24]

And there is more. Multiculturalists are trying to get Christmas renamed the "Winter Festival." While many Christians are trying to "Put Christ back into Christmas," as their slogan has it, the multiculturalists are trying to abolish the last vestige of Christmas by renaming it. Their objective is plainly to de-Christianize Christmas.

The de-Christianizing of Christmas is quickly taking hold in many department and discount stores, where, especially during the 1995 Christmas shopping season, traditional carols such as *Silent Night, The First Noel, Away in a Manger,* and *O Holy Night* were excised from many stores' traditional Christmas music selections that their shoppers have heard for many decades. All these carols mention Jesus Christ and the reason for his being born. In the name of toleration, Christmas carols are not tolerated.

Perhaps Christians need to boycott those stores that are banning the singing of the religious carols during the Christmas shopping season. If stores want to profit from this Christian holiday, they ought not to bite the hand that feeds them. Moreover, Christians would do well not to sit idly by as business leaders help multiculturalists destroy the "reason for the season," as one Christmas slogan puts it. One also wonders whether such business executives have ever thought about the long-range effects of their actions—namely, their practices may eventually eliminate Christmas altogether. For multiculturalists that would be a victory, but for countless businesses it would spell economic disaster, particularly for those businesses that reap a major share of their year's profits during the month of December.

Since the de-Christianizing of Christmas cannot be accomplished overnight, the ever-ready companions of multiculturalists, the media, are assisting wherever possible. *U.S. News and World Report*, for instance, published an article, "The Christmas Covenant," for the 1994 Christmas season. This piece devoted an entire column to the extremely rare birth of a white buffalo calf that had recently occurred in Janesville, Wisconsin. Next to a picture of Jesus Christ, the article shows the albino buffalo calf feeding on its mother's udder, and then it mentions the American Indian myth of the "White Buffalo Woman" who once "brought spiritual knowledge to a starving tribe, allowing its members to hunt buffalo across the Great Plains." The article then proceeds to cite an Oglala Lakota medicine man who says that "she [the 'white buffalo woman,' the calf] has returned and a great human reconciliation will occur."[25]

The multicultural message is obvious here—namely, Jesus Christ is not the only reconciler of humanity. The biblical message announced at Jesus' birth, "for to you is born in the city of David a Savior, who is Christ the Lord" (Luke 2;11), is on a par with the Indian myth of a white buffalo calf. The Indians have their reconciler too. Whether people worship an animal (white buffalo calf) or the person of Jesus Christ is of no consequence.

Down with All Christian Symbols

All these incidents reveal "how the high priests of multiculturalism now dictate our official icons," says Chavez.[26] To anyone familiar with multiculturalism, these actions are no surprise.

Thanks to some recent Supreme Court decisions, the multiculturalists have not lost any time in pursuing the removal and destruction of Christian symbols that irritate them. At the University of Central Arkansas, the multicultural correctniks had the campus chapel's three crosses removed and placed near a Christian mural where drapes would cover the mural and the crosses.[27] In a Grand Forks, North Dakota, high school students received an assignment telling them they could design a poster on any topic of their choosing. One student drew a poster that included a cross, the American flag, and the question: "Is the Son shining in your school?" The teacher gave the poster a perfect grade and displayed it in the school hallway with the other class posters. When the principal saw it, he ordered it removed, stating: "We have to be respectful of all religions and not place one over the other."[28]

U.S. West, one of the largest publishers of yellow pages in the country, tried to bar Christian symbols from its clients' ads. Two nursing homes,

one Catholic and another Lutheran, in St. Cloud, Minnesota, were told
to remove the crosses that were part of their advertisements before they
would be published. The firm later withdrew its directive.[29] In 1992 the
city of Rolling Meadows, Illinois, lost a five-year legal battle to keep the
insignia of a cross and a church that was part of the city's concrete seal
embossed on a 20–foot base of a flagpole outside of the city hall. A
federal court ordered the cross to be erased. So the city hired a workman
with a chisel and sander to expunge the two Christian symbols.[30] Another federal court judge ordered that two crosses be torn down that
made up some of the war memorials in San Diego and in La Mesa. The
judge also ordered the city of La Mesa to cease displaying a cross on its
police uniforms and city vehicles.[31]

The multiculturalist crusade against Christian symbolism is not restricted to Christian crosses. At Moorehead State University, officials recently wouldn't allow students to include a fish in a mural on their
dormitory's wall because the fish was an early Christian symbol.[32] In
Colorado, a federal court ordered a fifth-grade teacher in Denver not to
leave his Bible visibly on his desk.[33] In yet another school incident, a
picture of Jesus that hung on a wall for thirty years at Bloomingdale
High School in Kalamazoo, Michigan, was recently taken down "after
the U.S. Supreme Court refused to override a Michigan judge's court
order."[34]

In Hillsboro, Illinois, the American Civil Liberties Union has sued the
county for not removing a sign because of its words: "The World Needs
God." The sign was placed on the courthouse wall in 1936 by a Sunday
School teacher who thought it would drive the bootleggers out of town.
In February 1996, the county decided to remove the sign because it could
not pay additional court costs.[35]

Multiculturalism's passionate quest to remove all Christian symbols
from the public arena sometimes reveals its crusaders' considerable ignorance. Here is a case in point. "[F]ederal agents from the Department
of Housing and Urban Development (HUD) [recently] investigated *The
Statesman Journal* in Salem, Oregon, for publishing a drawing of [an
Easter] bunny in its real estate section."[36] Needless to say the bunny was
excised. Actually, the multiculturalists did Christianity a favor, for the
bunny is a pagan accretion that has nothing to do with Easter, the event
commemorating Christ's physical resurrection from the dead. The Easter
bunny has probably harmed Christianity's most significant festival more
than it has helped it.

A similar reversion to paganism was illustrated at the opening ceremonies of the 1994 Winter Olympics, held in Norway, when virtually
the entire world saw representations of pre-Christian-era pagan underground "beings" called *Vetters*. Had the Lutheran Church of Norway
(the nation's state church), which counts about 95 percent of its country's

population as Christians, had any input? Did the Olympic decision makers even consult the church? Why was it so important to focus on pagan mythology?

While the opening ceremonies showed a piece of Norway's history, no one mentioned Norway's great leader and hero, Olaf Haraldsson, better known as St. Olaf, who presided over his nation's first national assembly and moved it to adopt Christianity as the nation's religion.[37] When he abolished pagan practices such as "blood sacrifices, black magic, the 'setting out' of infants, slavery, and polygamy,"[38] his actions led to a rebellion in which he was slain in 1030.[39] Ironically, the multiculturally minded Olympics of 1994 honored the pagan religion that cost the king's life as he tried to civilize his nation, thus regressing a thousand years back to paganism.

THE PERSECUTION OF CHRISTIANS

Hate Crimes Against Christians

As of October 1992, multiculturalists had succeeded in getting twenty-seven states to pass laws against hate crimes. According to the U.S. Supreme Court in *R.A.V. v. St. Paul* (1992), many of these laws violate freedom of speech, contradicting the First Amendment. The Court (which for once was not on the side of multiculturalists) ruled unanimously that so-called hate speech cannot be punished.

Multiculturalists and their cohorts, though quick to label any criticism or rejection of their values or behavior as hate crimes, do not so name attacks on Christians and churches, even physical attacks. Nor does the mainstream media report such acts against Christians and the churches as hate crimes.

Specifically, in 1987 Andres Serrano, a lapsed Catholic, presented a photograph that he called *Piss Christ*, showing a crucifix submerged in human urine. It was displayed at several sites, including the Virginia Museum in Richmond in 1988. The Awards in the Visual Arts, an arm of the Southeastern Center for Contemporary Art, which receives federal funds from the National Endowment for the Arts, gave him a $15,000 "fellowship" for this piece of blasphemy.[40]

Had some artist submerged the Muslim crescent or the Jewish star of David in human urine the multiculturally sensitive media would have published editorial upon editorial in condemnation. Either act would have been declared a hate crime, but when Christian symbols are desecrated, all is silent from the media, revealing yet another case of reverse bigotry. Some may dismiss Serrano's *Piss Christ* as simply the work of an eccentric artist. But this so-called work of art has been honored and rewarded financially by established arts organizations. This anti-

Christian "art" and similar sacrilegious efforts are the work not just of some nonconforming artist but of many radicals who hate Christianity.

Recently, some feminists have argued that any art that demeans women is not art. If this is true regarding women, it is also true for other types of art. Dante once said that art was "visible speech." Either one of these definitions defines Serrano's *Piss Christ*, a piece of nonart, or really a "hate crime." A similar sacrilege was committed by John Fleck, who, in a play "publicly urinate[d] on a picture of Christ."[41]

Michael Medved, the national movie critic and Jewish author, presents numerous examples of how Hollywood in recent years has gone out of its way to malign and desecrate Christianity; at times it also attacks the Jewish faith. Because space does not permit summarizing all of his examples from his book *Hollywood vs. America*, I shall note only a few of his examples. Regarding *The Handmaid's Tale* (1990), a film that depicts life in an America ruled by Christian fundamentalists, Medved states: "As portrayed in the film, these religious zealots are considerably less lovable than Nazis, who at least had stylish uniforms to recommend them."[42] *The Rapture* (1991) shows a disappointed believer blowing her daughter's brains out with a revolver when the Rapture that was supposed to happen before Christ's second coming does not occur. She did this "while mumbling invocations to the Almighty."[43] One character in the film likens Christianity to drug addiction in that "you do God," not drugs.[44] Another movie, *At Play in the Fields of the Lord* (1991), manages to slander Catholics, Protestants, and Jews all at the same time. But the movie hits Christianity hardest because it is Christian missionaries who have invaded the Amazon rain forest and ruined the natives' culture. Christianity is equated with the superstitious beliefs of the jungle people. On the other hand, the movie is very careful not to offend adherents of native religions, treating them, Medved states "with far more respect than it accords any Western faith."[45] *Guilty as Charged* (1992) stars Rod Steiger who plays the part of a sadistic, murderous maniac who also is a Christian. He owns a slaughter house in which he electrocutes newly released prisoners. As part of the environment, "Crosses abound in this nightmarish world—prominently displayed in every cell and on the walls of the electrocution chamber."[46]

The anti-Christian biases of the movie industry, which is ever so careful to produce films that will not offend non-Christian groups or cultures, are summed up very well in Don Feder's book, *A Jewish Conservative Looks at Pagan America*. There Feder contrasts the movie *The Last Temptation of Christ* with *Muhammad, Messenger of God* and observes that Muhammad is neither seen nor heard on the screen in order not to offend Moslems. But in *The Last Temptation of Christ* no concern whatsoever is voiced as to whether Christians might be offended.[47] Jesus, who in the Bible is presented not merely as a prophet but also as the incarnate

God, is depicted in abject and blasphemous roles. He is portrayed as obsessed with sex, as voyeuristic, and as a charlatan who tries to impress his disciples, in one scene pulling out his bleeding heart to win their admiration. Feder calls the movie a "salacious slander," whereas Medved contends that the movie reveals "ideological agendas at work."[48]

The hatred directed against Christianity is not confined to the world of art and movies; it is also quite common on many university campuses. In July 1994 a professor at William Paterson College in New Jersey called the Pope a "racist c————-s————." Three months later the college's administration still had not acted to discipline the professor.[49] Sanford Pinsker, a Jewish professor at Franklin and Marshall College (Pennsylvania), maintains that " 'demonizing' Christians (a phrase at once oxymoronic and alas, accurate) is one of multiculturalism's darker sides."[50] Apparently, Christians make an "especially appealing target" on university campuses. As an example, he cites an incident at the University of Buffalo where pro-abortionist students tore down 14,400 tiny crosses, placed on campus by pro-life (Christian) students. The crosses symbolized the number of daily abortions in the United States. Nobody protested the violation of the nonabortionists' First Amendment rights. Instead, the campus newspaper urged students to spit on the pro-lifers and even to " 'Kick them in the head.' "[51] A staff writer of the campus paper editorialized: " 'just once I'd like to see someone blow up one of their churches."[52] Is this not the same kind of hate speech that multiculturalists condemn so vociferously when directed at minorities and homosexuals? Where were the university officials who, at this school and others, are always on the alert to discipline and even expel students who are "insensitive" to the non-Western or non-Christian groups?

Penalizing Christians

These hate-mongering incidents at colleges and universities are becoming more and more common across the nation's "fruited plain." In some instances, the dislike for Christians has gone beyond hate speech. Specifically, many Christians are actually being penalized by the self-proclaimed disciples of "sensitivity," multiculturalism's politically correct enforcers. In 1991 a Tennessee ninth-grader, Brittany Settle, received a grade of zero for writing a research paper about Jesus Christ. The student took the teacher's assignment at face value that said students could write on any "researchable" topic. But the teacher flunked the student's paper and dogmatically asserted that Brittany's topic "was not an appropriate thing to do in a public school."[53] The Settle family took the case to court, arguing that Brittany's right to free speech was at issue here. After the lower courts sided with the teacher, an appeal was made to the United States Supreme Court, but on November 27, 1995, the

Court declined to hear the case, letting the lower courts' decision stand. Brittany's father summed up the case: "It's open season on Christians."[54] He might have added, "in the name of 'tolerable' multiculturalism."

The anti-Christian crusade is rushing ever onward. The University of Virginia recently denied student activity funds to a student periodical, *Wide Awake*, printed by Christian students. The students of this publication argued that other religious groups, for example, the Muslim Student Association which publishes a magazine, *Al-Salam*, received student funds. The university's rationale was that the Muslim publication was a cultural publication and that *Wide Awake* was a religious one. In June 1995, the United States Supreme Court (in *Rosenberger v. Rector and Visitors of University of Virginia*) ruled in favor of the Christian students, stating that the university had denied free speech to the Christian students.[55]

The Christian College Coalition, a group that represents eighty-five church-related liberal arts colleges, "recently learned that most of its members would not be listed in a *Money* magazine guide to 'best college buys' because they discriminate on the basis of religion."[56] Phi Beta Kappa, the highly regarded national honor society, now "openly discriminates against institutions that have religious tests for faculty members."[57] And there is more. Ken Olson, a Lutheran clergyman, a psychologist, and a ritual-abuse expert in Phoenix, Arizona, who worked for the Arizona Child Protective Services, recently lost his psychologist's license because he engaged in prayer with a patient whose psychiatric problems had been caused by his parents' satanic-ritual abuse.[58] A Texas teacher in Waco was fired for praying in her classroom with a pupil who had an allergy problem.[59] Gordon Bailey, a high school football coach, has been ordered to leave the locker room when his players voluntarily pray before a game.[60]

During the Indiana State Parent Teachers Association (PTA) convention in the summer of 1994, the vice president of the national PTA referred to Christians who are active in politics as "stealth candidates."[61] When concerned, law-abiding Christians enter politics, the media brand them as the "religious right." One never hears about the "religious left," which is so influential in promoting the leftist policies dear to the media's reporters. It is quite apparent that a majority of the reporters who so freely use the "religious right" label have a strong dislike for Christianity. Their hatred is not surprising, for although 83 percent of the media elite, research shows, have been reared in a particular religion, eighty percent seldom or never attend church and nearly fifty percent claim no church membership.[62]

Given that so many have been raised in a certain religion, perhaps reporters and journalists are rebelling against their experiences as children, in which their parents may have compelled them to attend Sunday

School while they themselves stayed at home reading the Sunday news-paper and probably showing little or no knowledge, convictions, or prac-tices consistent with their church's teachings. Virtually every American pastor or priest sees this happen regularly. This conclusion regarding journalists is not pure speculation if one remembers that another study reported that most journalists "place themselves left of center [and] many are alienated from the 'system.' "[63] The church certainly is part of "the system." A similar explanation probably fits the movie producers and artists as well.

SILENCING ALL CHRISTIAN INFLUENCES

If Christianity cannot be attacked by tearing down its norms, erasing its symbols, demeaning it with derogatory comments, or publishing scat-ological "art," then it is given the silent treatment. The idea is to ignore it and all of the positive effects it has had on the world. School textbooks consistently use this approach.

Muting Christian Holidays

The *Anti-Bias Curriculum: Tools for Empowering Young Children* (1989) is a manual that urges teachers to eliminate "biases," beginning with kin-dergarten youngsters. One of its chapters, titled "Holiday Activities in an Anti-Bias Curriculum," purports to familiarize kindergartners with America's national holidays. The section titled "Thanksgiving," for ex-ample, begins by saying: "The history and customs of Thanksgiving highlight the complexities of disengaging, harmful bias from 'national' holiday celebrations."[64] It says nothing about why the Pilgrims (Chris-tians) held their first Thanksgiving in America. Nor does it mention that they thanked God, or for that matter, that millions of Americans still give thanks on this day. Instead, the discussion focuses on the American Indians' contribution to the "first Thanksgiving."[65]

As for Christmas, this manual states that it "reflects a specific religious belief system," but adds that "For children who are not Christian—be they Jewish, Buddhist, Muslim, atheist—Christmas can be a problem."[66] Thus there are instructions on how the Christmas holiday might be in-tegrated with Hanukkah, dancing around a Solstice tree, and the use of "Native American music." Candles and eggnog (two nonbiblical items) are the only Christmas items described. No reference is made to Jesus Christ or to his birth. The biblical meaning of Christianity is completely bypassed.

Unfortunately, the *Anti-Bias Curriculum* teachers' manual is not an iso-lated case among today's grade and high school textbooks. The spirit of multiculturalism has inspired all textbook writers to mute the significance(s) of all Christian holidays, as well as their influence on Western civilization.

Christianity and Hospitals

The history of hospitals shows that Christians established the first hospital. In pre-Christian Roman times, medical facilities (not hospitals as we think of them today) existed primarily for soldiers, gladiators, and slaves: "Manual laborers and other poor individuals had no place of refuge. Many feared death, and took little interest in the sick, but often drove them out of the house, and left them to their fate."[67] Nothing was available for the general populace or for the indigent until the early Christians established hospices. For instance, Callistus of Rome (died ca. 222), a Christian and a former slave, formally cared for the sick and the poor in the latter part of the second century. Roberto Margotta says: "In practical terms, the [early] Christians did much to relieve suffering. Hospices, called xenodochia, were built to shelter pilgrims and, in time, they became hospitals. The first great hospital was built by St. Basil of Caesarea in the year 370.[68]

The Christian stamp on hospitals is still evident today, as reflected in many of their names—Christian saints such as St. John's, St. Peter's, St. Mary's, St. Joseph's, and St. Vincent's; and Christian denominations such as Baptist, Lutheran, Methodist, and Presbyterian. These names show a continuous connection between Christianity and hospitals, which was present from their origin. They also reveal that from the beginning Christians were moved by Christ's words: "I was sick and you visited me" (Matthew 25:36). The early Christians did not consider their religion to be a mere intellectual exercise divorced from life.

So many Americans, however, know nothing about the ancient tie between hospitals and Christianity. They may think the Christian name is of only local significance, reflecting the prominence of a given church or denomination in the community. Thus people are ignorant of the centuries-old tie between hospitals and Christianity. Writers of so-called multiculturalist textbooks have given Christianity the silent treatment, in part out of ignorance, but for the most part quite deliberately. They tend to give far more credit to non-Christian religions. For example, one multiculturalist textbook for grade schools erroneously states that the Muslim "understanding of disease [about A.D. 1000] was far better than that of Christian Europe. They built hospitals and medical libraries."[69] But the Christian role in the first hospitals is ignored. Note here that the Muslims are said to have had a superior understanding of disease to that of Christian Europe. This statement shows an anti-Christian bias. Multiculturalists never say that Christianity had a better understanding of any phenomenon, for to make such a statement would be "insensitive" to other religions.

Christianity and the Origin of Universities

Christianity, primarily through its monasteries, created the universities as early as the twelfth century. One renowned historian, a strong critic of Christianity, writes: "The universities which began to appear at the end of the twelfth century and which multiplied in the thirteenth century were largely church foundations."[70] The earliest universities were established at Bologna, Paris, and Oxford.[71] But multiculturally based texts usually fail to include such facts.

The *World History* volume of the highly controversial *National Standards* (1994) in a qualified manner does state the Christian origin of universities, but detracts from the Christian contribution by trying to be multiculturally correct. It asks: "How did Muslim scholarship and universities influence their [the universities] development?"[72] Apparently, multiculturalists find it difficult to give Christianity unqualified credit for any of its contributions to the civilized world.

The Abolition of *Patria Potestas*

Multiculturalist writings make no reference to Christianity's influence in abolishing the ancient institution of *patria potestas,* which gave the Roman father absolute power over his family, even over life and death. Emperor Valentinian I outlawed this custom in A.D. 374 because, as a Christian, he respected the advice of Basil of Caesarea, a prominent leader in the early church who urged its abolition.[73] Outlawing *patria potestas* was Christianity's formal response to the horrors of family violence. This ancient custom—spelled out in one of the Twelve Tablets of Roman Law—permitted the father of a Roman family to practice infanticide, command his wife to have an abortion, and mistreat his wife and children without recourse from any social entity.

Many of the concerns expressed today regarding family violence originated in Christianity's condemnation of *patria potestas*. Multiculturalists overlook this fact and instead imply that the concern over family violence originated with modern liberal thought.

Christianity's Elevation of Women

Multiculturalists also fail to credit Christianity with improving the status of women. Most current textbooks give the impression that the rise in women's status is the result of modern, secular thought. The contrary is true, however. Early Christianity gave women unprecedented freedom and respect during the time of Christ and his apostles, welcoming women into its midst without their husbands' approval. This was very disturbing to the Greco-Romans. One scholar says: "Many [Roman] women, separate from their husbands or fathers, became Christians. Such behavior was repugnant to the Greco-Roman culture. The Roman institution of *manus,* along with other requirements, meant woman was to worship her husband's ancestral gods."[74]

To be sure, soon after the Apostolic era, the church often failed to maintain the freedom that Christ and the early Christians accorded women. Nevertheless, it still granted women a social status far superior to what they had been accorded in countries where Christianity was virtually absent or nonexistent. Multiculturalist writings, whether out of ignorance or intent, say nothing about Christianity having improved the once low status of women.

This omission is particularly noticeable because almost every grade school text today discusses the role of women in all areas of life. The *National Standards* texts, which use the method of asking teachers numerous questions in preparation for their classes, fail to ask a single question about the role of Christianity in improving the lot of women.

Christianity Civilized the Uncivilized

From its very beginning, Christianity introduced high moral standards into the Greco-Roman world, bringing honor to sex in marriage by rejecting adultery, fornication, and promiscuity; condemning divorce; and elevating the value of human life by opposing suicide, abortion, and infanticide: "The Western world in particular owes a great debt of gratitude to the Christian faith for the way it has changed the uncivilized tribes, peoples, and nations into a much more humane lot."[75]

These moral contributions, however, are not found in today's multiculturalist school textbooks. In the mid-1980s Robert Bryan surveyed a number of high school textbooks used in Montgomery County, Maryland, and found "a remarkable consensus to the effect that after 1700 Christianity has no historical presence in America."[76] When Christianity is finally noted, Bryan says, it is commonly mentioned in a negative way.

The anti-Christian posture is gaining momentum while multiculturalists deceitfully tell the public they value all cultures. As pointed out in previous chapters, multiculturalists love all cultures except the Euro-American culture. They have an especially passionate dislike for anything that reflects the influence(s) of Christianity. This negative disposition drives their efforts to eradicate Christianity's norms, values, and symbols from American culture. It is a modern political purge, done methodically and deceptively under the cloak of multiculturalism.

The multiculturalists' purging efforts to remove Christian values, norms, and symbols from American public life are no mere attempts to alter American culture. Rather, it is an attack on civilization itself. As Fernand Braudel recently observed, "Throughout the history of the West, Christianity has been at the heart of the civilization it inspires, even when it has allowed itself to be captured or deformed by it.[77] Even eighteenth-century rationalism, which attacked the foundations of Christianity was derived from it.[78] Ironically, the ideology of multiculturalism, which also attacks Christianity, is itself a distorted derivation of Christianity.

To challenge the multiculturalist purges is no easy task. As Michael Warder has said: "If you stand up and speak a modicum of common sense against the cultural left [the multiculturalists], be prepared. You will be called 'ignorant,' 'racist,' 'Nazi,' 'homophobe,' 'anti-feminist,' 'anti-environment,' or a 'money grubbing religious bigot.' "[79]

NOTES

1. Martin Luther, "Against the Heavenly Prophets in the Matter of Images and Sacraments," *Luther's Works,* trans. Bernhard Erling and ed. Conrad Bergendoff (Philadelphia: Muhlenberg Press, 1958), 40:98.

2. Martin Luther, "Temporal Authority: To What Extent It Should Be Obeyed," *Luther's Works,* trans. J. J. Schindel, rev. and ed. by Walther I. Brandt (Philadelphia: Muhlenberg Press, 1962), 45:128.

3. Martin Luther cited in Paul Althaus, *The Ethics of Martin Luther,* trans. Robert C. Schultz (Philadelphia: Fortress Press, 1972), p. 27.

4. Jay Livingston, *Crime and Criminology* (Englewood Cliffs, N.J.: Prentice Hall, 1996), p. 149.

5. United States Federal Bureau of Investigation data reported in *Statistical Abstracts of the United States, 1964* (Washington, D.C.: U.S. Department of Commerce, 1964), p. 148. See also *Statistical Abstracts of the United States, 1995* (Washington, D.C.: U.S. Department of Commerce, 1995), p. 199.

6. *Statistical Abstracts, 1995,* p. 73.

7. Ibid., p. 77.

8. William Bennett as cited in Rush Limbaugh, *See, I Told You So* (New York: Pocket Books, 1993), p. 84.

9. William Foxwell Albright, in *American Spiritual Biographies: Fifteen Self Portraits* ed. Louis Finkelstein (New York: Harper and Brothers, 1948), p. 177.

10. Dennis Prager, "Homosexuality, the Bible, and Us—a Jewish Perspective," *The Public Interest* (summer 1993): 61.

11. Ibid., p. 70.

12. George Weigel, "The New Anti-Catholicism," *Commentary* (June 1992): 25.

13. John Leo, "The Gay Tide of Catholic-Bashing," *U.S. News and World Report,* 1 April 1991, 15.

14. Marlin Maddoux, "When They Attacked One Church, They Attacked Yours," *Point of View Newsletter,* 27 May 1994.

15. Leo, "The Gay Tide," p. 15.

16. Ibid.

17. Judith Reisman, cited in "Gay Magazine Publishes Picture of Christ," *Lambda Report* (February/March 1995): 7.

18. Jeff Yarbrough, cited in ibid.

19. "Des Moines Parents Force Scuttling of Pro-Gay Curriculum," *Lambda Report* (February/March 1995): 10.

20. *Statistical Abstracts of the United States, 1994* (Washington, D.C.: U.S. Department of Commerce, 1994), p. 70.

21. Linda Chavez, "Aztec Idols, Yes; Mary and Jesus, No?" *USA Today*, 7 December 1994, 11A.

22. Ibid.

23. "Seasonal Displays/Prohibition on Religious Matter," *Postal Bulletin*, 27 October 1994, 3.

24. Sarah McCarthy, "High Court Rulings Make Holidays Dull," *Human Events*, 14 April 1995, 16.

25. Jeffrey L. Sheler, "The Christmas Covenant," *U.S. News and World Report*, 19 December 1994, 67.

26. Chavez, "Aztec Idols," p. 11A.

27. DKL, "Endnotes," *Campus Report* (November 1993): 2.

28. "Principal Bans Religious Poster," *Christian American* (May/June 1995): 9.

29. "Yellow Pages Remove and Then Put Back Religious Symbols," *Religious Rights Watch* (April 1994): 1.

30. "City Removes Cross from Seal," *Jacksonville (Illinois) Journal-Courier*, 2 November 1992, 5.

31. "Crossfire," *Chronicles* (March 1992): 39.

32. Pat Robertson, "The Turning Tide," *The New York Guardian* (November 1993): 1.

33. Ibid.

34. "Jesus Portrait Removed from Public School," *Christian American* (April 1995): 18.

35. "Board Won't Fight Sign Removal," *Jacksonville (Illinois) Journal-Courier*, 3 March 1996, p. 2.

36. McCarthy, "High Court Rulings," p. 16.

37. D. James Kennedy and Jerry Newcombe, *What If Jesus Had Never Been Born?* (Nashville, Tenn.: Thomas Nelson, 1994), p. 164.

38. Sverre Steen, *Langsomt ble Landet vaart Eget* [Slowly the land became ours], passage translated by Kristi Saebo Newcombe (Olso, Norway: Cappelens Forlage, 1967), pp. 52–53. Cited in Kennedy and Newcombe, *What If Jesus Had Never Been Born?*, pp. 146–165.

39. Kenneth Scott Latourette, *A History of Christianity* (New York: Harper and Brothers, 1953), p. 388.

40. Richard Bolton, ed., *Culture Wars: Documents from Recent Controversies in the Arts* (New York: New Press, 1992), p. 343.

41. Michael Medved, *Hollywood vs. America: Popular Culture and the War on Traditional Values* (New York: HarperCollins Publishers/Zondervan, 1992), p. 27.

42. Ibid.

43. Ibid., 58.

44. Ibid.

45. Ibid., pp. 60, 61.

46. Ibid., pp. 60–61.

47. Don Feder, *A Jewish Conservative Looks at Pagan America* (Lafayette, La.: Huntington House, 1993), p. 149.

48. Medved, *Hollywood vs. America,* p. 48.

49. Nino Langiulli, "The Weed of Diversity Bears Bitter Fruit," *Catalyst* (September 1994): 14–15.

50. Sanford Pinsker, "Lost on Campus: Civility, Rational Debate," *The Christian Science Monitor,* 30 November 1995, 19.

51. Ibid.

52. Ibid.

53. Tony Mauro, "Court Upholds 'Zero' On Christ Report," *USA Today,* 28 November 1995, 1A.

54. Ibid.

55. Scott Jaschik, "High Court Bars University of Virginia from Denying Funds to Religious Newspaper," *Chronicle of Higher Education,* 7 July 1995, A25.

56. George M. Marsden, "Church, State and Campus," *New York Times,* 26 April 1994, A19.

57. Ibid.

58. "Pyschologist Loses License for Performing Exorcism," *Religious Rights Watch* (December 1993): 1.

59. Ibid., p. 2.

60. Ibid., p. 1.

61. *Greenwood and Southside Challenger,* 13 July 1994, 4.

62. L. Brent Bozell III and Brent H. Baker, eds., *And That's the Way It Isn't* (Alexandria, Va.: Media Research Center, 1990), p. 44.

63. S. Robert Lichter, Stanley Rothman, and Linda S. Lichter, *The Media Elite* (Bethesda, Md.: Adler and Adler, 1986), p. 294.

64. Louise Derman-Sparks and the A.B.C. Task Force, *Anti-Bias Curriculum: Tools for Empowering Children* (Washington, D.C.: National Association for the Education of Young Children, 1989), p. 87.

65. Ibid.

66. Ibid., p. 92.

67. John Jefferson Davis, *Your Wealth in God's World,* cited in Kennedy and Newcombe, *What If Jesus Had Never Been Born?,* p. 144.

68. Roberto Margotta, *The Story of Medicine; Man's Struggle Against Disease— From Ancient Sorcery to Modern Miracles of Vaccines, Drugs, and Surgery* (New York: Golden Press, 1968), p. 102.

69. James A. Banks et al., *The World: Past and Present* (New York: Macmillan/ McGraw-Hill, 1993), p. 371.

70. Joseph Reither, *World History at a Glance* (Garden City, N.J.: Dolphin Books, 1965), p. 194.

71. Latourette, *A History of Christianity,* p. 552.

72. *National Standards: World History,* Charlotte Crabtree and Gary B. Nash, project co-directors (Los Angeles: National Center for History in the Schools, 1994), p. 145.

73. Matthew Bunson, "Patria Potestas," *Encyclopedia of the Roman Empire* (New York: Facts on File, 1994), p. 315.

74. Alvin J. Schmidt, *Veiled and Silenced: How Culture Shaped Sexist Theology* (Macon, Ga.: Mercer University Press, 1989), p. 92.

75. Kennedy and Newcombe, *What If Jesus Had Never Been Born?* p. 157.

76. Robert Bryan, *History, Pseudo-History, Anti-History: How High School Textbooks Treat Religion* (Washington, D.C.: Learn, 1988 [?], p. 3.

77. Fernand Braudel, *A History of Civilization*, trans. Richard Mayne (New York: Penguin Books, 1994), pp. 333–334.

78. Ibid.

79. Michael Warder, "The Politics of Cultural Wars," *Vital Speeches of the Day* (August 1993): 655.

Chapter 11

With "Friends" like These . . .

Treat your friend as if he might become an enemy.

Publilius Syrus

Nearly every American is familiar with the words of this chapter's title. But how well do Americans know their multiculturalist "friends"? Many prominent U.S. leaders, whom the nation trusts to preserve and protect its cultural heritage, norms, and values naively promote multiculturalism in education, business, and religion. Indeed, with friends like these, who needs enemies?

LIBERAL COLLEGE/UNIVERSITY ADMINISTRATORS

Leaders in colleges, universities, and other educational contexts kowtow to the politics of multiculturalism in part because many see themselves as "liberal" or "progressive." Indeed, professors and presidents at many higher educational institutions are usually very liberal in comparison to society at large. Some are also Marxist. The liberal environment on many campuses is so pronounced that conservative professors, usually a small minority, often keep their convictions to themselves. They feel intimidated among the conformist-minded "intellectuals," who are quick to laugh at anyone whose thinking or politics differs from their own and who is seen as intellectually out of touch.

It is from such faculties that most college or university administrators, especially presidents and deans, are selected. Ordinarily, a known conservative professor has about as much chance of becoming a president

or chancellor of a university or college as any of us has in winning a
state lottery. Since liberal professors are in the majority on most campuses, they possess a lot of political clout in the presidential selection
processes. Those who are selected to serve on presidential screening or
search committees are commonly like-minded liberal associates or colleagues. Thus, the people chosen as presidents and deans are commonly
from the liberal end of the continuum. And so during the last two decades when the radically liberal ideology of multiculturalism gained
dominance on the campuses, most presidents and deans went along with
what their liberal faculty members wanted. Multiculturalism therefore
had easy entry into American education.

Their liberal orientation prompts many college/university presidents
and vice presidents to appease multiculturalists on their faculties. Here
the recent case at Yale University in 1995 comes to mind. A billionaire
alumnus contributed $20 million to the university, specifying that the
amount be spent on developing courses in Western history and culture.
The multiculturalists soon orbited around the president and the administration. Because of their anti-Western prejudices, developing additional
courses in Western history and culture would be tantamount to committing the greatest heresy on campus. Courses in Western culture, the
multiculturalists demanded, needed to be reduced or eliminated from
the curricula, not added to or strengthened. Of course, the Yale administration acquiesced to the hard-core multiculturalists and returned the
donor's money.[1]

As observed in Chapter 6, the acquiescence of Stanford University's
president to leftist faculty demands resulted in a reduced number of
courses in Western civilization. In addition, a new eight-track course,
under the rubric of Culture, Ideas, and Values (CIV), was ushered in.
The president, Donald Kennedy, and advocates of the CIV deceptively
announced that little had really changed vis-à-vis the previous offerings.
They stated that selections from Plato and from the Bible were still being
read, but what they did not tell the students or the alumni was that some
of the CIV sections taught that Genesis was rife with sexism and made
St. Paul politically correct by saying that he may have been a homosexual. Shakespeare is still studied, but *The Tempest* is now viewed from a
"slave's perspective" and is made to serve as an instructive lesson in
Western imperialism. . . . Students learn that World War II was racist but
not sexist—that is, until the dropping of the bomb, which was phallo-
centric.[2]

Stanford's Donald Kennedy also created a special office to promote
multiculturalism on campus. This office, known as the Office for Multicultural Development, "is a millenarian project aiming at a sweeping
social revolution that would force [in Kennedy's words] 'new thinking

and new structures which would incorporate diversity' onto recalcitrant faculty and students."[3]

At the University of Cincinnati, President Mary Ellen Ashley argues that a person "of another race cannot be a 'racist' unless he/she has social power."[4] Translation of this erroneous comment means that only whites can be racists because they have social power. When Donna Shalala—now in President Clinton's cabinet—was head of the University of Wisconsin at Madison, she argued that covert racism at the universities is now as bad as overt racism was in the country thirty years ago. As chancellor, she introduced "The Madison Plan," which mandated the acceleration of multiculturalism, no matter what the cost. The plan looked like "an academic version of Stalin's Five Year Plans."[5]

Once the purpose of college/university education was to teach students to examine, think, analyze, and understand the accumulated knowledge of the past and present. Today, education is being redefined by multiculturalists who see themselves as missionaries who have to convert their students to their leftist perspective. This posture is derived largely from the Marxist *Weltanschauung* that permeates so much of multiculturalist thinking, including educators. Karl Marx argued that it was inadequate to interpret and understand the world, and that it had to be changed. So an increasing number of educators see it as their task to convert students to multiculturalism and thus change the world. The presidents and deans in higher education have been the multiculturalists' best friends.

Many articles in scholarly publications openly advocate that colleges and universities are to be sociopolitical change agents. This message is apparent in the article titled "Access, Equity, and Cultural Diversity: Rediscovering the Community College Mission."[6] Note that the accent is now on colleges and universities having a "mission." They are to act as missionaries, and their mission is to change the world by introducing "diversity" and other multiculturalist objectives.

THE NATIONAL EDUCATION ASSOCIATION (NEA)

Your child(ren)'s grade school teacher may very well be a member of this leftist political group that masquerades as a professional education organization with over two million teachers. Does this mean that your children's teachers are also radical? No, not necessarily, but it does mean that if they are not like the NEA leadership, the organization's leaders are using them to achieve their radical goals.

As an organization committed to multiculturalism, the NEA is actively promoting abortion on demand, homosexuality, political correctness, Affirmative Action, and any program that is decidedly left of center. Recently, in Fairfax County, Virginia, the organization promoted a sex education video that contained a ninth-grade lesson on homosexuality conveying the message that homosexuality is an acceptable way to live.[7] The NEA also has a gay and lesbian caucus group that sets much of the NEA's agenda. At its national convention in 1994, the caucus group officially received bright-pink ribbons attached to their delegate passes.[8] The 1995 convention did more of the same. It approved an array of radical resolutions that homosexuality be part of sex education in schools, that "domestic partners" be eligible as dependents, that moments of silence in schools be banned, that preschools have "diversity" programs, and so on.[9]

At the 1994 convention, its president delivered a speech that one reporter said "was full of contempt for views held by conservatives and Christians."[10] The organization passed a resolution saying that its teachers "must move from cultural awareness to cultural activism."[11] Here too we see Marx's philosophy rearing its ugly head.

Like so many other leftist organizations that are forever preaching toleration but cannot tolerate opposing views or criticism directed against them, the NEA is also of that ilk. In June 1993, *Forbes* magazine published a highly critical article on the NEA calling it the National Extortion Association. For this article, the NEA president removed *Forbes* from the list of periodicals that its members may purchase at special rates.[12] Rush Limbaugh has called the NEA the "Michigan Mafia" that "has displaced the United Auto Workers as the principal power in Michigan politics."[13]

So if hard-working, loyal American parents think their children's teachers, many of whom belong to the NEA, are in good hands, and that this organization helps and encourages teachers to foster and preserve their country's heritage, they need to take another look. With friends like the NEA, patriotic American parents need no enemies.

ELEMENTARY AND HIGH SCHOOL LEADERS

Although there is no need to repeat examples of historical distortions and anti-Western culture in textbooks from Chapter 5 here, all Americans are urged to take an active interest in examining their children's textbooks. Parents and local school boards can no longer rely on educational leaders at the state or district level to adopt policies or textbooks consistent with the traditional American norms and values. Nor can they any longer take it for granted that their children will be exposed to a truthful history of their country. Often, as has already been shown, significant historical facts are either withheld or distorted in order to achieve multiculturalist ends.

For example, the teaching of Afrocentrism (briefly noted in Chapter 6) is being introduced into more and more American schools. This multiculturalist, race-based, often factually false ideology is conspicuously evident in the *African American Baseline Essays,* which first made their appearance in the Multnomah School District of Portland, Oregon, in 1987. These essays, often referred to as the Portland Baseline Essays, now used in many schools, focus on six areas of learning: art, social studies, language arts, mathematics, science, and music. In each of these sections, an all-out effort is made to advance Afrocentrism, often at the expense of well-established facts.

Here are some examples. Throughout the essays, Africa, a continent, is equated with ancient Egypt, a country. This is a geographical error. Second, the essays (as do some other Afrocentric writings) bluntly portray Egypt as a black country: "Egypt was a Black [*sic*] nation."[14] This claim, as Mary Lefkowitz, a scholar of the classics, has said, "is misleading in the extreme."[15] Frank Snowden, a black classicist, refers to the ancient Egyptians, in contrast to the Nubians and Kushites, as "lighter skinned,"[16] not black. Another egregious claim made by the essays is that the great ideas and philosophical works in the ancient world, for which the early Greeks and Romans (Europeans) are credited, first originated in Africa and therefore were essentially stolen from Africa. Here is how the essays state this claim: "The Europeans not only colonized most of the world, but also began to colonize information about the world and its people." Again: "The people now called Africans not only influenced the Greeks and the Romans, but they also influenced the early world before there was a place called Europe."[17] Thus Western civilization had its roots in Africa.

These are just some of the "data" found in the essays taught to black and white students in numerous schools today. The essays are also filled with a good deal of ethnocentrism. One citation reads: "African scholars are the final authority on Africa."[18] This is like saying that one cannot evaluate or study the dynamics of marriage and the family unless one is married.

As noted earlier, numerous educational leaders have tried to introduce materials into the grade and high schools that unsuspecting parents do not anticipate. In some instances parents do get wind of behind-the-scenes tactics, as happened in New York City and Des Moines, Iowa. In both areas, parents were able to stop the efforts but virtually at the last hour. In how many other places have these stealth-like plans succeeded?

NAIVE BUSINESS CORPORATIONS

Multiculturalism is invading businesses and corporations by way of "diversity" and "politically correct" training programs. Don Feder lists the following corporations as opening their doors to multiculturalism: Mobile, Apple Computer, Xerox, Digital Equipment, Procter and Gamble, and AT&T. These businesses have become "major players in the diversity game."[19] Feder also notes that 40 percent of American businesses are engaged in some form of diversity training, and in some instances diversity consulting firms charge "$500,000 for the first year of a three-to-five-year commitment."[20] Linda Chavez writes that many diversity "consultants are paid as much as $10,000 a day to train managers to 'value diversity.' "[21]

With such exorbitant fees, the neo-Marxian multiculturalists are smiling as they fleece these businesses while also undermining the very foundation that has made American corporations successful. That foundation is Western capitalism whose principles have always stressed the productivity and competitive skills of workers, not their skin color, sex, or ethnicity.

That corporations are capitulating to multiculturalism is tragic enough, but in addition many of these expensive diversity programs have greatly undermined their employees, particularly white males. White males are often subjected to humiliating "sensitivity sessions" that seek to make them conscious of diversity. Some of these sessions force individuals to accept the homosexual "life-style," agree with radical feminism, or assume guilt for "injustices" that white males have perpetrated. Quite often, these sessions also highlight the "abuses" of the church that many "diversity" trainers project from their negatively perceived church experiences onto the employees for a big fee.

The *New York Times* recently reported that the Ford Foundation underwrote diversity efforts by giving $150,000 to train faculty to teach diversity awareness.[22] The Ford Foundation has also given millions of dollars to several Hispanic groups such as the National Council of La Raza, the Mexican American Legal Defense and Education Fund (MALDEF), ASPIRA, and others. A number of other corporations such as Kellogg, Anheuser-Busch, and Coors have joined Ford in funding Hispanic groups.[23] The funds received from these firms do not go to assimilate but rather to separate Hispanics from the mainstream of American life and culture by underwriting bilingual programs, for instance. In reality, these corporations are contributing to what Arthur Schlesinger calls the "disuniting of America." Linda Chavez states that these groups, funded by the Ford Foundation, may consider themselves to be on the cutting edge of social change, but they are not helping Hispanics become part of the American mainstream like other immigrant groups preceding them. These groups, together with their self-appointed leaders, do not represent rank-and-file Hispanics. Moreover, they give more and more Hispanics a socialistic entitlement mind-set. "The only groups that benefit from such misguided policy objectives are those that broker the policies in the first place."[24]

Burger King has a vice president of Diversity Affairs, and Hoechst

Celanese requires that its management officers join organizations in which they will be a minority.[25] IBM in San Jose held a day when its workers dressed in various ethnic costumes and performed ethnic dances.[26] And Xerox's CEO is quoted as saying: "Diversity is no fad with us."[27]

Having employees dress in ethnic costumes, along with promoting diversity in other contexts, in time is merely an example of symbolic ethnicity, by which individuals see ethnic background as a vestige of their ancestral past. It is nostalgia and is not really taken seriously. At this symbolic level, ethnicity is harmless, but once it moves beyond this level it becomes serious. Thus what seems good on paper may in the future result in ethnic and racial strife both in the workplace and on the street.

THE ROLE OF RADIO, PRESS, AND TELEVISION

Among the numerous, avid supporters of multiculturalism are the mass media. In the name of diversity, the media are filling minority groups, especially young black Americans, with anger.

Every day these kids . . . are told they have no chance in America . . . they have no opportunity whatsoever because they are minorities and because other people live exclusively to keep them down. And who is filling these people's heads? . . . It is those who are self-appointed leaders and saviors of these people who constantly pummel them day in and day out with this negativity. . . . They grow up resenting success, while they have not been taught how to find it themselves.[28]

In the fall of 1993, *Time* magazine published a special issue that included a teaching guide devoted to what it called "Celebrating Diversity."[29] This was a mass media attempt to spread the doctrine of multiculturalism. Numerous other publications, *Change, Tikkun, The Nation, The Chronicle of Higher Education,* and others, have tried to cast a positive light on multiculturalism.

Television is probably multiculturalism's best media friend. It has been showing error-filled, propaganda-like productions in order to make American Indians feel good and white men feel guilty. In May 1995, the Public Broadcasting System (PBS) aired Ric Burns' production "The Way the West Was Lost and Won, 1845–1893" in four 90–minute segments. This presentation was filled with political correctness designed to atone for the white man's evils committed against the Indians, or rather "Native Americans." To be sure, the white settlers' sins against the Indians are not excusable. But this production transformed the American Indians into saints who had miraculously escaped man's fall into sin. What the white man did was evil, but a very different morality was shown when the program "defend[ed] the murder of hundreds Minnesota farmers in the New Ulm area by Sioux warriors in 1862 as a justified 'uprising.' "[30]

A spate of other television programs bashing the white man have recently been aired. In April 1995, Kevin Costner's "500 Nations" was channeled into the homes of millions of Americans, presumably to convert viewers to his politically correct view of American history. One reporter found that the TV rankings of the first two parts of Costner's "500 Nations" were so poor that as of mid-1995 the "network [hadn't] announced when the final two parts will be shown."[31] Is the bashing of the white-man's culture beginning to backfire? Perhaps multiculturalists like Costner are unwittingly making white men aware of what multiculturalism is really all about—namely, an attempt to berate and eventually destroy the traditional American culture.

When viewing presentations that are filled with animosity toward the Euro-American culture, one sees alienated, angry multiculturalists projecting their perceived alienation and anger onto the American public at large. Because of their alienation, they are in search of meaning. One way to achieve that quest is to trash and bash the society and the culture from which they are alienated.

LIBERAL, NAIVE CHURCHES

Many years ago, H. Richard Niebuhr, in his *Christ and Culture* portrayed several ways in which the church has presented Christ and his teaching in history vis-à-vis culture: the Christ against culture, the Christ above culture, and the Christ of culture.[32] In the last-named instance, the church conforms to the worldly culture. This is what is happening in many of America's mainline denominations with regard to multiculturalism.

In 1990, almost two years before the five hundredth anniversary of Christopher Columbus's discovery of America, the governing board of the National Council of Churches (NCC), an organization decidedly left-of-center, sided with multiculturalism as it condemned Columbus's accomplishments. The NCC passed the following resolution: "For the descendants of the survivors of the subsequent invasion, genocide, slavery, 'ecocide,' and the exploitation of the wealth of the land, a celebration is not an appropriate observance of this anniversary."[33] Moved by the spirit of multiculturalism, the NCC further stated that the arrival of Columbus in America was a "historical tragedy" requiring the entire Christian church "to repent of its complicity."[34] These statements were part of what the NCC called "A Faithful Response to the 500th Anniversary of the Arrival of Christopher Columbus." The NCC also condemned Christian missionaries for "destroying native religious beliefs"[35] of the American Indians. In taking this position, apparently this liberal church federation, which still uses the word "Christian" in its official name, believes the ideology of multiculturalism is more compelling than Christ's command to his followers. He told his disciples: "Go therefore and make disciples of all nations, baptizing them in the name of the Father and of the Son and of the Holy Spirit" (Matthew 28:19).

In Chapter 10, I discussed how Christian and biblical norms, symbols, and values are attacked by the secular arm of multiculturalism. In the case of the NCC, a federation of liberal churches is attacking Christianity from within. With "friends" like these, the Christian church needs no enemies.

Barely a major denomination in the United States has not in some way bowed before the shrine of multiculturalism. Recently, the Presbyterian Church (USA) gave $66,000 to a conference of radical feminists held in Minneapolis, Minnesota, in 1993. This conference tried to re-image God by praying to an imaginary goddess Sophia. Some of the speakers "angrily denounced the Christian church, charging that its teachings about Jesus Christ constitute the chief source of oppression, human violence, racism, sexism, classism, and the abuse of the earth."[36]

Radical feminists from various Protestant denominations attended the re-imaging conference. In true multiculturalist fashion, the conference tried to give radical feminists a god (goddess) that would be more compatible with the feminist subculture. Instead of praying to Jesus Christ, they prayed: "Our maker Sophia, we are women in your image: . . . with nectar between our thighs we invite a lover, we birth a child; with our warm body fluids we remind the world of its pleasure and sensations."[37] One participant, a featured speaker and an officeholder of the World Council of Churches, said she favored her "culture's religion which has 722 gods and goddesses."[38]

At its 1993 convention, the Evangelical Lutheran Church in America (ELCA) took its turn in embracing multiculturalism. In so doing, it trashed the rich tradition of the Lutheran liturgy by introducing an American Indian "smudging" ritual as part of its worship at the Kansas City convention. This rite used smoldering sweet grass, sage, and cedar, an American Indian version of incense. A feminist clergy preached on "inclusiveness" by castigating the Euro-American whites in the ELCA for being too exclusive; they were afraid of "losing [their] denominational and ethnic identity."[39] In response to this politically correct sermon, one observer noted that ironically the speaker thought it necessary to exclude those of European descent by accusing them of not being part of the "Native Americans, the Rajans, the Gonzales," and so on.[40]

The ELCA's publishing house, Augsburg Fortress Press, recently mailed a brochure encouraging congregations to use "multicultural resources to plan and enhance [parish] worship service." In keeping with the multiculturalist focus, the brochure departs radically from traditional

Lutheran language by suggesting one of its publications called *Planning Revivals in African American Contexts.* Lutherans have never practiced or advocated emotional revival-type worship. But evidently, the urge to merge with multiculturalism is so strong in the ELCA that traditional Lutheran practices are expendable.

The United Methodist Church in its *Youth* magazine (December 1994) carried a positive article on Kwanzaa.[41] Apparently, the denomination not only seeks to be multiculturally correct, but it also intends to indoctrinate its future leaders into multiculturalism, including Afrocentrism.

Not surprisingly, liberal churches have climbed aboard the bandwagon of multiculturalism. What is surprising is that conservative churches, out of ignorance and credulity, are doing so too. For example, the Lutheran Church—Missouri Synod (LCMS), which most religious analysts classify as theologically conservative, has no women clergy, believes in the inerrancy of the Bible, supports capital punishment, opposes abortion, and rejects homosexuality.

Yet in 1993, the Board for Parish Services of the LCMS published a teacher's manual, *Black History Multicultural Materials,* which was designed for use in the denomination's numerous parochial schools. The manual provides a "list of 24 classroom ideas and 7 suggestions for working with parents" to promote multicultural education. Some of the "ideas" direct teachers to apply "the knowledge of lifestyles and customs of cultures learned in class," to "honor the holidays of the cultures in the community," to "plan a cultural awareness week with other teachers," to have "a bilingual resource person," and so on. The manual also makes much of the Harriet Tubman story, which virtually every multicultural textbook cites today.

Recently, the president of the LCMS, Alvin L. Barry, wrote: "[W]e are truly being called to be a multicultural church body and all that implies."[42] With public knowledge that Barry strongly opposes the ordination of women, the homosexual lifestyle, and the pro-abortion movement, and that he supports continued Christian missionary work in other countries, we can only conclude that he does not know what multiculturalism is and does.

This same conservative church body (the LCMS) recently had its Lutheran Hour coordinator of multicultural outreach put a positive accent on multiculturalism. It also revealed a good measure of naivete concerning this radical ideology. One report quoted the director as saying that "the knowledge of other cultures can enrich our understanding of the Bible." Moreover, the "Ethiopian custom of eating from a common bowl relates to the Biblical custom of table fellowship and connects with the doctrine of close communion."[43] It is painfully obvious that the director has accepted one of the false portraits of multiculturalism discussed in

Chapter 2—namely, that it is a phenomenon that merely teaches Americans about other cultures.

Liberal churches knowingly advance the agenda of multiculturalism, and conservative churches do so naively. In either instance, the Trojan horse of multiculturalism is slowly conquering America and its institutions, including its churches.

NOTES

1. Jacques Steinberg, "Yale Returns $20 Million to an Unhappy Patron," *New York Times*, 15 March 1995, A1.

2. David Sacks, "Donald Kennedy: The College President as Political Surfer," in *Surviving the PC University* ed. Peter Collier and David Horowitz (Studio City, Calif.: Second Thoughts Books and Center for the Study of Popular Culture, 1993), p. 32.

3. Ibid., p. 33.

4. Collier and Horowitz, *Surviving the PC University*, p. 57.

5. Ibid., p. 56.

6. Pauline E. Kayes, "Access, Equity, and Cultural Diversity: Rediscovering the Community College Mission," in *Multicultural Education: Strategies for Implementation in Colleges and Universities* ed. J. Q. Adams and Janice R. Welsch (Macomb, Ill.: Staff and Curriculum Developers Association, 1992), 2: 85–106.

7. Peter LaBarbara, "NEA Pushes Homosexual Agenda," *Christian American* (May/June 1995): 8.

8. "Gay & Lesbian Caucus Targets Youth: First Graders Must Be Taught Tolerance," *Education Reporter* (August 1994): 1.

9. Phyllis Schlafly, "If NEA Delegates Get Their Way," *Washington Times*, weekly edition, 7–13 August 1995, 33.

10. "Prez Mocks Religious Conservatives," *Education Reporter* (August 1994): 1.

11. "New Business Items Adopted," *Education Reporter* (August 1994): 4.

12. "National Education Association Holds Annual Convention," *Business/Education Insider* (Washington, D.C.: Heritage Foundation, 1994), p. 3.

13. Rush Limbaugh, "The National Education Association," *The Limbaugh Letter* (1994): 5.

14. *African American Baseline Essays* (Portland, Ore.: Portland Public Schools, 1987; revised 1990), p. A6.

15. Mary Lefkowitz, "Not Out of Africa," *The New Republic*, 10 February 1992, 35.

16. Frank Snowden, *Before Color Prejudice* (Cambridge, Mass.: Harvard University Press, 1983), p. 73. See also his *Blacks in Antiquity: Ethiopians in the Greco-Roman Experience* (Cambridge, Mass.: Harvard University Press, 1970).

17. Ibid., p. SS1.

18. Ibid., p. SS4.

19. Don Feder, "Diversity Training: P.C. in Corporate America," *AFA Journal* (May 1994): 20.

20. Ibid.

21. Linda Chavez, "Demystifying Multiculturalism," *National Review*, 21 February 1994, 26.

22. Michel Winerip, "Faculty Angst over Diversity Courses Meets Student Zeitgeist at U. Mass," *New York Times*, 4 May 1994, A13.

23. Linda Chavez, *Out of the Barrio: Toward a New Politics of Hispanic Assimilation* (New York: Basic Books, 1991), p. 79.

24. Ibid., p. 83.

25. Faye Rice, "How to Make Diversity Pay," *Fortune*, 8 August 1994, 82.

26. Ibid., p. 84.

27. Ibid.

28. Rush Limbaugh cited by Reed Irvine, "Notes from the Editor's Cuff," *AIM Report* (December 1993): A.

29. "Celebrating Diversity," *Time* (Special Issue, fall 1993).

30. Rick Marin, "The Other 'Civil War,'" *Newsweek*, 8 May 1995, 62.

31. Woody West, "Series' PC Myth-Making Turns Indians into Saints, Whites into Savages," *Washington Times*, weekly edition, 15–21 May 1995, 23.

32. H. Richard Niebuhr, *Christ and Culture* (New York: Harper and Row, 1951).

33. Cited in James Muldoon, "The Columbus Quincentennial: Should Christians Celebrate It?" *America*, 27 October 1990, 300.

34. Ibid.

35. Editorial, "Repenting of America 1492–1992," *First Things* (October 1990): 5.

36. Susan Cyre, "PCUSA Funds Effort to Re-create God," *The Presbyterian Layman* (January/February 1994): 1.

37. "Weird Stuff," *Forum Letter*, 18 February 1994, 2.

38. Cyre, "PCUSA Funds," p. 10.

39. "Religious Scapegoats," *Forum Letter*, 7 October 1993, 3.

40. Ibid.

41. Mendi Dessalines Shirley Lewis, "What Does Kwanzaa Mean?" *Youth* (December 1994): 10–13.

42. Alvin L. Barry, "From the President: A Convention Overview," *The Lutheran Witness* (August 1994): 26.

43. "Cultural Diversity Is Subject of 'Hour' Special for New Year's," *The Lutheran Layman* (November 1995): 19.

Chapter 12

America's Fight for Its Soul

I'd rather see America save her soul than her face.

Norman Mattoon Thomas

The French philosopher, Ernest Renan, once observed that "A nation is a soul, a spiritual principle" and that two things constitute its soul. One is "its common possession of a rich legacy of memories; the other is the present consensus, the desire to live together, the will to continue to value the heritage that has been received undivided.... To have shared glories in the past, a common will in the present, to have done great things together, to want to do them still."[1]

This description has especially been true of the United States for at least 200 years. To Renan's definition I would add that America's soul also reflects strong spiritual values and beliefs, undergirded by Judeo-Christian norms and morality that have been largely interpreted and applied in the light of Christian principles.

In 1787, the Continental Congress passed the Northwest Ordinance Act which, among other things, required the teaching of religion and morality in its schools. Article III stated: "Religion, morality, and knowledge being necessary to good government and the happiness of mankind, schools and the means of education shall be forever encouraged." Every student of American history knows that "religion" in Article III meant the Christian religion, not just any religion.

The multiculturalist attack on America's culture, which seeks to reject the natural/moral law, biblical values, and Christian symbols, is an attack not just on the nation's longstanding morality but also on its soul.

Thus America is not merely competing with some alternative cultural values but is engaged in an all-out war to preserve its soul. For inspiration and courage to fight and win the war against multiculturalism, the nation needs to restore its long-held beliefs and values.

AMERICA THE PROMISED LAND

Since the early 1600s, America's founders and leaders have seen the nation in a biblically spiritual light. The Pilgrims viewed America as divinely chosen by God, much as the ancient Israelites saw the land of Canaan as they came to it from Egypt.

The American concept of the Promised Land was not confined to the Pilgrims. It has been elucidated repeatedly throughout the nation's history by men such as Benjamin Franklin, John Adams, and Thomas Jefferson, whom the Continental Congress on July 4, 1776, appointed to a special committee "to bring a device for a seal of the United States of America."[2] At Jefferson's urging, the committee formally presented a drawing depicting America as the new Israel. This sketch portrayed Americans, like the children of Israel, being led by a cloud during the day and by a pillar of fire by night in pursuit of the Promised Land. Although this design was not adopted, it clearly shows that the concept of seeing America as the Promised Land was not just confined to the Pilgrims.

Abraham Lincoln saw America as the Promised Land when he said the United States was "the world's last best hope." So did the Jewish immigrant to the United States in the 1970s, when upon hearing and seeing rebellious Marxist students on a university campus publicly demonstrating and shouting, "Ho, Ho, Ho Chi Minh," he asked: "Don't they know they live in paradise?"[3]

To the multiculturalists America is not the Promised Land, but a despised land because it has practiced cultural "imperialism" and "oppression," and continues to do so. For example, it significantly altered and even caused some cultures of the American Indians to disappear. Moreover, it still foists the "Euro-American" culture on its many immigrants. This is why the multiculturalists work so feverishly to make America a multiculturalist society because only then, according to them, will it cease to be culturally oppressive.

AMERICA PROVIDENTIALLY PRESERVED

To the Pilgrims and to prominent Americans after them, God did not just lead them to the Promised Land; He also providentially preserved it for them. Nowhere is this more evident than in some of the extraordinary, fortuitous events and incidents that occurred during the country's War of Independence. From a military perspective, the Americans should never have won that war, but they did. Many Americans, including George Washington, believed that God often intervened in that war to save the nation.

One such intervention occurred at Dorchester Heights, Massachusetts, on the night of March 4, 1776. On this night, as George Washington planned to fortify this hill, a thick fog developed below, while on top of the hill the moon shone brightly, enabling the Americans to arm the hill's top with cannons and other weapons. The British from across the bay could not see what was happening on the hill. The next morning they were flabbergasted to see Dorchester Heights militarily fortified. General William Howe said: "The rebels have done more in one night than my whole [British] army would have done in months."[4]

Seeing Washington's army and artillery located on Dorchester Heights, General Howe decided to ready his men to row across the water to Dorchester Heights with the next tide to attack Washington and his Patriots. But while waiting for the tide, a hurricane-like storm arose, making it impossible for the British soldiers to row to the peninsula. One British soldier described the storm as having "a wind more violent than anything I ever saw." The storm did not abate until the next morning, when Howe saw that the extra time had allowed the Americans to fortify their positions even more firmly. A few days later he withdrew his army from Boston to New York. The Americans took Boston without a single casualty. Washington recognized the hand of God in what happened those two eventful days by saying it was "a remarkable interposition of Providence."[5] Two hundred years later, James Flexner, a modern historian of Washington and the War of Independence, also saw the events at Dorchester Heights as acts of God (see his article, "Providence Rides a Storm").[6]

Washington's heralded success in crossing the Delaware River in the predawn hours of Christmas Day 1776 was yet another time when a violent storm, creating near-zero visibility, made it impossible for the British sentries to see Washington's flotilla coming in to attack. The British soldiers (Hessians, really) were caught off guard, and in less than an hour the battle was over. The victory vastly improved American morale. Summing up this significant feat, Peter Marshall and David Manuel write: "Was it a fluke, as Washington's detractors, now themselves in disfavor, mutter? Or was it, as General Henry Knox (one of Washington's military logistics experts) wrote, that 'Providence seemed to have smiled upon every part of this enterprize' "?[7]

The Patriots had yet other signs of divine intervention during the war. At the Battle of Princeton in January 1777, Washington galloped to the front lines of the battle and shouted: "Fire." He did this on his highly visible white horse, making him a conspicuous and easy target for the

British, who were only yards away. Soldiers were falling all around him. Flexner reports: "Washington's aide, Colonel Edward Fitzgerald, covered his face with his hat, for he could not bear to see the Commander in Chief killed. When, all the guns having emptied, the firing ceased, Fitzgerald lowered his hat. Around him, many men were writhing in their last agonies. But Washington sat solidly on his horse, untouched."[8]

The Princeton incident was not the only time Washington benefited from divine intervention. At the Battle of the Monongahela, near Fort Duquesne (now Pittsburgh), more than twenty years before the War of Independence, the twenty-three-year-old Washington had two horses killed under him and four bullet holes rip through his coat.[9] Fifteen years after that battle, an Indian chief called a council and recalled that he had commanded his warriors in this battle to take aim at the tall, young soldier, whom he saw as more dangerous than other redcoats because he used the tactics of Indian warriors. The chief continued:

Our rifles were leveled, rifles which, but for him, knew not how to miss. . . . 'Twas all in vain; a power mightier far than we shielded him from harm. He cannot die in battle. I am old . . . but ere I go, there is something that bids me to speak in the voice of prophecy. Listen! The Great Spirit protects that man, and guides his destinies—he will become the chief of nations, and a people yet unborn will hail him as the founder of a mighty empire.[10]

In all of these experiences, Washington recognized God's intervening action. He also saw the hand of God in the interception of Major John Andre, Benedict Arnold's messenger. "In no instance," said he, "since the commencement of the War has the interposition of Providence [one of Washington's favorite words for God] appeared more conspicuous than in the rescue of the Post and Garrison of West Point from Arnold's villainous perfidy."[11]

These noteworthy examples of prominent Americans who believed that God had providentially preserved the nation in some of its most critical hours in history do not sit well with multiculturalists. To believe that God preserved the country is contrary to the "vision of the anointed," as Thomas Sowell would say.[12] Why would God preserve a racist, sexist nation? Moreover, the very concept of providential guidance is repugnant to multiculturalists. It carries too much Judeo-Christian freight.

REPUBLICAN VIRTUES

The firm belief that America is the Promised Land and that God often intervened to preserve it motivated the Founding Fathers to embark on a bold, new venture. In 1787 they hammered out a federal Constitution during a hot, humid summer in Philadelphia. At the end of this convention, someone asked Benjamin Franklin: "What kind of government are we going to have?" He responded: "A republic, if you can keep it."

We will never know for sure what Franklin meant, and we may debate the matter. His remark probably stemmed from his knowledge of history, especially of how the Roman republic failed, and perhaps also the thinking of his French friend, Voltaire, who believed that all republics end in tyranny.[13] Apparently, Franklin believed that a republican government could endure only if its leaders and people were given to moral virtues. They needed to obey God's moral laws—a quality that the republic of ancient Rome sadly lacked.

Similar to Franklin's conviction are the words of another Founding Father, Thomas Jefferson, who said: "I think that our government will remain virtuous."[14] Another Founder, Benjamin Rush, also believed virtue was vital to the American republic: "the only foundation for a useful education in a republic is to be laid in Religion [sic]. Without this there can be no virtue, and without virtue there can be no liberty, and liberty is the object and life of all republican governments."[15]

A recent observer states that the Founders believed that "If public virtue declined, the republic declined, and if it declined too far, the republic died."[16] They recognized that the United States would endure only if its people lived honest, morally upright lives. Once the practice of virtue gave way to moral and cultural relativism, as multiculturalism espouses, Americans, according to Franklin, Rush, and others, would lose their republic, their freedom, and the blessings that their once Promised Land bestowed.

If the American republic can endure only by being morally virtuous, then it is vitally important that America conquer the forces of multiculturalism that are jettisoning the nation's longstanding moral norms, especially the Ten Commandments, which have been the foundation of American virtue from the nation's beginning. How long can the republic remain virtuous when its standards for virtue may no longer be taught or even posted in America's public schools? When the morality contained in these Commandments is relativized or rejected by growing numbers of its citizens and leaders, it is not surprising to see why America is experiencing a moral meltdown. Crime rates are near an all-time high, a third of the nation's children are born out-of-wedlock, divorce rates are the highest in the civilized world, abortionists kill one-third of America's conceived babies, family violence is atrociously high, and homosexuality is being socially legitimated without shame. Much of the populace, and even many of the country's highest leaders in government, live as though there were no moral law, no God, and no sense of shame. Indeed, as the Ten Commandments are being erased from America's schools and public buildings, they also are disappearing from the people's convictions, leading to the loss of republican virtues. Undeniably, America's soul is on the precipice.

ATTACKS ON AMERICA'S NATIONAL SYMBOLS

During the last 200 years, the United States not only developed impressive national symbols, but its citizens have also deeply internalized their meanings. These symbols are being attacked by multiculturalists directly and indirectly in ways that the public often does not recognize.

"We, The People"

For two centuries every school child has been taught the words, "We, the people," the first three words of their nation's Constitution. These words proclaim that the nation is a republic, that public thing (*res publica*), whose people rule themselves by giving consent to those who govern them, as opposed to being ruled by a monarch or dictator who lacks such consent.

In the currently rabid quest for multiculturalism, not only is there the desire to reject America's Western culture, but also there is the goal to undermine what Americans have always meant by the words "We, the people"—namely, a majority of the people rule. But now some want to replace the rule of the majority with weighted voting rights for racial and minority groups, or "peoples," as the multiculturalists say. Weighted voting gives a minority voter more than one vote for a candidate or issue.

The widespread furor over President Clinton's nomination of Lani Guinier in 1993 to a government post resulted largely over this issue. Guinier favored weighted voting. Clinton's nomination of Guinier was an example of what he meant in his inauguration speech when, like a true multiculturalist, he said: "Each generation of Americans must define what it means to be an American." It appears that one way to redefine America is to replace the first three words, "We, the people," of the country's Constitution, with "We, the peoples."

So when multiculturalists say they want to introduce cultural diversity by giving special attention to different "peoples," much more is involved here than what many might think. The eventual goal is to attack the very nerve center of the nation, its Constitution. This historical, and longest continually functioning, constitution spells out the republican concept of "We the people," not "peoples," as sovereign, and many multiculturalists aim to change it.

If multiculturalists should someday succeed in replacing the word "people" in the Constitution with "peoples," America will become an arena of unassimilated tribal groups primed for racial and ethnic conflicts. The very thing multiculturalists fault America for, namely, racism and discrimination, would inevitably get worse, not better.

Shortly before his death in 1994, Russell Kirk warned: "Should the multiculturalists have their way, culture, with us Americans a century and a half later, would end in heartache—and anarchy."[17] This may well be an understatement because if the current growth of multiculturalism is not checked and reversed, the heartache and anarchy that Kirk talks about will happen much sooner.

"E Pluribus Unum"

In 1782, when the United States officially accepted these Latin words that Thomas Jefferson borrowed from Virgil's poem, *Moretum,* as its motto, it did more than merely adopt a slogan. It reflected its identity. The slogan *E Pluribus Unum* declared that out of many people—immigrants from all over the world—the nation formed one united people. *E Pluribus Unum* has been such an integral part of the United States that the phrase is embossed on every American coin. The many became one by means of America's melting pot.

For 200 years Americans took *E Pluribus Unum* for granted. It was an American thing. But then came the multiculturalists in the 1980s and 1990s. Despising cultural assimilation, they long for *E Pluribus Plures* (keeping the many as many). They want "diversity," so that every immigrant group can retain its culture and language. *E Pluribus Unum* is "cultural oppression."

If there are any doubts regarding the good *E Pluribus Unum* has done for America, one only needs to remember Canada's tragic experience. The country is unraveling as its leadership bows to all kinds of demands of its cultural and subcultural groups. No institution has been left untouched. A few years ago, the Royal Canadian Mounted Police (RCMP), of which I was once proudly a member, even capitulated to Canada's multiculturalist mania. One of its regular members, a Sikh, demanded the right to wear a turban in place of the stetson hat that accompanies this police force's famous scarlet tunic. The Sikh won his case in the name of multiculturalist diversity. More than a century of the RCMP's pride and honor was sacrificed on the altar of multiculturalism. One person's deviancy (now called "diversity") was more important than the *esprit de corps* of thousands of other Mounties, which for more than a century was a hallmark of this world-renowned police force. This Canadian example illustrates a common stance of multiculturalists; namely, that when non-Western cultures impose their cultural customs on their host countries, it is only being multicultural, but when the assimilated citizens reject such customs, it is "oppression" or "bigotry."

If America loses the ability to assimilate the many (*plures*) into one united nation, it will become like Canada and other divided countries. When that happens, America will have lost its soul. It will then be a tribalistic country in which each group will selfishly seek its own ethnocentric norms, mores, and other foreign interests, eventually producing serious social and cultural conflicts, and probably even physical violence.

"One Nation Under God"

When Thomas Jefferson penned the Declaration of Independence, he specifically used the words "God" and "Creator." Ever since then, Washington, Adams, Madison, Lincoln, and other U.S. presidents have not hesitated to mention and honor God in public addresses. This is a distinctive American practice.

When George Washington took the oath of office as the country's first president, he concluded by saying "So Help Me God," even though these words were not part of the formal oath in the Constitution. Every president has invoked these words ever since. This practice shows that American presidents see the nation as dependent on God, as being under His providential care.

Most Americans know that the nation's Pledge of Allegiance contains the words "one nation under God." Although these words were not part of Francis Bellamy's original version of 1892, Congress added them in 1954.

The phrase "one nation under God" is contrary to the spirit of multiculturalism. It is "offensive" to the atheists, agnostics, secular humanists, and others who make up the roster of multiculturalism. One critic recently suggested that the pledge should be rewritten, not only because of its reference to God, but also because it was an "exercise in chauvinism."[18]

"In God We Trust"

The belief that the nation's destiny is linked to God has been so pronounced that in 1865 Congress even authorized that the words "In God We Trust" be inscribed on some of the nation's coins. In 1908 Congress required all coins to bear this inscription, and in 1955 this phrase had to be printed on paper currency too.

In 1956 Congress declared "In God We Trust" to be the nation's official motto. The phrase comes from one of the stanzas of Francis Scott Key's *Star-Spangled Banner*, penned in 1814.

The American reverence for God is also evident in one of the nation's favorite songs, *God Bless America*, written by Irving Berlin, who came to America as an immigrant. He loved America and its melting pot which made him an American. He was so pleased that he wrote this song in which all Americans ask God to bless their great nation.

Multiculturalists object to the word "God" because they say it offends atheists and secularists and because they know that to most Americans God does not mean just any god, but the God of the Bible. Such a view of God is too exclusive for serious-minded multiculturalists.

"ONE NATION . . . INDIVISIBLE"

In 1892, when Francis Bellamy, with the memory of the Civil War, wrote his version of the Pledge of Allegiance, he asked Americans to keep their nation united. One divisive experience for the country was more than enough.

Bellamy's noble goal of national indivisibleness is now being threatened by the growth of multiculturalism, whose ideology aggressively fosters many potentially divisive behaviors. Multiculturalists are encouraging immigrants not to assimilate, promoting bilingualism, making Americans color-conscious, labeling people homophobes if they disapprove of homosexuality, bashing white males, advocating "diversity" programs, and attacking America's many symbols.

Unity is never attained by accenting differences; any thought to the contrary is utopian. What family would remain united if the differences of each member were continually emphasized? America's unity has been the product of maximizing the characteristics its people had in common, not by highlighting cultural or ethnic differences.

HYPHENATING ALL AMERICANS

In recent years, multiculturalists have done a good job of hyphenating Americans. While this is not a new practice, in the past governmental entities did not encourage or promote it, as it does today, in keeping with the spirit of multiculturalism. In some instances, bureaucrats in the federal government have recently coined new hyphens. The designation "Hispanic-American" came into being in 1978 when the Office of Management and Budget (OMB) in Washington, D.C., came up with this classification. Another recent coinage is the hyphen "Asian-American." And an even more recent one is today's "African-American" designation for American blacks. This hyphen was first launched at the African-American Summit in New Orleans in April 1989 by Ramona H. Edelin, the president of the National Urban Coalition.[19]

The mass media insist on hyphenating Americans, especially those from minority cultures. They rigidly refer to blacks as "African-Americans," in spite of research showing that most blacks in the United States prefer to be called black if a distinction must be made. One survey in 1991, conducted by the Joint Center for Political and Economic Studies, a group that focuses on black issues, found that 72 percent of America's blacks preferred to be known as black and only 15 percent preferred African-American.[20] This preference makes a lot of sense because for most black Americans, their ancestors came here 200 to 300 years ago. Thus they know little about African cultures. Moreover, Africa is a continent with 53 countries and some 800 different languages.

Hyphenating Americans does not bind Americans together. Instead, it segregates them into groups, and it also qualifies people's commitment to America. This is why President Theodore Roosevelt in the early 1900s opposed the practice. Unequivocally, he said:

A hyphenated American is no American at all. This is just as true of the man who puts "native" before the hyphen as of the man who puts German or Irish or English or French before the hyphen. American is a matter of the spirit of the soul. Our allegiance must be purely to the United States. We must unsparingly condemn any man who holds any other allegiance.[21]

Hyphenating Americans runs counter to long-established American practice. No one during World War I called General Pershing a German-American, and no one during World War II referred to General Eisenhower as a German-American. And America was the better for it.

When General Norm Schwartzkopf led the American troops in the Gulf War of 1992, he was not referred to as a German-American, and rightly so. His German descent was of no consequence. Similarly, when General John Shalikashvili, President Clinton's chairman of the Joint Chiefs of Staff, appears on television he is not identified as a Polish-American. Then why do the media refer to General Colin Powell as African-American whenever it's convenient? After all, he is as much of an American as is Schwartzkopf or Shalikashvili. To ask the question is not to be insensitive, as many multiculturalists are quick to respond. To the contrary, it is probably insensitive not to accord Powell, or any other noteworthy member of a American minority group, the same degree of American status that is given to other Americans.

There are additional reasons for not hyphenating Americans. They are not identified as hyphenated Americans on their passports. Also, when American soldiers go overseas, they are not referred to as African-American, German-American, or Irish-American but as American soldiers. The sooner the hyphenating ends, the better it will be for all Americans and for the continuing unity of the nation.

ATTACKS ON AMERICA'S NATIONAL PRIDE

Multiculturalists are dedicated to expunging all references to the nation's glorious accomplishments, and this includes the country's national pride. They detest America's national pride, which they regard as "chauvinistic," and are succeeding in many of their attempts to erase American pride. In Portland, Oregon, in March 1994, they persuaded the city to reject a newly fashioned sculpture of a pioneer family on the Oregon Trail that depicted a white pioneer husband pointing confidently to the horizon ahead, a mother holding her deceased daughter's doll, and their son clutching a Bible. The sculpture, *Promised Land*, by David Manuel illustrated American pride.

An editorial in the *Seattle Post-Intelligencer* cited the opinion of an art professor from Oregon State University who saw the sculpture as an affront to multiculturalism. He stated: "I'm not sure we need any more memorials to the dominant culture."[22] So the sculpture had to go.

Efforts to diminish the nation's pride leaves loyal Americans only two choices: succumb to the anti-American ideology and politics of multiculturalism, and thereby engage in a type of national masochism, or fight for their nation's soul in order to preserve its long-held values.

THE DECLINE OF JUDEO-CHRISTIAN MORALITY

Multiculturalism's attack on the Judeo-Christian or biblical morality and values, as delineated in Chapter 10, is an assault on America's moral infrastructure. Once this system of morality, with its age-old and proven results, crumbles, the nation is doomed. This system has undergirded the nation's freedoms, rights, and economic opportunities. Loyal Americans need to ask multiculturalists a simple question: "Show us another system of 'morality' equal to the Judeo-Christian morality that has served a nation better." There is none.

In the past some Americans did on occasion violate some Judeo-Christian norms and values, but even in their weakest moments, they never questioned the validity of those norms. They knew that these norms came from God, whom they honored by inscribing His name on their coins, public buildings, pledge of allegiance, and patriotic songs. Today that has changed. Now we see widespread deviations from these norms, and in addition there are even public forums and organizations that advocate and promote open departure from them. For instance, there are numerous pro-abortion, pro-homosexual and pro-lesbian groups, and at least one national pedophilic organization.

If the legitimating of behavior that violates the natural/moral law continues in America, the destruction of the nation's soul is inevitable. With regard to America's moral decline as a result of sexual promiscuity, Paul Cameron says: "At no time in history has a society departed so quickly and so radically from traditional norms, and at no time in history has such conduct been so dangerous."[23]

America may self-destruct as have so many nations in the past. We need recall only what happened to the golden age of ancient Greece, to the once mighty Roman Empire, and to Hitler's Third Reich which he thought would last a thousand years. All three fell because they approved and practiced behavior contrary to the natural/moral law. Consider Hitler's Germany. The Nazis gained power in 1933. Two years later, notes Kevin Abrams (a Canadian of Jewish descent), they removed the term "unnatural" from the German Criminal Code with regard to its definition of homosexuality.[24] Abrams also shows that the Nazi regime was run and operated by a disproportionate number of homosexuals. Arrests of homosexuals were limited and selective, and the arrests that were made served as a facade to make the German people, industrial leaders, and the Prussian Officer Corps think that the Nazis opposed homosexual behavior.[25] Hitler's "S.S. guards and officers [who] would repeatedly rape pink triangle prisoners, and Jewish and Gypsy boys," says Heinrich Heger, an Austrian author and homosexual, who was arrested and used sexually by the Nazis in a concentration camp. Heger also writes: "The SD-SS would use sadomasochism on a daily basis."[26]

To warn the United States about its deteriorating morality is not to be an alarmist, bigoted, or homophobic. The homophobic label, I might note, is often erroneously pinned on anyone who opposes homosexuality or sees it as a violation of the natural/moral law. The label homophobia is used to intimidate all those who see homosexual behavior as morally wrong. As Thomas Sowell has shown, the "anointed" often use the term as "a way of avoiding substantive debate."[27]

Moreover, is it homophobic to fear *not* the homosexual but one of today's most common effects of homosexual behavior, namely, AIDS? Most people know that the majority of AIDS cases in the United States occur among practicing male homosexuals. Similarly, it can be argued that it is not homophobic to dislike and disagree with the radically different view that many confirmed homosexuals have of the world. "A man confirmed in homosexual behavior," says Michael Jones, "will have a radically different view of the world than someone else, say, one who tries to follow the Christian view of sexuality as being inextricably bound with procreation and limited in expression to a partner in marriage."[28] Consistent with this assessment is Gertrude Himmelfarb's observation that the economic philosophy of John Maynard Keynes, a homosexual, was influenced by his sexual values. To him the classical economic theory that lay behind the British and American reluctance to engage in deficit financing was a Puritan hang-up of those who cared about their children's future.[29]

When critics resisted Keynes's concept of deficit financing because of its long-term dangers, he replied in words that have now become well-known. "In the long-run we are all dead," he said. These words reveal more than what meets the eye or ear. In other words, why should a confirmed homosexual be concerned about deficit financing and its long-term effects? He will not have offspring who will someday have to bear the burden of his country's national deficit.

America must not let itself be fooled into believing multiculturalism's message that there is no absolute code of right or wrong, and that all morality is culturally relative. Much of this ideology is currently promoted under the label of "values clarification," a method used now in many public schools. It may sound good, but it is flagrantly relativistic. It teaches students that there is no right or wrong. They are merely asked to express their "values," feelings, ideas, and beliefs to others in terms of their own subjective value systems. Those who express their values in light of the Ten Commandments or the Judeo-Christian ethic frequently are seen as out of step and are ridiculed.

Multiculturalism's values clarification, or multi-morality, is both wrong and dangerous. It preaches that the Ten Commandments are at best only one system of morality and that ultimately any behavior is acceptable, as long as it has some group or subcultural support. Thus no group's or culture's behavior may be criticized, much less penalized. The end result of such a system is moral anarchy.

MULTICULTURALISM'S NEO-PAGANISM

Statistics reveal that 81 percent of Americans identify with Christianity;[30] nonetheless, multiculturalists continue to remove biblical norms from the public school curricula and to expunge Christian symbols from tax-supported public buildings. Similar efforts are not directed against non-Christian or neo-pagan religious groups. Indeed, some instances special efforts are made to implement and support non-Christian practices or symbols (see Chapter 10).

The bias in favor of pagan religious values, in opposition to Christian values and symbols, is also evident in some recent movies, for instance, *The Lion King* and *Pocahontas*. Both films favorably dispense neo-pagan beliefs. *Pocahontas*, widely touted as a "multicultural" film, pays high tribute to the pantheistic beliefs of the Pohatwan tribe. It has Grandmother Willow (a talking tree) tell Pocahontas that sacred spirits reside in plants, rocks, wind, earth, and so on. "All around you are spirits, child. If you listen, they will guide you," says Grandmother Willow. Thus the pantheistic beliefs of American Indians are supported by multiculturalism, while Christianity is discriminated against in numerous movies.

From its earliest years, Christianity has always condemned pantheism for at least two reasons. First, it fails to distinguish God from His created works, and second, it sees every earthly element and creature as divine. Multiculturalists revived pantheism in *The Lion King* and *Pocahontas*, and also subtly used these movies to infiltrate the formative minds of young children with beliefs contrary to Christianity. Ironically, pantheism, once a hallmark of uncivilized societies is today being repackaged in what is called "New Age" beliefs—all part of the multiculturalist agenda.

Americans can be fooled by these seemingly harmless movies only at their own peril. Films like these are subtle attacks on Judeo-Christian values. It is part of the multiculturalist design to undermine and destroy the Judeo-Christian components of the Euro-American culture and thus another way of endangering America's soul.

THREATS TO AMERICA'S SCHOOLS

As all Americans know, the price of liberty is eternal vigilance. One place where they really must be vigilant is in their public schools, on both the elementary and secondary levels. As noted in Chapters 2 and 5, multiculturalists have infiltrated American schools by pushing their ideology onto teachers and students through their textbooks, which are strongly biased against American culture. Similar to other left-wingers before them, multiculturalists know that they will more likely achieve their goals if they can invade the schools with their ideology.

Some Americans are indeed vigilant on the public school front, as Chapters 6 and 10 show with regard to their having stopped the schools of New York City and Des Moines, Iowa, from adopting materials promoting homosexuality. This kind of vigilance needs to operate on all levels of society, however.

Also with regard to the school front, Americans must become active in restoring the teaching of American history as it used to be taught for generations, when textbooks and teachers taught students about the heroic acts and contributions of men like Patrick Henry, Paul Revere, and others, rather than omit them from texts as is presently true in many instances. Textbooks need to begin giving credit again to Western/Judeo-Christian philosophy and to return to the insights that the Founding Fathers used to found and shape the nation's institutions. Schools must cease pandering to the anointed minorities by teaching unsubstantiated claims as historical facts in order to make them feel good. Ethnic cheerleading has no place in American schools. Teachers are obliged to teach their students about the really significant individuals and events of American history, those that have stood the test of time.

Teachers need to teach students that God gave the United States great presidents when they were most needed—for instance, Washington, Jefferson, Lincoln, Roosevelt, Truman, Eisenhower, and Reagan. These men were not afraid to lead. They filled Americans with pride. They knew that what they were doing was right, and they had no doubts that their decisions would be good for the nation. They did not apologize for acts they never committed, as multiculturalists have persuaded many of our current leaders to do.

THE WHITE-GUILT SYNDROME

The phenomenon of white guilt has enabled non-Western cultural groups to receive special privileges that no previous groups in America's history have ever received in the past. The time has come for white Americans, who comprise 76 percent of the country's population, to reject the white-guilt syndrome.

White guilt needs to be rejected for several reasons. First, the socioeconomic problems that minority groups experience today are not the fault of the white majority. Second, even if their problems were in part the result of the white majority, blaming others never helps the disadvantaged overcome difficulties. A group that sees itself as victim leads to self-pity, not to character building, self-respect, and self-determination. It leads to looking for special benefits and privileges that only serve to delay progress and development. Third, no white Americans alive today can rightfully be blamed for the enslavement of blacks in the eighteenth and nineteenth century, unjust and evil as it was. Nor can the past injustices that American Indians experienced, also more than 100 years ago, be blamed on the present generation of whites. The sins that were committed by some white Americans in the past are not the sins of the present generation. To take ownership of ancestral injustices, which are so readily handed out by multiculturalists, is not only irrelevant but also masochistic. It also does not help the respective minorities in the least.

And so, Americans need to cast off the mantle of white guilt that multiculturalists and radical minority leaders have draped around so many. Minorities today would do well to recall the experience of many minorities of the past, the Germans, the Irish, the Italians, the Poles, the Greeks, most of whom came to America in poverty. Unfortunately, they too were often victims of prejudice and discrimination, and sometimes severely so. But they overcame these obstacles, not by claiming victim status, but by taking advantage of America's unequaled freedoms and economic opportunities. They were content with having equal opportunity which they did not confuse with equal outcome or results, as many leftist politicians tell minority groups today. Ironically, these one-time (old) minorities are now part of the "evil" white majority, which, multiculturalists say, has helped create the "oppressive" Euro-American culture that subjects today's minorities to all sorts of inequalities.

FROM TOLERATION TO ACCEPTANCE TO COERCION

America has long tolerated different views. Its Constitution's First Amendment made toleration a hallmark of freedom. The framers of the

Constitution, however, never had the slightest intention of equating tolerance with acceptance. Unfortunately, with the help of multiculturalist propaganda, many Americans now are making this erroneous equation. Hence various behaviors, some of them immoral, which once were only tolerated, are now accepted and socially legitimated.

It is one thing to tolerate something and quite another to accept that which is tolerated. When the latter happens, the distinction between moral and immoral behavior essentially disappears, nullifying the Judeo-Christian standard of morality. Absolute norms and values vanish, everything is morally relative, and facts are irrelevant. When this occurs, the stage is set for a national nightmare, and the rise of coercive power is all but inevitable. Once there is no more absolute truth, or the possibility of it, rational arguments are no longer effective, nor are they tolerated. Coercive power becomes the only means for those who want their ideology—their truth—to prevail.

Ironically, at that juncture cultural relativity comes to an end. Now the relativists become arbitrary absolutists. This is what happened in Nazi Germany and in Communist Russia. To a degree, some of this is already evident with the "politically correct" enforcers on college/university campuses, where many students are being disciplined and expelled for not conforming to the ideology of multiculturalism. America has recently taken long strides toward accepting what it once merely tolerated. And as is often true, when this happens, the next move is toward coercive power. It seems that the nation is beginning to move in the latter direction as many in its midst are forcing a "politically correct" multiculturalist agenda on its people.

LEARN FROM CANADA'S FAILED EXPERIMENT

Multiculturalism does not work because it is a utopian dream at best and a political nightmare at worst. If there is any doubt, just look to modern Bosnia, Sri Lanka, and Chechnya. But they are so distant that these multiculturalist catastrophes may not seem to have any relevance to our future cultural and political stability. So we need to look to our northern neighbor with whom we share a 3,000–mile boundary, Canada.

As noted earlier (in Chapter 8), Quebec, which never assimilated Canada's majority culture, representing 75 percent of the population, is on the verge of seceding from Canada. While it reluctantly remains within the confederation, it continues to demand to be recognized as a "distinct society" within the country. But there is more in the winds.

In May 1996 the Parti Quebecois (PQ) at its provincial convention (called "national convention" by the French) voted to have its leader Premier Lucien Bouchard carry out "a more strenuous enforcement of existing language laws."[31] If the PQ, the party in power, actually legislates this convention's resolution, Quebec will then likely enforce Bill 101 and Bill 178 (passed in 1977 and 1988, respectively). The former bill severely restricts access to English schools, except for children who have at least one parent who was educated in English. Children of non-English immigrants must attend French-speaking schools. This bill also requires all businesses with more than 100 employees to have programs promoting French. The bill also provides for a language police (*Commission de protection de la langue francaise*) that enforces the bill's demands. During the last several years the language police, however, has been rather inactive, ever since the Liberal party took office. This party has maintained a less rigid stance on the language issue. Now that the PQ is in office again, it remains to be seen whether Bouchard will really take "a more strenuous enforcement" posture. If he does, it will spawn more political conflict and divisiveness, stretching the frail and tender threads of Canada's confederation (union) perhaps to the breaking point.

The multiculturalist Pandora's Box in Canada has unleashed other problems, one of which is the Canadian Indians' demand for sovereignty in large portions of the country. In the fall of 1995, the Shuswap Nation in the province of British Columbia was demanding sovereignty over a certain portion of land. Its protagonists armed themselves and carried signs declaring they were "Sovereignists Not Terrorists." More recently, in winter 1996, the 6,000 Nisga'a Indians, also in British Columbia, demanded and received from the provincial government 772 square miles of the Nass Valley. As part of the agreement, they will "set up their own court for minor offenses and their own police force."[32] In the meantime, British Columbia has forty-seven other Indian groups vying for sovereignty rights, which has prompted some reports that the Indians are "staking claim to virtually the entire province."[33]

If Canada has not been able to make multiculturalism work, and it has not, the United States cannot be expected to do it better. Shortly before he left office in 1993, Prime Minister Brian Mulroney of Canada, in an American television interview, enviously referred to the United States as a "melting pot nation" in contrast to Canada. His comment should be kept in mind, and the ideological multiculturalists who seek to destroy the people's unity should be rebuffed.

It is noteworthy that a survey of Canadians in late 1995 found that a lot of Canadians did not think "Canada will be around by the year 2000."[34] So, America must learn from Canada's failed experiment.

AMERICA, DO IT AGAIN!

Given the numerous ways in which multiculturalism has already undermined the American culture, the future does not look bright. Yet, I am still optimistic that "the land of the free and home of the brave" will overcome multiculturalism and thus preserve its soul.

There are several reasons for my optimism. First, Americans are by nature an optimistic people. It is the spirit of optimism that helped make America great, and it is this spirit that can defeat and silence the negative, anti-American message of the multiculturalists.

Second, the Patriots won the War of Independence against insurmountable odds. As noted above, logistically and militarily, they should never have won that war. At the appropriate time, France came to the aid of the Patriots, a number of other providential events occurred, and America gained its independence.

Third, the Founding Fathers hammered out a written Constitution in 1787, at a time when thirteen fledgling states lacked both economic and political coherency. The young nation was floundering. That Constitution, which British Prime Minister Gladstone said was "the most wonderful work ever struck off at a given time by the brain and purpose of man," is still in force today, making it the longest enduring, continuously operative governmental document in history. No other human document has given any nation more stability and its citizens more freedom, rights, and opportunities in all human history. That Constitution may in no small way help it preserve its soul. For instance, many of the speech codes written and promoted by the "politically correct" disciples of multiculturalism on many of our college/university campuses have recently been declared unconstitutional by the United States Supreme Court. This is a major setback for the multiculturalists.

Fourth, as a nation, the United States survived the Civil War. Torn in two, it reunited and abolished slavery by passing the Thirteenth Amendment to the Constitution less than a year after the war's end. In 1868, the states ratified the Fourteenth Amendment, barring abridgment of citizen privileges or immunities. Two years later (1870) the states ratified the Fifteenth Amendment making it illegal to deny or curtail the right to vote on the basis of a person's race or color.

Fifth, America survived the Great Depression. During those difficult years the aggressive forces of communism in the 1930s were unable to make any significant inroads into America's hardworking, patriotic working force. The nation slowly overcame its economic problems, and it became the key player in World War II.

Sixth, without U.S. economic and military power the Allies would never have won World War II. U.S. soldiers helped defeat both the Nazis and the Japanese in 1945, and so the United States became a world power. Its citizens became more united than ever, as well as a justly proud people.

Seventh, America overcame the corrosive social chaos of the 1960s produced by the Vietnam War resistance and other radical social movements. Leftist radicals attacked the government by scurrilously calling it "the system." They hoped to destroy it, along with its capitalistic economy and supportive institutions. But the constitutional system, with its checks and balances, though severely tested in those tumultuous years, endured. It withstood the Marxist assault that lay behind much of this social rebellion.

Eighth, the United States won the Cold War against Soviet communism. This difficult, protracted struggle against the "Evil Empire," as President Reagan called it, finally came to an end after he built up the military defense forces, including the promotion of a "Star Wars" defense system, as the leftists derisively called it. The inefficient, bureaucratically corrupt system of the Soviet Union's communist government could not compete with the free enterprise capitalistic system.

As the twentieth century entered its last decade, communism in the Soviet Union and Eastern Europe collapsed. Had it not been for the leftists in our midst, who minimized the U.S. role in the downfall of communism, the American people would today be as proud of this great achievement as they were of winning World War II.

Ninth, the United States has always been a relatively conservative nation compared to Canada, England, France, or Italy, which are all considerably more socialistic and less freedom oriented. This conservative posture, for example, has kept America from adopting wholesale socialistic policies, the Social Security retirement system and Medicare notwithstanding. It has enabled a higher percentage of people to succeed than anywhere else in the world.

The United States' conservative posture is especially evident in presidential and congressional elections. For instance, most liberal members of the Democratic party do not identify themselves as liberal when running for office; if they did, they would rarely get elected. Prior to the 1992 election, Bill Clinton called himself a "new Democrat," which cleverly hid his liberal, multiculturalist agenda from the voters. It is the nation's conservative history that hopefully will enable it to defeat multiculturalism.

Tenth, if America sincerely returns to the Judeo-Christian morality and its corresponding values, which is the heart-and-core of its culture—it can still save its national soul. The words that Moses spoke to Israel over 3,000 years ago must be heeded: "Know therefore that the Lord your God is God, the faithful God who keeps his covenant and steadfast love with those who love him and keep his commandments, to a thousand generations, but he repays those who hate him to their faces, to destroy them. . . . Therefore you shall keep the commandments and the statutes and the judgments which I am commanding you today, to do them" (Deuteronomy 7:9–11).

Although these words were addressed to the ancient Hebrews, they apply to America too. It will not survive as a nation if it ignores this admonition. The pages of history are littered with ruined civilizations that thought they could reject the natural/moral law, the Judeo-Christian ethic. The nation must not violate God's moral standards, as is increasingly true today, in the name of multiculturalism. Indeed, "Culture rises with morality and falls with it too."[35]

As a nation, the United States also needs to heed the words of Solomon who declared: "Righteousness exalts a nation, but sin is a reproach to any nation" (Proverbs 14:34). Both Solomon's and Moses' words are reflected in those of William F. Albright: "God will keep His covenant with His people, if His people obey the divine commands."[36]

Finally, as America fights multiculturalism, it must remember its past victories. It attained those victories because its people were willing to correct their flaws as they feared and respected God's moral law. This message is not a new one. The United States heard it a century ago from Katharine Lee Bates, the writer of *America the Beautiful*, who pointedly told the nation: "America! America! / God mend thine ev'ry flaw, / Confirm thy soul in self-control, / Thy liberty in law." So in the manner of its past, America can do it again. God bless America!

NOTES

1. Ernest Renan, "Qu'est qu'une Nation?" in *French Literature of the Nineteenth Century* ed. R. F. Bradley and R. B. Mitchell (New York: F. S. Crofts, 1935), p. 284.

2. Worthington C. Ford, ed., *Journals of the Continental Congress, 1774–1789* (Washington, D.C: U.S. Government Printing Office, 1906), pp. 517–518.

3. Leonard Kriegel, "Boundaries of Memory: Liberals, Patriotism, and Melting Pots," *Virginia Quarterly Review* (winter 1995): 34.

4. "Washington's First Victory," *Boston Globe*, 7 March 1976, 65. Cited in Peter Marshall and David Manuel, *The Light and the Glory* (Old Tappan, N.J.: Fleming H. Revell, 1977), p. 299.

5. Cited in James Thomas Flexner, *George Washington in the American Revolution* (Boston: Little, Brown, 1967), p. 76.

6. James Thomas Flexner, "Providence Rides a Storm," *American Heritage* (December 1967): 13–17, 98–99.

7. Marshall and Manuel, *The Light and the Glory*, p. 318.

8. Flexner, *George Washington*, p. 185.

9. George Bancroft, *History of the United States of America* (Boston: Little, Brown, 1879), 3: 72.

10. Cited in William Johnson, *George Washington, The Christian* (Nashville, Tenn.: Abingdon Press, 1919), pp. 41, 42.

11. George Washington, "To Lieutenant Colonel John Laurens," in *The Writings of George Washington from the Original Sources, 1745–1799*, ed. John C. Fitzpatrick (Washington, D.C.: U.S. Government Printing Office, 1937), 20: 173.

12. Thomas Sowell, *The Vision of the Anointed* (New York: Basic Books, 1995).

13. Erik von Kuehnelt-Leddihn, *Leftism Revisited: From Sade and Marx to Hitler and Pol Pot* (Washington, D.C.: Regnery Gateway, 1990), p. 67.

14. Thomas Jefferson, *Works*, ed. H. A. Washington (New York: Derby and Jackson, 1859), 2: 332.

15. Benjamin Rush, "A Plan for the Establishment of Public Schools" (Philadelphia, 1786), reprinted in *Essays on Education in the Early Republic* ed. Frederick Rudolph (Cambridge, Mass.: The Belknap Press of Harvard University Press, 1965), p. 10.

16. Forrest McDonald, *Novus Ordo Seclorum: The Intellectual Origins of the Constitution* (Lawrence, Kans.: University of Kansas Press, 1985), p. 71.

17. Russell Kirk, *America's British Culture* (New Brunswick, N.J.: Transaction, 1993), p. 92.

18. Ralph Buchsbaum, "Is There a Better Pledge?" *The Humanist* (May/June 1990): 36.

19. "Social Science and the Citizen," *Society* (May/June 1991): 2.

20. Ibid.

21. Theodore Roosevelt, "American, Hyphenated," in *The Roosevelt Encyclopedia* ed. Albert Bushnell Hart and Herbert Ferleger (New York: Roosevelt Memorial Association, 1941), p. 16.

22. Editorial, "Portland's Statue Flap," *Seattle Post-Intelligencer*, 13 March 1994, E2.

23. Paul Cameron, *Exposing the AIDS Scandal* (Lafayette, La.: Huntington House, 1988), p. 11.

24. Kevin E. Abrams, "The Other Side of the Pink Triangle," *Lambda Report* (August 1994): 8.

25. Ibid., p. 9.

26. Cited by Abrams, in ibid.

27. Thomas Sowell, *The Vision of the Anointed: The Self-Congratulation as a Basis for Social Policy* (New York: Basic Books, 1995), p. 217.

28. Michael Jones, *Degenerate Moderns: Modernity as Rationalized Sexual Behavior* (San Francisco: Ignatius Press, 1993), pp. 58–59.

29. Gertrude Himmelfarb, "From Chapham to Bloomsbury: A Genealogy of Morals," *Commentary* (February 1985): 41.

30. *Statistical Abstract of the United States 1994* (Washington, D.C.: U.S. Department of Commerce, 1994), p. 70.

31. Barry Came, "We're Ready to Fight," *Maclean's*, 13 May 1996, 28. See also Diane Francis, "Challenging Quebec's Language Law," *Maclean's*, 25 March 1996, 13.

32. Robin Ajello, "Bittersweet Victory," *Maclean's*, 26 February 1996, 24.

33. Ibid.

34. Desmond Morton, "The Road Ahead," *Maclean's*, 18 March 1996, 10.

35. Jones, *Degenerate Moderns*, p. 86.

36. William Foxwell Albright, "The Vision Fulfilled," in *America and the Holy Land* ed. Moshe Davis (Westport, Conn.: Praeger, 1995), p. 38.

Selected Bibliography for Further Reading

BOOKS CRITICAL OF MULTICULTURALISM

Atlas, James. *Battle of the Books: The Curriculum Debate in America.* New York: W. W. Norton, 1990.

Auster, Lawrence. *The Path to National Suicide: An American Essay on Immigration and Multiculturalism.* Monterey, Va.: American Immigration Control Foundation, 1990.

Bennett, William. *Devaluing of America: The Fight for Our Culture and Our Children.* New York: Touchstone Books, 1994.

Bernstein, Richard. *Dictatorship of Virtue: Multiculturalism and the Battle for America's Future.* New York: A. A. Knopf, 1994.

Bolton, Richard, ed. *Culture Wars: Documents from Recent Controversies in the Arts.* New York: Free Press, 1992.

Brimelow, Peter. *Alien Nation.* New York: Random House, 1995.

Chavez, Linda. *Out of the Barrio: Toward a New Politics of Hispanic Assimilation.* New York: Basic Books, 1991.

Cheney, Lynne. *Telling the Truth: Why Our Culture and Our Country Stopped Making Sense—And What We Can Do About It.* New York: Simon and Schuster, 1995.

Collier, Peter, and David Horowitz, eds. *Surviving the PC University.* Studio City, Calif.: Second Thought Books and Center for the Study of Popular Culture, 1993.

D'Souza, Dinesh. *Illiberal Education.* New York: Free Press, 1991.

———. *The End of Racism: Principles for a Multiracial Society.* New York: Free Press, 1995.

Feder, Don. *A Jewish Conservative Looks at Pagan America.* Lafayette, La.: Huntington House Publishers, 1993.

Gitlin, Todd. *The Twilight of Common Dreams: Why America Is Wracked by Culture Wars.* New York: Metropolitan Books, 1995.
Gross, Paul, and Norman Levitt. *Higher Superstition: The Academic Left and Its Quarrels with Science.* Baltimore, Md.: Johns Hopkins University Press, 1994.
Hunter, James Davison. *Before the Shooting Starts.* New York: Free Press, 1994.
Kimball, Roger. *Tenured Radicals.* New York: Harper and Row, 1990.
Medved, Michael. *Hollywood v. America: Popular Culture and the War on Traditional Values.* New York: Harper and Row, 1992.
Nelson, Brent. *America Balkanized.* Monterey, Va.: American Immigration Control Foundation, 1994.
Porter, Rosalie. *Forked Tongue.* New York: Basic Books, 1990.
Schlesinger, Arthur J. *The Disuniting of America: Reflections on a Multicultural Society.* New York: W. W. Norton, 1991.
Sowell, Thomas. *The Vision of the Anointed.* New York: Basic Books, 1995.
Thibodaux, David. *Political Correctness: The Cloning of the American Mind.* Lafayette, La.: Huntington Publishing House, 1992.

BOOKS FAVORING MULTICULTURALISM

Aguirre, Adalberto, and Jonathon H. Turner. *American Ethnicity: The Dynamics and Consequences of Discrimination.* New York: McGraw-Hill, 1995.
Asante, Molefi Kete. *Afrocentricity.* Trenton, N.J.: Africa World Press, 1989.
Bernal, Martin. *Black Athena: The Afroasiatic Roots of Classical Civilization.* Vol. 1. New Brunswick, N.J.: Rutgers University Press, 1989.
Dathorne, O. R. *In Europe's Image: The Need for American Multiculturalism.* Westport, Conn.: Bergin and Garvey, 1994.
Delage, Denys. *Bitter Feast: Amerindians and Europeans in Northeastern North America, 1600–64.* Vancouver: University of British Columbia Press, 1993.
Fish, Stanley. *There's No such Thing As Free Speech, and It's a Good Thing Too.* New York: Oxford University Press, 1994.
Kaplan, Amy, and Donald E. Pease, eds. *Cultures of the United States Imperialism.* Durham, N.C.: Duke University Press, 1993.
Kymlicka, Will. *Multicultural Citizenship: A Liberal Theory of Minority Rights.* Cambridge: Oxford University Press, 1995.
Lind, Michael. *The Next American Nation: The New Nationalism.* New York: Free Press, 1995.
Matsuda, Mari J. *Words That Wound: Critical Race Theory, Assaultive Speech and the First Amendment.* Boulder, Colo.: Westview Press, 1993.
Nelson, David., et al. *Multicultural Mathematics.* Cambridge: Oxford University Press, 1993.
Nieto, Sonia. *Affirming Diversity: The Sociopolitical Context of Multicultural Education.* New York: Longmans, 1992.
Sale, Kilpatrick. *The Conquest of Paradise: Christopher Columbus and the Columbian Legacy.* New York: A. A. Knopf, 1990.

Takaki, Ronald. *A Different Mirror: A History of Multicultural America.* Boston: Little, Brown, 1993.

Wilson, John J. *The Myth of Political Correctness: The Conservative Attack on Higher Education.* Durham, N.C.: Duke University Press, 1995.

Index

About the Author

ALVIN J. SCHMIDT is Professor of Sociology at Illinois College in Jacksonville. A former Canadian, he is the author of numerous articles and several books, including *Veiled and Silenced: How Culture Shaped Sexist Theology* (1989) and *Fraternal Organizations* (1980), and has served as consulting editor for *Dictionary of Cults, Sects, and Religions of the Occult* (1993).